Hilton Head
Entertains

Nancy Pruitt—Editor

Artwork by West Fraser

Proceeds for the benefit of
Hilton Head Preparatory School.

This cookbook is a collection of our favorite recipes,
which are not necessarily original recipes.

Published by: Hilton Head Preparatory School

Copyright© Hilton Head Preparatory School
8 Fox Grape Road
Hilton Head Island, South Carolina 29928

Edited, Designed and Manufactured in the
United States of America by:
Favorite Recipes® Press
P. O. Box 305142
Nashville, Tennessee 37230
1-800-358-0560

Library of Congress Number: 91-36462
ISBN: 0-87197-320-0

First Printing: 1991   10,000 copies
Second Printing: 1993   10,000 copies

DEDICATION

The guiding idea leading to the design of this book is the long remembrance of a beautiful Southern lady, Mrs. Joseph Bacon Fraser, known to her friends as Becky. It was the wish of this committee to produce a cookbook which would reflect the elegance and beauty of this very special person and would be a tribute to her selfless and generous contributions for the betterment of Hilton Head Island. She exemplified the epitome of Southern hospitality which she graciously extended to family, friends and strangers who were in actuality "friends she had not met."

The committee's many hours of work were a labor of love, joyfully committed, and the result is **Hilton Head Entertains***, which is lovingly dedicated to Carolyn B. "Becky" Fraser.*

HILTON HEAD ENTERTAINS

The population of Hilton Head Island is a composite of people from many geographical locations and many walks of life; the forms of entertaining are just as varied. Some hostesses enjoy doing their own cooking and decorating. Others prefer to hire caterers. Still others open cans or stop by the local delicatessen or take-out counter. The result is the same, however, and the important thing is that people have a good time and keep returning to the island to enjoy our brand of "potpourri" entertainment.

We hope that you will like the way this book presents the menus and recipes of island hostesses and the suggestions for the unique ways they entertain. Although it presents the various events and functions special to Hilton Head Island, you can adapt them to your locale and enjoy them anywhere.

CONTENTS

HILTON HEAD PREP

The proceeds from the sale of this cookbook will benefit Hilton Head Preparatory School. This is an independent, coeducational, college preparatory school for students in grades one through twelve. It is celebrating twenty-five years of excellent independent education in the Hilton Head area.

The school is located on forty-six acres on the southern tip of Hilton Head Island, two blocks from the Atlantic Ocean and adjacent to the 600-acre Sea Pines Forest Preserve. Ideally situated forty minutes from both Savannah, Georgia, and Beaufort, South Carolina, the growing community is two hours south of historic Charleston, South Carolina.

Hilton Head Prep is accredited by the Southern Association of Colleges and Schools and is the only fully accredited independent school in the Hilton Head community. All courses are taught in view of the fact that the school's primary purpose is to prepare students for college, and 100% of its graduates go to colleges and universities all over the nation.

The unique coastal climate and environment of the area afford students many special educational and recreational opportunities. The school offers a variety of clubs, extra-curricular activities and inter-scholastic sports. Unique programs include an Interim Study Program which offers opportunities for independent study, career apprenticeship, and cultural trips. Other programs include peer tutoring, a model United Nations group, artists-in-residence, and many others.

Many parents and friends of Hilton Head Prep students have generously contributed their time and recipes to this cookbook project. Without them the book would not have been possible. Although we have not attempted to list every contributor, a special thanks goes to each of them.

Entertaining

Hilton Head Style

HERITAGE WEEK

Hilton Head Island is a golfer's dream, especially in the spring when the pros gather on our Harbour Town golf course in Sea Pines for the famous MCI Heritage Classic golf tournament. During Heritage Week everyone opens his home and heart for a week of nonstop entertaining at brunches, lunches, cocktails, buffets or cookouts.

OPEN VILLAS

Artichoke Rice Salad*
Heritage Peachy Baked Ham*
Sesame Chicken Drumettes*
Copper Pennies*
Assorted Fruits
Gingerbread Squares*
"Golf Tee" Ice Cream Cones

FAIRWAY FUN OPEN HOUSE

Part of the charm of this menu are the creative decorations. The cold cuts are arranged on the platter to resemble a golf bag. The slaw is served in a golf ball ice bucket. The sandwich rolls are served in baskets with Heritage Plaid napkins and the centerpiece is a loaf of bread in the shape of an alligator with a golf ball in its mouth.

Assorted Cold Cuts
Seven-Day Slaw*
Patio Beans*
Marinated Vegetable Salad*
Assorted Sandwich Rolls
Fudge Squares*
Oatmeal Cookies

DO IT YOURSELF GRILL-OUT

For this easy menu, the host and hostess provide the hot grill and all the fixings and encourage guests to do their own thing.

Heritage Hot Dogs and Hamburgers
Grilled Chicken*
Salad Bar   Homemade Dressings
Assorted Buns
Heritage Heavenly Hash

HERITAGE BOOTH TREASURES

Sloppy Joes-for-a-Crowd*
Chili Dogs
Barbecue
Double Shot Brownies*
Heritage Chocolate Chip Cookies*

LUNCHEON FOR THE PROS' WIVES

The golf pros love to bring their families to our island because we roll out the red carpet to entertain their families. Fun activities and reliable sitters are provided for the children, so Mom is free to follow Dad or enjoy an event such as this island luncheon.

Sea Pines Seafood Casserole*
Hot Wine Fruit Salad*
Asparagus Vinaigrette*
Poppy Seed Bread*
Mile-High Strawberry Pie*

FAMILY CIRCLE
TENNIS TOURNAMENT

Harbour Town is the scene of the annual ladies' pro tennis tournament. It is a great time to entertain at brunch or lunch before the matches or at a Sunday night snack supper to watch reruns of the final matches on the VCR.

FAMILY CIRCLE BRUNCH

Fresh Fruit Salad Compote*
Baked Ham   Link Sausage
Scrambled Eggs   Jiffy Biscuits*
Jams   Jellies

TENNIS PRO LUNCH

Sausage and Wild Rice*
Overnight Bran Muffins   Tennis Ball Bread*
Carolina Cantaloupe

HARBOUR TOWN LUNCH

Sausage Quiche*
Carolina Cheese Grits*   Spiced Fruit*
Mimosas*   Assorted Muffins

SUNDAY NIGHT SNACK SUPPER

Southern Chili*   Mexican Corn Bread*
Tossed Salad
Forget-Me-Not Carrot Cake*

GARDEN OF EDEN LUNCHEON

This is a lovely menu for entertaining your tennis or golf foursome. Everything can be prepared in advance and served when the match is over. The pie is easy to make; do the cheesecake only if your friends are worth the trouble!

Congealed Chicken Salad*
Fresh Fruits in Season   Pineapple Muffins*
Maple Pecan Pie* or
White Chocolate Cheesecake*

The optional placement of dessert silver above the plate is convenient when service is limited or when the hostess is doing the serving herself at an informal luncheon or supper.

SERENDIPITY AT SUNSET

The peacefulness and beauty of a Hilton Head sunset cannot be surpassed, and there is no better way to enjoy it than with good friends, a cool drink and a delicious buffet.

Stupendous Sausage Balls*
Shrimp Butter*   Crackers
Layered Mexican Dip*   Chipped Beef Spread*
Spinach Balls*   Vidalia Onion Dip*
Cool Drinks of Your Choice

HILTON HEAD HIGH TEA

It's high time we reinstate the High Tea. Hilton Head is once again enjoying this elegant form of entertaining. Traditionally, teas are given to honor someone such as a bride, a debutante, a new neighbor or graduating seniors and their mothers. Invitations to a high tea are written or engraved on the face of a folded note or inside, if the name or monogram of the hostess is on the face.

The table for a formal tea should be as large as possible in order to hold a silver tea service. It is usually placed at the end of the table farther away from the main door in order to serve as the focal point. The punch bowl for a cold beverage is usually at the other end of the table or on a small side table. The table should be covered with a white lace or linen cloth with an overhang of 18 to 20 inches. Napkins should match the cloth. Fresh flowers should be used for the centerpiece.

Proper foods to serve at a tea are tiny sandwiches, bite-sized savories, scones, sweet cakes and cookies. These should be arranged on plates and placed on both sides of the table.

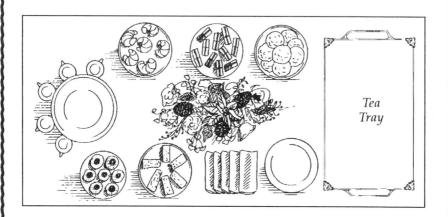

Tea Tray

SETTING A TEA TABLE

The tea tray or trolley holds a pot of very hot water, a full teapot of freshly-made tea, a cream pitcher, a sugar bowl and a small plate of thin lemon slices. The pourer is usually a special friend or relative of the hostess or honoree. She will fill the teacup 2/3 full and add cream, hot water, sugar or lemon to suit individual tastes.

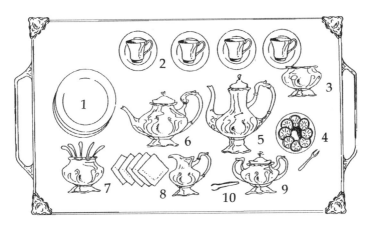

1 stacks of plates	6 tea
2 cups and saucers	7 spoon bowl
3 waste bowl	8 cream pitcher
4 thin slices of lemon, lemon fork	9 sugar bowl
5 very hot water	10 sugar tongs

TEA FOR THE SENIORS

*This menu was served at a formal tea honoring
the Prep senior girls and their mothers.*

Checkerboard Sandwiches*
Open-Faced Gingered Fruit Tea Sandwiches*
Cheese Tarts*
Man-Made Strawberries*
Tiny Iced Brownies
Debutante's Tea*

TROUSSEAU TEA

*The bride enjoys sharing the delights of her trousseau
with her close friends at a Trousseau Tea. It is usually given
by a grandmother or close relative at the bride's home so
all may view the trousseau treasures.*

Cherry Sandwiches*
Open-Faced Garden Sandwiches*
Date Wheels*
Cheese Tarts*
Pecan Tassies*
Cheese Straw Crispies*
Strawberry Tree with Confectioners' Sugar
Mints   Spiced Nuts
Tea   Punch

TEDDY BEAR TEA

*Little girls learn to be young ladies and have a wonderful
time entertaining dolls or mommies at this never-to-be-forgotten
Alice in Wonderland afternoon. The Bear-Face Sandwiches
are made with thinly spread peanut butter and jelly,
raisins for eyes and a cherry slice mouth.*

Victorian Rose Tea
Surprise Cupcakes*
Scones*   Jam
Bear-Face Sandwiches
Raisin Nut Wheels*

THE YANKEES ARE COMING

This is a dinner prepared by a Hilton Head resident, originally from Georgia, when Yankee friends come to visit. Her husband considers it a furthering of the guest's education.

Fried Chicken*

Milk Gravy   Rice

Fried Okra*

Black-Eyed Peas

Pear Relish*

Biscuits

Sweet Potato Pie*

Real Southern Pecan Pie*

DOCKSIDE DINING

This menu features recipes and foods that are special to the island and capture the essence of entertaining on Hilton Head.

Plantation Pecans*

Hilton Head Boiled Peanuts

Calibogue Shrimp and Grits*

Daufuskie Deviled Crabs*

Sea Pines Corn Pudding* in Tomatoes

Radicchio Pecan Salad*

Garlic-Blue Cheese Mayonnaise*

Low Country Biscuits*

Melrose Conserve*

Churned Peachy Ice Cream*

Heritage Chocolate Chip Cookies*

Carolina Iced Coffee*

BLACK TIE BIRTHDAY

When a special person has a birthday, he should be treated to a royal feast. This menu should make anyone feel special.

Black Olive Soup*
Three-Lettuce Salad* in Lettuce Crowns
Lobster-Stuffed Tenderloin*
Fresh Asparagus   Pimento Garni
Potato Puff Casserole*   Sour Cream Biscuits*
Hummingbird Cake*

AFTER-BALLET COFFEE

This is an easy and unique form of entertaining. All of the ingredients are placed in groups on tables. Recipes are written on elegant scrolls set amidst the necessary ingredients. Large pitchers of regular and decaffinated coffee are provided, and guests are encouraged to "mix their own." Silver baskets of bonbons and mints complete this repast.

Irish Coffee*   Mexican Coffee*
Café Swisse Mocha*   Latin American Coffee*
Italian Coffee*   Café Brûlot*
Bonbons*   Mints

HOME FROM THE HUNT DINNER

*Hilton Head Island is a game preserve, so hunters travel
to mainland fields to bag their game. Island hostesses use
this method of entertaining to share their wealth or, as
one honest wife says, to clean out the freezer.*

Ducks Burgundy*

Marinated Goose*

Company Venison Stroganoff*

Dove Pie*   **Quail in Mushroom Sauce***

Green Beans   Wild Rice with Wine*

Low Country Biscuits*

Prune Cake*   **Coffee**

JUBILEE COCKTAIL PARTY

*Jubilee is one of the main fund-raisers held by parents
of Prep students and marks the beginning of the Christmas
social season. It combines a Festival of Trees, a Dinner Dance
and a Live Auction. This cocktail party, catered by a
Prep parent, is one of the items in the auction.*

Rum Sausages*

Spinach Dip* in Round Bread Bowl

Crab Meat Dip*   **Timbales**

Vegetable Platter   Dip

Brie in a Pastry*

Chicken Salad in Cocktail Puffs*

Chicken Nuggets   Chili Meatballs*

Shrimp Mousse*

Jubilee Ham   Sour Cream Biscuits*

Strawberry Cheese Ring*   **Gingersnaps***

CHRISTMAS EVE BRUNCH

A Hilton Head Hostess shares the following: "One of the most unforgettable memories of childhood is the excitement of Christmas Eve Day. This annual party for our children's friends and their parents helps to channel that excitement and prolong the pleasure of the season."

Holiday Fruit Salad*

Heavenly Ham

Limpa Rolls   Angel Biscuits

Cheese Grits-Sausage Casserole*

Miniature Cinnamon Pastries*

Peanut Butter Bonbons

Crème de Menthe Brownies

Old-Fashioned Shortbread

Coffee Punch*

Fresh Orange Juice   Mulled Cider

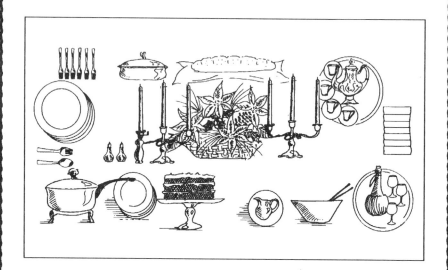

SETTING A BUFFET TABLE

CHRISTMAS DINNER

*This menu is for a Christmas dinner "the island way"
and features Hilton Head favorites and specialties.*

Oyster Soufflé
Cran-Orange Wreath*
Turkey À La Champagne
Corn Bread Dressing with Mushrooms
Cranberries and Rice*
Sweet Potato Soufflé in Orange Cups
Green Beans Wrapped in Bacon
Refrigerator Yeast Rolls*
Mincemeat Tarts   Fuzzy Navel Pie*
Coffee Punch*   Deviled Pecans*

To carve a turkey, place it on a platter with legs to the carver's right. Cut through between the thigh and body and remove the entire leg (usually with the hand). Slice the dark meat from the leg on an auxiliary platter. You may sever the joint between the thigh and drumstick.

Insert the fork across the breastbone; cut off the wing. Place wing to one side before carving the white meat.

Carve the breast downward in thin even slices. Finish one side before turning the turkey to carve the other side.

NEW YEAR'S DAY OPEN HOUSE

On Hilton Head Island, we encourage family entertaining. This is our version of a "Ring Out the Old, Ring in the New" Open House. One menu is for the kids' table and one menu is for the adults' table, but no law says you can't sample both.

YOUNG AT HEART OPEN HOUSE

Slow Cooker Sloppy Joes
Small Dinner Rolls
Peanut Butter and Jelly Triangles
Chex Party Mix*
Popcorn Balls
Cinnamon Brownies*
Gingersnaps*
Christmas Punch*

HEARTFULLY YOUNG OPEN HOUSE

Sea Island Pickled Shrimp*
Smoked Oyster Roll
Sausage-Stuffed Mushrooms*
Ham Biscuits
Layered Mexican Dip*
Date Wheels*
Chocolate-Covered Fruitcake*
Assorted Bonbons*
Eggnog*

Becky's
Favorites

VIDALIA ONION DIP

Yield: 6 cups

1 cup white vinegar
1 cup sugar
1 cup water
1 tablespoon celery seed

1 tablespoon celery salt
3 or 4 Vidalia onions, chopped
1 cup sour cream
1 cup mayonnaise

Mix first 5 ingredients in bowl. Add onions. Marinate in refrigerator overnight. Drain onions. Add sour cream and mayonnaise; mix well.

CHICKEN AND RICE SALAD

Yield: 6 servings

2 cups cooked rice
1/4 cup chopped onion
2 tablespoons oil
1 teaspoon curry powder
2 cups chopped cooked chicken

2 cups frozen peas, thawed
1 1/2 cups chopped celery
Pineapple, grapes and almonds
3/4 cup mayonnaise
Salt and pepper to taste

Combine rice, onion, oil and curry powder in bowl; mix well. Marinate in refrigerator overnight. Add chicken, peas, celery, pineapple, grapes, almonds, mayonnaise, salt and pepper; mix well. Serve on bed of lettuce or watercress. Garnish with toasted almonds.

SUPERB BAKED CRAB

Yield: 6 servings

3 tablespoons butter
1/4 cup flour
1 teaspoon seasoned salt
1 cup milk
1 1/2 teaspoons onion flakes
1/3 cup Sauterne

2 egg yolks
1 tablespoon lemon juice
1 tablespoon chopped parsley
1   2-ounce can mushrooms
1/4 cup grated Parmesan cheese
1 pound crab meat, flaked

Melt butter in saucepan. Stir in flour, seasoned salt and milk. Add onion flakes. Cook until thickened, stirring constantly. Stir in wine. Beat egg yolks slightly in bowl. Stir a small amount of hot sauce into egg yolks; stir egg yolks into hot sauce. Cook over very low heat for 5 minutes, stirring constantly; do not boil. Stir in lemon juice, parsley, mushrooms and half the cheese. Mix in crab meat. Spoon into shallow baking dish; sprinkle with remaining cheese. Broil 4 inches from heat source until light brown. Serve at once.

PATIO BEANS
Yield: 8 servings

1 can butter beans, drained
1 can kidney beans, drained
1 can baked beans
4 slices bacon, chopped
1 onion, chopped

1 cup Cheddar cheese cubes
Parmesan cheese to taste
1/2 cup packed brown sugar
1/3 cup catsup
1 tablespoon Worcestershire sauce

Combine all ingredients in baking dish; mix well. Bake at 350 degrees
for 20 minutes or until bubbly.

EGGPLANT PARMIGIANA
Yield: 6 to 8 servings

3 cloves of garlic, minced
1 onion, minced
1 tablespoon oil
1   20-ounce can tomatoes
1¹/4 teaspoons salt
1/4 teaspoon pepper
1   8-ounce can tomato sauce
1/4 teaspoon thyme

2 medium eggplant, peeled,
   thinly sliced
1 egg, beaten
1/4 cup dry bread crumbs
1/4 cup grated Parmesan cheese
8 ounces mozzarella cheese,
   shredded
1/4 to 1/3 cup Parmesan cheese

Sauté garlic and onion in oil in skillet. Add tomatoes, salt and pepper. Simmer for 10 minutes. Add tomato sauce and thyme. Simmer
for 20 minutes. Dip eggplant into egg; coat with mixture of bread
crumbs and 1/4 cup Parmesan cheese. Arrange in baking dish. Add
2/3 of the sauce. Top with mozzarella cheese, remaining sauce and 1/3
cup Parmesan cheese. Bake at 350 degrees for 30 minutes.

ONION PIE
Yield: 4 to 6 servings

4 slices bacon, crisp-fried
2 cups sliced Vidalia onions
1 unbaked pie shell
3 eggs, slightly beaten
1¹/2 cups half and half

3/4 cup shredded Swiss cheese
1 tablespoon chopped parsley
1/4 teaspoon dry mustard
3/4 teaspoon salt
1/8 teaspoon pepper

Sauté onions in bacon drippings in skillet. Spoon into pie shell;
crumble bacon over top. Combine remaining ingredients in bowl;
mix well. Pour over bacon. Bake at 375 degrees for 45 minutes.

BRAN BREAD

Yield: 24 servings

1 cup shortening
³/₄ cup sugar
1¹/₂ teaspoons salt
1 cup boiling water
1 cup bran cereal

2 envelopes dry yeast
1 cup lukewarm water
2 eggs
5¹/₂ to 6 cups sifted unbleached
  flour

Combine shortening, sugar, salt and boiling water in large bowl; mix well. Stir in cereal. Cool to lukewarm. Dissolve yeast in lukewarm water in bowl. Add to cereal mixture with eggs; mix well. Add 3 cups flour. Beat for 5 to 10 minutes or until elastic. Add remaining flour 1 cup at a time, mixing well after each addition. Place in greased bowl, turning to coat surface. Chill for 24 hours. Divide into 2 portions. Roll into rectangles on lightly floured surface. Roll as for jelly rolls, tucking ends under; place seam sides down in greased loaf pans. Bake at 450 degrees for 10 minutes. Reduce oven temperature to 350 degrees. Bake for 30 minutes longer. Remove to wire rack to cool.

HUMMINGBIRD CAKE

Yield: 16 servings

3 cups flour
2 cups sugar
1 teaspoon baking soda
1 teaspoon cinnamon
1 teaspoon salt
3 eggs, beaten
1¹/₂ cups oil
1 8-ounce can crushed
   pineapple
2 cups chopped bananas

1 cup chopped pecans
1¹/₂ teaspoons vanilla extract
¹/₂ cup butter or margarine,
   softened
8 ounces cream cheese, softened
1 1-pound package
   confectioners' sugar
1 teaspoon vanilla extract
1 cup chopped pecans

Mix flour, sugar, baking soda, cinnamon and salt in large bowl. Add eggs and oil; mix just until moistened. Stir in undrained pineapple, bananas, 1 cup pecans and 1¹/₂ teaspoons vanilla. Spoon into 3 greased and floured 9-inch cake pans. Bake at 350 degrees for 30 minutes or until layers test done. Cool in pans for 10 minutes. Remove to wire rack to cool completely. Cream butter and cream cheese in mixer bowl until smooth. Add confectioners' sugar; beat until fluffy. Mix in 1 teaspoon vanilla. Spread between layers and over top and side of cake. Sprinkle with 1 cup pecans.

Appetizers
& Sandwiches

CHEESE LOG
Yield: 16 servings

16 ounces cream cheese,
  softened
2 cups grated Cheddar cheese
1 small wedge of Roquefort
  cheese
1 roll garlic cheese
l large package bleu cheese

1/3 cup Parmesan cheese
1/4 cup Worcestershire sauce
1 cup chopped pecans
1 cup chopped black olives
Minced parsley
Paprika to taste

Combine cheeses, Worcestershire sauce, pecans and olives in bowl.
Shape into log. Roll in parsley and paprika. Chill until serving time.

Marilyn McNeely

TANG CHEESE BALL
Yield: 16 servings

16 ounces cream cheese,
  softened
3 tablespoons Tang

1 cup chopped pecans
1 cup chopped dates
1/4 cup chopped pecans

Combine cream cheese, Tang, 1 cup pecans and dates in bowl. Shape
into ball. Roll in remaining 1/4 cup pecans.

Louise S. Hunter

SMOKED SALMON ROLL
Yield: 16 servings

1 pound salmon, drained,
  deboned
8 ounces cream cheese, softened
1 tablespoon lemon juice
2 teaspoons grated onion

1 teaspoon horseradish
1/4 teaspoon salt
1/4 teaspoon liquid smoke
1/2 cup chopped pecans
3 tablespoons chopped parsley

Combine first 7 ingredients in bowl; mix well. Chill for several hours.
Shape into 2x8-inch log. Roll in mixture of pecans and parsley. Serve
with crackers.

Deb Halloran

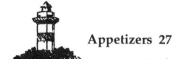

SHRIMP CHEESE BALLS

Yield: 8 servings

6 ounces cream cheese,
    softened
1¹/₂ teaspoons prepared
    mustard
1 teaspoon grated onion

1 teaspoon lemon juice
Dash of pepper
Dash of salt
1 4-ounce can shrimp, drained
²/₃ cup chopped salted nuts

Combine first 6 ingredients in bowl; mix well. Stir in shrimp. Chill.
Shape into ¹/₂-inch balls. Roll in nuts.

Barb Smith

ARTICHOKE HORS D'OEUVRES

Yield: 12 servings

1 cup mayonnaise
1 cup Parmesan cheese
1 small can mushrooms,
    drained

1 large can whole artichokes,
    drained

Combine mayonnaise and cheese in bowl. Stir in mushrooms and
artichokes. Place on nonstick baking sheet. Bake at 375 degrees for
20 minutes or until golden brown. Serve hot with crackers.

Debbie McKinley

HOT CHEESE DIP

Yield: 16 servings

¹/₂ to ³/₄ cup chopped onion
1 tablespoon butter
2 cups grated Cheddar cheese

8 ounces cream cheese,
    softened
1 cup mayonnaise

Sauté onion in butter in skillet. Combine with remaining ingredients
in bowl. Spoon into 1¹/₂-quart baking dish. Bake at 350 degrees for
20 to 30 minutes or until lightly browned. Serve hot with crackers.

Louise S. Hunter

CRAB MEAT DIP

Yield: 32 servings

2 onions, chopped
2 green bell peppers, chopped
1/4 cup butter
6 tablespoons flour
6 tablespoons butter, softened
1 cup half and half

2 pounds crab meat
1 large can sliced mushrooms
1 teaspoon thyme
1 teaspoon curry powder
1/2 cup sherry

Sauté onions and bell peppers in 1/4 cup butter in skillet. Combine flour, remaining 6 tablespoons butter and half and half in bowl. Stir in vegetables. Add remaining ingredients. Serve from chafing dish with toast points or pastry shells.

Jo Gross Huffman

OVEN-BAKED CRAB DIP

Yield: 12 servings

16 ounces cream cheese,
    softened
1/3 cup mayonnaise
1 tablespoons confectioners'
    sugar
1 tablespoon Chablis
1/2 teaspoon prepared mustard

1/4 teaspoon onion powder
1/4 teaspoon garlic salt
1/4 teaspoon salt
12 ounces fresh crab meat,
    drained, flaked
Paprika to taste

Combine first 8 ingredients in bowl. Stir in crab. Spoon into lightly greased 1-quart baking dish. Sprinkle with paprika. Bake at 375 degrees for 15 minutes.

Lynn Ruggles

LUSCIOUS LAYERED CRAB DIP

Yield: 12 servings

2 6-ounce cans white crab
    meat, drained, flaked

8 ounces cream cheese, softened
Cocktail sauce

Combine crab meat and cream cheese in bowl; mix well. Chill until serving time. Top with cocktail sauce.

Lynn Baughman Asnip

HOT CRAB MEAT APPETIZER

Yield: 4 servings

8 ounces cream cheese,
  softened
1 6-ounce can crab meat,
  drained, flaked
2 tablespoons finely chopped
  onion

1 tablespoon milk
½ teaspoon creamy horseradish
Salt and pepper to taste
Dash of Worcestershire sauce
½ cup toasted sliced almonds

Combine first 7 ingredients in bowl. Spoon into shallow baking dish. Top with almonds. Bake at 375 degrees for 15 minutes. Serve hot with bite-sized fresh vegetables or crackers.

Chris Mauro

EGGPLANT APPETIZER

Yield: 12 servings

⅓ cup olive oil
3 cups chopped peeled
  eggplant
⅓ cup chopped green bell
  pepper
1 onion, chopped
2 cloves of garlic, crushed
½ cup chopped mushrooms

1 can tomato paste
¼ cup water
2 tablespoons red wine vinegar
½ cup sliced Spanish olives
1½ teaspoons sugar
½ teaspoon oregano
⅛ teaspoon pepper
1 teaspoon salt

Heat oil in skillet. Add eggplant, green pepper, onion and garlic. Cook, covered, for 10 minutes, stirring occasionally. Stir in mixture of mushrooms, tomato paste and water. Add remaining ingredients. Simmer, covered, for 30 minutes or until eggplant is tender. Chill, covered, overnight. Serve hot or cold with crackers.

Dorothy Collins

Radish Rose—Select round radishes. Cut thin slice from each end. Cut 4 or 5 thin petal-shaped slices around outer edge from top to bottom, leaving bottom intact. Chill in iced water until petals open.

GUACAMOLE

Yield: 6 servings

1 large avocado, peeled, finely chopped
3 small green onions, chopped
2 tablespoons lemon juice

1/2 10-ounce can tomatoes and green chilies, drained
1/8 teaspoon salt

Combine all ingredients in bowl; mix well. Place avocado pit in center of dip; cover tightly to prevent darkening before serving. Serve with corn chips.

Lee Boone

LAYERED MEXICAN DIP

Yield: 24 servings

2 or 3 ripe avocadoes
1/8 teaspoon lemon juice
1 bunch green onions with tops, chopped
2 cups sour cream
1 8-ounce jar picante sauce

2 ripe tomatoes, chopped
2 small green bell peppers, chopped
8 ounces Monterey Jack cheese, grated

Mash avocadoes in 9-inch pie plate. Sprinkle with lemon juice. Layer remaining ingredients in order given. Chill, tightly covered, for 4 to 12 hours. Serve with tortilla or corn chips.

Lisa Pruitt

SHRIMP BUTTER

Yield: 24 servings

2 pounds boiled shrimp
1 pound unsalted butter
1/2 cup pitted black olives

2 tablespoons lemon juice
2 tablespoons capers

Combine all ingredients in food processor container. Process until blended. Spoon into favorite mold. Chill until serving time.

Ron Hodge

SPINACH DIP
Yield: 24 servings

2   10-ounce packages frozen
   chopped spinach
2 packages dry vegetable soup
   mix
2 onions, chopped

2 cans water chestnuts, chopped
2 cups sour cream
2 cups mayonnaise
1 small jar pimentos
1/2 teaspoon Tabasco sauce

Combine all ingredients in bowl; mix well. Chill for several hours to overnight. Serve in hollowed-out round loaf of bread.

Susan Kesler

SMOKY VEGETABLE DIP
Yield: 12 servings

1 large carton sour cream
1 cup grated sharp Cheddar
   cheese

1 package dried green pea soup
   mix
Liquid hickory smoke to taste

Combine all ingredients in bowl. Chill until serving time. Serve with bite-sized fresh vegetables.

Caroline G. McGee

APRICOT-PEACH SPREAD
Yield: 16 servings

1   16-ounce jar apricot
   preserves
1   16-ounce jar peach preserves
2 tablespoons dry mustard

1   5-ounce jar prepared
   horseradish
8 ounces cream cheese,
   softened

Combine preserves, dry mustard and horseradish in bowl; mix well. Serve over cream cheese with crackers.

Jan Elizabeth Baughman Hunter

ARTICHOKE SPREAD

Yield: 12 servings

1 cup mayonnaise
1 cup grated Parmesan cheese

1 can artichoke hearts, drained,
chopped

Combine all ingredients in bowl; mix well. Spoon into baking dish. Bake at 350 degrees until top is crusty. Serve with crackers.

Elaine Fulton

AVOCADO-CRAB MEAT SPREAD

Yield: 10 servings

2 ounces cream cheese, softened
2 tablespoons Worcestershire
  sauce
2 tablespoons chopped fresh
  parsley

$^1/_4$ cup mayonnaise
1 teaspoon dry mustard
Juice of 1 lemon
2 avocadoes, chopped
$^1/_2$ cup crab meat

Combine first 5 ingredients in bowl. Stir in lemon juice. Add avocadoes and crab meat; mix well. Serve with crackers.

Ronelle Plocher

CRAB MOLD

Yield: 30 servings

2 envelopes unflavored gelatin
$^1/_4$ cup cold water
1 can tomato soup
8 ounces cream cheese
1 cup chopped celery
1 cup chopped onion

1 cup chopped green bell
  peppers
1 cup mayonnaise
1 pound frozen crab meat,
  thawed

Soften gelatin in water in bowl. Combine with soup and cream cheese in double boiler. Cook until heated through, stirring frequently. Add remaining ingredients. Spoon into mold. Chill overnight. Unmold onto serving plate. Serve with crackers.

Maurine L. Holmes

CHIPPED BEEF SPREAD

Yield: 12 servings

8 ounces cream cheese,
  softened
2 tablespoons milk
1/2 cup sour cream
1 package chipped beef,
  shredded

2 tablespoons onion flakes
1/4 cup finely chopped green
  bell pepper
1/2 teaspoon garlic salt
1/2 cup coarsely chopped pecans
2 tablespoons butter

Combine first 3 ingredients in bowl. Stir in beef. Add onion flakes, green pepper and garlic salt; mix well. Spoon into baking dish. Heat pecans with butter in saucepan. Sprinkle over chipped beef mixture. Bake at 350 degrees for 20 minutes. Serve with crackers.

Betty Gustafson

ARTICHOKE SQUARES

Yield: 12 servings

2 6-ounce jars marinated
  artichoke hearts
1 small onion, finely chopped
1 clove of garlic, minced
4 eggs, beaten
1/4 cup dry bread crumbs
1/4 teaspoon salt

1/8 teaspoon pepper
1/8 teaspoon oregano
1/8 teaspoon Tabasco sauce
8 ounces Cheddar or Swiss
  cheese, grated
2 tablespoons minced parsley

Drain liquid from 1 jar artichokes into skillet; dispose of remaining liquid. Chop artichokes; set aside. Sauté onion and garlic in skillet until transparent. Combine with remaining ingredients in large bowl; mix well. Spoon into buttered 7x11-inch baking dish. Bake at 350 degrees for 30 minutes. Cool in pan. Cut into 1-inch squares. Serve cold or warm.

Nancy Miller

Bacon Roll-Ups

Yield: 16 servings

¹/₄ cup margarine
¹/₂ cup water
1¹/₂ cups herb-seasoned
   stuffing mix

1 egg
¹/₄ pound hot sausage
¹/₂ to 1 pound bacon

Combine first 5 ingredients in bowl. Chill thoroughly. Shape into 1-inch logs. Wrap each with bacon; secure with wooden picks. Place on baking sheet. Bake at 325 degrees for 20 minutes, turning once.

Louise Levzow

Baked Brie Bites

Yield: 8 servings

2 French sourdough rolls
Margarine
¹/₂ cup packed brown sugar

15 ounces Brie, cut into thin
   wedges
¹/₄ cup chopped almonds

Cut round ends from rolls; discard. Cut each roll into four ¹/₂-inch slices. Spread margarine over 1 side of rolls. Combine brown sugar and almonds in bowl. Layer half the almond mixture on bread. Top each with Brie and remaining almond mixture. Place on ungreased baking sheet. Bake at 375 degrees for 6 to 7 minutes or until heated through. Serve with dry white wine.

Valerie Curry

Brie in a Pastry

Yield: 12 servings

1 package frozen puff pastry,
   thawed
1 whole round Brie cheese

¹/₂ cup chopped green onions
¹/₂ cup chopped pecans
1 egg yolk

Divide pastry into 2 portions. Place Brie on 1 portion. Top with onions and pecans. Cover with remaining pastry; seal edges. Brush with egg yolk. Freeze for 2 hours. Place on baking sheet. Bake at 425 degrees until golden. Let stand for 1 hour. Place on serving plate; cut into wedges.

Ron Hodge

CHEESE STRAW CRISPIES
Yield: 24 servings

1 cup butter, softened
2 cups sifted flour
8 ounces sharp cheese, shredded

¼ teaspoon salt
¼ teaspoon red pepper
1½ cups rice cereal

Combine first 5 ingredients in bowl. Stir in cereal. Shape into quarter-sized balls. Place on greased baking sheet. Flatten with fork dipped in flour. Bake at 350 degrees for 10 minutes. May sprinkle with paprika or dry onion soup mix for different flavors.

Janie Wilkerson

CRAB MEAT RAVIGOTE
Yield: 6 servings

1 pound crab meat
2 tablespoons chopped sweet
  pickles
2 tablespoons lemon juice
¼ teaspoon salt

1 hard-boiled egg, chopped
1 teaspoon chopped parsley
¼ cup mayonnaise
2 tablespoons chopped olives
¼ teaspoon paprika

Mix first 6 ingredients in serving dish. Spread mixture of mayonnaise and remaining ingredients over crab mixture. Chill in refrigerator.

Gloria Carmines

HILTON HEAD CRABGRASS
Yield: 20 servings

1   10-ounce package frozen
  chopped spinach
1 onion, finely chopped
1 carrot, grated
½ cup butter
10 ounces flaked crab meat

⅓ to ¾ cup Parmesan cheese
⅓ cup dry sherry or white wine
1 teaspoon lemon juice
1 clove of garlic, minced
Salt, pepper and garlic salt to
  taste

Cook spinach partially in saucepan; drain. Sauté onion and carrot in butter in skillet until tender but not brown. Add remaining ingredients. Cook until heated through. Serve from chafing dish on French bread toast or melba rounds.

June Minske

KELLY BUFFALO WINGS

Yield: 30 servings

1 cup melted butter
1 teaspoon lemon juice
1/2 bottle of gourmet barbecue
   sauce
1 1/2 teaspoons Tabasco sauce

Worcestershire sauce to taste
1 teaspoon basil
4 packages dry Italian
   seasoning
60 chicken wings, cooked

Combine first 7 ingredients in bowl. Coat chicken wings with sauce. Place on baking sheet. Bake at 350 degrees for 10 minutes.

Dan Kelly

COCKTAIL PUFFS

Yield: 24 servings

1/4 cup butter
1/2 cup boiling water
1/2 cup flour

Dash of salt
2 eggs

Melt butter in boiling water in saucepan. Add flour and salt, stirring vigorously. Cook over low heat until mixture forms soft ball, stirring constantly. Cool slightly. Add eggs 1 at a time, beating well after each addition. Drop by teaspoonfuls onto ungreased baking sheet. Bake at 400 degrees for 20 minutes. May fill with chicken salad, crab meat, cream cheese, mustard and sardines or other favorite fillings.

Teri Keith

CHEX PARTY MIX

Yield: 6 3/4 cups

6 tablespoons melted butter or
   margarine
1 teaspoon seasoned salt
4 teaspoons Worcestershire
   sauce

2 cups Corn Chex
2 cups Rice Chex
2 cups Wheat Chex
3/4 cup salted mixed nuts and
   pretzel sticks

Combine first 3 ingredients in baking pan. Add cereal, mixed nuts and pretzels; stir to coat well. Bake at 250 degrees for 45 minutes, stirring every 15 minutes. Spread on paper towel to cool.

Lynn Clanton

CHILI MEATBALLS

Yield: 25 servings

1 egg
1/2 cup water
1/2 cup seasoned bread crumbs
1 cup grated cheese
1 1/2 teaspoons chili powder

2 teaspoons salt
1 pound ground chuck
1 cup barbecue sauce
1 cup grape or strawberry jelly

Beat egg with water in bowl. Stir in next 4 ingredients. Add ground chuck; mix well. Shape into 50 quarter-sized balls. Place in shallow pan. Bake at 350 degrees for 15 minutes. Combine barbecue sauce and jelly in saucepan. Cook until jelly is melted, stirring frequently. Serve over meatballs.

Louise Levzow

SAUSAGE-STUFFED MUSHROOMS

Yield: 24 servings

1 cup chopped onions
2 cloves of garlic, minced
1   10-ounce package frozen
    spinach, thawed, drained
2 tablespoons butter

1 pound sausage
16 ounces Swiss cheese,
    shredded
24 very large mushrooms

Sauté onions, garlic and spinach in butter in skillet until onions are clear; drain. Brown sausage in skillet, stirring until crumbly; drain. Combine spinach mixture, sausage and cheese in bowl; mix well. Stuff mushrooms with mixture; place in baking dish. Bake at 450 degrees until brown.

Ron Hodge

Fluted Mushroom—Select firm, round white mushrooms. Rub gently with lemon juice to prevent discoloration. Press the flat tip of a knife into the center of the mushroom cap in a star design. Continue making indentations in rows around mushroom cap.

STUFFED MUSHROOMS

Yield: 8 servings

3 pints mushrooms
3/4 cup mayonnaise
1 medium onion, grated
10 slices crisp-fried bacon

Dash of seasoned salt
1 1/2 cups shredded extra-sharp
  Cheddar cheese

Cut off mushroom stems; discard. Rinse mushrooms; drain on paper towels. Combine mayonnaise, onion, crumbled bacon and seasoned salt in bowl; mix well. Stuff mixture into mushrooms; sprinkle with cheese. Place mushrooms in baking dish. Bake, covered with foil, at 325 degrees for 10 minutes. Remove foil. Bake for 5 minutes longer.

Eola Fienning

OLIVE CHEESE BALLS

Yield: 36 servings

1 1/4 cups flour
8 ounces Cheddar cheese,
  shredded

1/2 cup melted butter
36 stuffed green olives

Combine flour and cheese in bowl; mix well. Add butter; mix well. Shape 1 teaspoon mixture into ball around each green olive. Place 2-inches apart in ungreased baking pan. Bake at 400 degrees for 15 to 20 minutes or until brown. Serve hot.

Katie Robertson

SCALLOPED OYSTERS

Yield: 25 servings

8 ounces butter-flavored
  crackers, crumbled

1/2 cup melted butter
1 quart oysters, drained

Combine cracker crumbs and butter in bowl; mix well. Spray 9x13-inch baking dish with nonstick cooking spray. Sprinkle half the buttered crumbs in baking dish. Place oysters, not touching, on crumbs; top with small sprinkle of crumbs. Bake at 400 degrees for 10 minutes or until light brown. Serve in baking dish with cocktail picks.

Marjory J. Fowler

EXCEPTIONAL PÂTÉ

Yield: 48 servings

1/2 cup chopped onion
3 tablespoons butter
1 small tart apple, peeled,
  chopped
3 tablespoons butter

1 pound chicken livers
2 tablespoons whipping cream
2 tablespoons butter, softened
1/2 teaspoon salt
1/4 teaspoon pepper

Sauté onion in 3 tablespoons butter in skillet until clear. Add apple. Cook until apple is very soft, stirring frequently. Remove to food processor container. Melt 3 tablespoons butter in skillet. Add chicken livers. Cook until brown but still pink inside, stirring frequently. Add chicken livers and cream to food processor container. Process until creamy and smooth; add additional cream if necessary for desired consistency. Stir remaining 2 tablespons butter into pâté. Add salt and pepper; mix well. Chill until serving time. Serve with crackers. May store in refrigerator for up to 2 days or freeze.

Pat A. Lusk

LIVER PÂTÉ MOLD

Yield: 50 servings

1 envelope unflavored gelatin
1/4 cup cold water
1   10-ounce can beef consommé
8 ounces liver sausage roll,
  softened

8 ounces cream cheese,
  softened
1 tablespoon mayonnaise
2 tablespoons finely chopped
  parsley

Soften gelatin in cold water in bowl. Combine with consommé in saucepan. Heat until gelatin is melted, stirring frequently. Spray mold with nonstick cooking spray. Pour 1/4 cup consommé into mold. Chill until firm. Combine liver sausage roll and cream cheese in mixer bowl; mix well. Add mayonnaise and parsley; beat well. Add remaining consommé; beat well. Pour over congealed layer. Chill until firm. Unmold onto serving plate. Serve with crackers.

Carol Lewis

Rum Sausages

Yield: 50 servings

8 packages little smokie
  sausages
1 1-pound package brown
  sugar

1 cup rum
1 small bottle of soy sauce

Brown sausages in skillet, stirring frequently; drain. Combine brown sugar, rum and soy sauce in large saucepan; mix well. Bring to a boil, stirring frequently. Simmer for 5 minutes, stirring occasionally. Add sausages. Simmer for 15 minutes, stirring occasionally. Serve in chafing dish with picks. May be stored in refrigerator for several days or frozen.

Jo Huffmann

Stupendous Sausage Balls

Yield: 120 servings

1½ pounds ground lean pork
1 pound cooked ham, ground
2 cups cracker crumbs
2 eggs, beaten
1 cup milk
Salt or MSG to taste

1 cup packed light brown sugar
1 teaspoon dry mustard
½ cup vinegar
½ cup hot water
¼ cup raisins

Combine pork, ham, cracker crumbs, eggs, milk and salt in bowl; mix well. Shape into walnut-sized balls; place in baking dish. Bake at 350 degrees for 10 minutes. Combine brown sugar, dry mustard, vinegar, hot water and raisins in bowl; mix well. Pour over sausage balls. Bake for 40 minutes longer.

Claudia Ware

MARINATED SHRIMP

Yield: 12 servings

3 pounds medium shrimp,
   boiled, peeled
2¹/₂ to 3 teaspoons celery seed
1 bottle of capers
1 large onion, thinly sliced
20 bay leaves
1¹/₂ to 2 cups oil

1 cup warmed vinegar
2 teaspoons salt
Dash of Tabasco sauce
¹/₄ cup Worcestershire sauce
1 tablespoon Grey Poupon
   mustard

Arrange shrimp in 2 layers in shallow dish. Sprinkle with celery seed, undrained capers, onion slices and bay leaves. Process oil, vinegar, salt, Tabasco sauce, Worcestershire sauce and mustard in blender until smooth and well mixed. Pour over shrimp. Marinate, covered, in refrigerator for 2 days to 1 week. Drain; serve with picks and crackers.

Anne Bradley

TASTY MARINATED SHRIMP

Yield: 12 servings

3 pounds cooked shrimp,
   peeled
3 medium onions, sliced
5 bay leaves
1¹/₂ tablespoons whole cloves
1¹/₄ cups oil

³/₄ cup white vinegar
1¹/₂ teaspoons salt
2¹/₂ teaspoons celery seed
2¹/₂ tablespoons capers with
   liquid
1 large clove of garlic, minced

Layer shrimp and onion slices in shallow dish, crushing bay leaves and whole cloves over each layer. Combine oil, vinegar, salt, celery seed, capers and garlic in bowl; mix well. Pour over shrimp. Marinate, covered, in refrigerator for 24 hours, turning after 12 hours. Drain shrimp; place on bed of ice in red-tip lettuce-lined bowl. Serve with picks. This is always a big hit with our guests, no matter how often we serve it.

Nina B. Suddath

SHRIMP MOUSSE

Yield: 2 servings

1 envelope unflavored gelatin
1/4 cup water
1 10-ounce can tomato soup
8 ounces cream cheese
2 6-ounce cans shrimp

1/2 cup chopped green bell
  pepper
1/2 cup chopped onion
1/2 cup chopped celery
1 cup mayonnaise

Soften gelatin in water. Heat tomato soup and cream cheese in saucepan over low to medium heat until smooth. Add gelatin; mix well. Remove from heat; add shrimp, green pepper, onion, celery and mayonnaise. Pour into bowl. Chill overnight.

Sharon Spears

SPINACH BALLS

Yield: 60 servings

2 10-ounce packages frozen
  chopped spinach, thawed,
  drained
2 cups stuffing mix
2 medium onions, chopped
1/2 cup celery or water chestnuts
6 eggs, beaten

3/4 cup melted butter
1/2 cup grated Parmesan cheese
1 teaspoon garlic salt
1/2 teaspoon pepper
1/2 teaspoon thyme
Dash of Tabasco sauce

Combine spinach, stuffing mix, onion, celery, eggs, butter, cheese, garlic salt, pepper, thyme and Tabasco sauce in bowl; mix well. Chill in refrigerator for 2 hours. Shape into 1 1/2-inch balls; place in baking dish. Bake at 350 degrees for 20 minutes. May be frozen.

Nancy Pruitt

Hors d'Oeuvres Basket—Fill a lovely basket with fresh vegetable and breadstick dippers or with fruit and cookies. Nestle bowls of dip among the goodies.

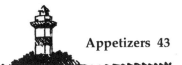
STRAW AND HAY

Yield: 8 servings

4 ounces white linguine
4 ounces green linguine
Salt to taste
1/2 cup butter
8 ounces cooked ham, cut into
  thin strips

3/4 cup cooked peas
1 2-ounce jar sliced
  mushrooms, drained
2 egg yolks, well beaten
1 cup whipping cream
1 cup grated Parmesan cheese

Cook white and green linguine in boiling salted water in heavy 6-quart saucepan until just tender; drain. Add butter, ham, peas and mushrooms; mix well. Beat eggs yolks and cream in bowl with whisk until foamy. Add gradually to linguine mixture, stirring gently. Add half the cheese. Cook over medium heat until mixture is thickened, stirring constantly. Sprinkle with remaining cheese.

Phyllis Modell

DEVILED PECANS

Yield: 4 servings

2 tablespoons margarine
1 tablespoon A-1 sauce

Dash of salt
1 cup pecan halves

Melt margarine with A-1 sauce and salt in saucepan. Stir in whole pecans until coated. Spread on baking pan. Bake at 325 degrees for 20 to 30 minutes or until toasted.

Jan Peeples

OYSTER CRACKERS

Yield: 20 servings

16 ounces oyster crackers
1 cup oil
1 teaspoon garlic powder
1 teaspoon onion powder

1 envelope buttermilk ranch
  salad dressing mix
2 teaspoons dillweed

Place oyster crackers in large bowl. Mix remaining ingredients in small bowl. Pour over crackers; mix well. Store in airtight container in refrigerator.

Marianne Kirkpatrick

ROAST BEEF SANDWICHES AU JUS

Yield: 2 servings

2 individual loaves French
  bread
Mayonnaise
Horseradish or horseradish
  sauce
8 ounces thinly sliced deli
  roast beef

1 can beef consommé or broth
1 tablespoon butter
1 teaspoon lemon juice
2 teaspoons sherry

Slice bread into halves lengthwise. Spread cut sides evenly with mayonnaise and horseradish. Pile roast beef on bottom halves; top with remaining bread. Wrap with plastic wrap. Pour consommeé into 2 ramekins. Add butter and lemon juice to each. Microwave, covered with plastic wrap, on High for 1½ minutes. Stir in sherry. Microwave sandwiches on High for 45 seconds. Serve immediately with sauce for dipping.

Sue West

SICILIAN SANDWICHES

Yield: 2 servings

1 pound thinly sliced top
  sirloin breakfast steaks
2 tablespoons olive oil
¼ cup Italian salad dressing
1 green bell pepper, cut into
  strips

1 onion, sliced
1 large tomato, cut into wedges
2 individual loaves French
  bread
1 cup shredded mozzarella
  cheese

Cut sirloin into strips. Brown for 3 minutes in mixture of olive oil and salad dressing in large skillet. Add green pepper, onion and tomatoes. Slice bread into halves lengthwise. Spoon meat mixture onto bottom halves or onto all halves to serve open-face. Top with cheese. Microwave each sandwich on High for 1¼ minutes or until cheese melts.

Sue West

SLOPPY JOES FOR-A-CROWD

Yield: 40 servings

5 pounds ground beef
5 large onions, chopped
5 envelopes Sloppy Joe mix
5 1-quart bottles of barbecue
   sauce

5 1-quart bottles of water
40 sandwich buns

Brown ground beef with onions in large stockpot, stirring frequently; drain. Sprinkle Sloppy Joe mix over top. Stir in barbecue sauce and water. Simmer for 30 minutes. Spoon into buns.

Kitty McNeely

CHICKEN AND PEPPERS IN PITAS

Yield: 4 servings

2 large whole chicken breasts,
   skinned, boned
3 tablespoons soy sauce
2 teaspoons cornstarch
1 tablespoon sherry
1/8 teaspoon sugar
1/8 teaspoon garlic powder

2 medium green or red bell
   peppers, cut into 1/4-inch
   wide strips
8 ounces mushrooms, sliced
5 tablespoons oil
1/2 cup water
2 pita rounds, cut into halves

Rinse chicken and pat dry; cut each breast into halves. Slice chicken into 1/8-inch slices with knife held almost parallel to cutting surface. Combine with soy sauce, cornstarch, sherry, sugar and garlic powder in bowl; mix well. Sauté green peppers and mushrooms in 2 tablespoons oil in 12-inch skillet over medium-high heat for 2 minutes or until tender-crisp. Remove to bowl with slotted spoon. Add remaining 3 tablespoons oil and chicken mixture. Stir-fry for 5 minutes or until chicken is tender. Add sautéed vegetables and water. Bring to a boil, stirring to deglaze skillet. Serve in pita rounds.

Nancy Stephens

CHICKEN SALAD SANDWICHES

Yield: 8 servings

2 cups chopped cooked
  chicken or turkey
3/4 cup shredded American
  cheese
1 cup chopped celery
1 tablespoon prepared mustard
1 tablespoon lemon juice
1/2 cup mayonnaise

16 slices white bread
3 eggs
1 cup milk
1/2 teaspoon salt
Butter for browning
  sandwiches
1 can cream of mushroom soup
  (optional)

Combine chicken, cheese, celery, mustard, lemon juice and mayonnaise in bowl; mix well. Spread on half the bread; top with remaining bread. Beat eggs with milk and salt in bowl. Dip sandwiches in batter. Brown on both sides in butter in large saucepan or on griddle. Place on warm serving plates. Heat soup in saucepan until bubbly. Spoon over sandwiches.

Pam Welch

CROQUE MONSIEUR

Yield: 8 servings

1 loaf French bread
Sliced ham
1 cup peanut oil or melted
  butter

3/4 cup flour
2 cups milk
3/4 cup shredded Gruyère
  cheese

Cut French bread into 1-inch slices. Arrange in lightly buttered baking pan. Layer ham over bread. Blend oil and flour in saucepan. Cook for several minutes, stirring in milk gradually. Cook until thickened, stirring constantly. Stir in cheese until melted. Pour over bread and ham. Bake at 350 degrees for 15 minutes.

June Ahrendt

CHEESY SANDWICHES

Yield: 32 servings

1 8-ounce jar maraschino
   cherries
16 ounces cream cheese,
   softened

1/4 cup sugar
1 loaf fresh white bread

Drain cherries, reserving 1/4 cup juice. Reserve 5 cherries for garnish. Combine remaining cherries with cream cheese, reserved cherry juice and sugar in blender container; process until smooth. Cut 4 small rounds from each slice of bread. Cut half the rounds into smaller rings. Spread cherry filling on larger rounds. Top with rings. Cut reserved cherries into slivers. Garnish tops of sandwiches.

Nancy Pruitt

CHEESE AND OLIVE SANDWICHES *Yield: 4 to 6 servings*

2 cups shredded sharp
   Cheddar cheese
1/2 cup chopped black olives
2/3 cup mayonnaise
1 tablespoon lemon juice

1 teaspoon chili powder
1 teaspoon garlic powder
12 to 18 slices bread
Softened butter

Combine cheese, olives, mayonnaise, lemon juice, chili powder and garlic powder in bowl; mix until smooth. Spread bread with butter, then with cheese mixture. Stack 3 slices of bread together for each sandwich; place on baking sheet. Bake at 400 degrees for 10 to 15 minutes or until bubbly. Cut diagonally and serve immediately.

Connie D. Herrman

Pimento Cheese Sandwich Spread
Yield: 4¹/2 cups

1 pound sharp Cheddar cheese,
    shredded
¹/2 cup (or more) mayonnaise

1 4-ounce jar chopped
    pimento

Combine cheese, mayonnaise and pimento in bowl; mix well. Store in refrigerator for up to 4 weeks; use as needed for sandwiches. May substitute mayonnaise-type salad dressing for mayonnaise if preferred. May add 1 tablespoon sugar, ¹/2 cup pickle relish, 4 slices crumbled crisp-fried bacon or 2 tablespoons grated onion.

Louise Levzow

Raisin Nut Sandwich Spread
Yield: 4 cups

1 lemon, grated
1 cup sugar
1 egg
1 tablespoon butter

1 cup mayonnaise
1 cup chopped pecans
1 cup raisins

Combine lemon, sugar, egg and butter in saucepan. Cook until thickened, stirring constantly. Add mayonnaise, pecans and raisins; mix well. Store in airtight container in refrigerator; use as needed for sandwiches.

Janie Wilkerson

Strawberry Ribbon Sandwiches
Yield: 4 cups filling

16 ounces cream cheese,
    softened
2 cups strawberry preserves

¹/2 cup chopped nuts
White bread
Whole wheat bread

Combine cream cheese, preserves and nuts in bowl; mix well. Chill in refrigerator overnight. Trim crusts from bread. Stack 1 slice of white bread between 2 slices whole wheat bread for each sandwich, spreading filling between slices. Cut into 4 or 5 slices.

Jo Gross

GINGERED FRUIT TEA SANDWICHES *Yield: 5 cups filling*

24 ounces cream cheese,
  softened
1/2 cup cream
3 tablespoons lemon juice
1 teaspoon seasoned salt

1/4 cup finely chopped candied
  ginger
1 to 1 1/2 cups finely chopped
  dates
1/2 cup finely chopped pecans

Combine cream cheese with cream, lemon juice and seasoned salt in bowl; mix until smooth. Add ginger, dates and pecans; mix well. Cut bread as desired. Spread with fruit mixture. Serve open-face.

Janie Wilkerson

STRAWBERRY BLINTZ SANDWICHES *Yield: 4 servings*

8 slices white bread
1/2 cup creamy peanut butter
1 cup creamed cottage cheese
1 teaspoon grated lemon rind
2 eggs

1/4 cup milk
Margarine for browning
  sandwiches
1 cup strawberry jam or
  preserves

Spread bread evenly with peanut butter. Combine cottage cheese and lemon rind in bowl; mix well. Spread on half the bread. Top with remaining bread. Beat eggs with milk in bowl. Dip sandwiches 1 at a time into egg mixture. Brown sandwiches 1 at a time on both sides in margarine in large skillet over medium-high heat. Melt jam in small saucepan over low heat. Spoon over sandwiches. These are a special breakfast treat.

Barbara DeLoach

Radish Mum—Select round radishes. Trim off root ends. Make several thin crosswise cuts almost to the bottom of radish. Make additional cuts perpendicular to first cuts. Chill in iced water until radish opens.

DOUBLE-DECKER TEA ROUNDS

Yield: 12 servings

3 ounces cream cheese, softened
1 teaspoon sour cream
1 tablespoon grated cucumber
1/4 teaspoon curry powder
1/4 teaspoon salt
16 slices fresh bread

1 1/2 ounces cream cheese, softened
1/2 teaspoon sour cream
1 1/2 teaspoons finely chopped pimento
1/4 teaspoon salt

Combine 3 ounces cream cheese, 1 teaspoon sour cream, cucumber, curry powder and 1/4 teaspoon salt in bowl; mix well. Cut 12 rounds of bread with 2-inch cutter. Spread with cucumber mixture. Combine 1 1/2 ounces cream cheese, 1/2 teaspoon sour cream, pimento and 1/4 teaspoon salt in bowl; mix well. Cut 12 rounds from remaining bread with 1-inch cutter. Spread with pimento mixture. Place on larger rounds. Chill, covered with waxed paper and damp towel, for 30 minutes or longer. Garnish with sprig of watercress, dill, parsley or toasted nut.

TWO-TONE TEA ROUNDS

Use whole wheat bread, Boston brown bread or other dark bread for larger rounds and white bread for smaller rounds.

SWEET-TOOTH TEA ROUNDS

Substitute apricot marmalade for cucumber in spread for larger rounds and apple jelly for pimento in spread for smaller rounds.

CHICKEN OR SEAFOOD TEA ROUNDS

Spread larger rounds with minced chicken salad or finely minced lobster or crab meat blended with mayonnaise. Spread smaller rounds with anchovy butter.

Open-Faced Sandwiches

Use different cookie cutters and breads to make decorative bite-sized shapes for open-faced sandwiches. Filling can be applied with a piping tube and different tips. Just remember to keep them small, dainty and pretty. Try some of the following ideas:

Creamy Orange Sandwiches

Combine equal parts of softened cream cheese and orange marmalade. Spread on small squares of date-nut bread and garnish with slivers of orange rind.

Garden Sandwiches

Spread bread with cream cheese blended with mayonnaise. Top with a tiny slice of salad tomato, green pepper or cucumber. Add fresh dill to the cream cheese for the cucumber sandwiches.

Paté Sandwiches

Spread various patés on triangles of rye or pumpernickel bread.

Shrimp Butter Sandwiches

Spread shrimp butter on a round of cracked wheat bread. Top with a sliver of shrimp.

TEA SANDWICHES

*Tea sandwiches should be dainty, pretty, tasty and easy to eat.
The possibilities are endless. Try some of these suggestions:*

TEA WHEELS

Cut whole wheat bread with 1½-inch cutter. Use doughnut-hole cutter to remove centers of half the circles, making rings. Spread larger rounds with filling of choice; top with rings.

RIBBON SANDWICHES

Trim crusts from white bread and whole wheat bread. Alternate 2 slices white bread and 1 slice whole wheat bread for each sandwich, spreading filling of choice between slices. Wrap tightly in waxed paper and damp towel. Chill for 1 hour or longer. Cut from top to bottom into ½-inch slices.

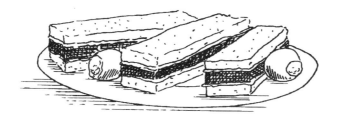

RIBBON SANDWICH FILLINGS

For bleu cheese filling, combine 1/2 cup softened butter, 1 teaspoon prepared mustard, 1 1/2 teaspoons grated onion and 1/4 cup crumbled bleu cheese. For variety, add grated cucumber and substitute chopped watercress for bleu cheese. For fruit fillings, combine butter, cream cheese and grated orange rind or mix apple butter, cream cheese and softened butter.

CHECKERBOARD SANDWICHES

Make 4-layer ribbon sandwiches, pressing layers together; wrap with foil. Chill for several hours. Cut each stack into 1/2-inch slices. Spread cut sides of slices with filling. Restack in 3 layers. Chill, wrapped in foil, for several hours. Cut stacks as desired.

PIMENTO TRIANGLES

Trim crusts from bread and spread with pimento cheese or other filling of choice. Cut diagonally into 4 triangles. Arrange with points up on serving plate.

SANDWICH ROLLS

Trim crusts from loaf of unsliced bread. Slice bread lengthwise as thin as possible. Spread generously with filling of choice. Roll each slice of bread from narrow end as for jelly roll to enclose filling. Arrange seam side down on serving plate. Chill, covered with waxed paper and damp towel, for 1 hour or longer.

SANDWICH RINGS

Freeze sandwich rolls. Cut into 1-inch slices. Place on serving plate. Let stand for 20 minutes to thaw before serving.

Punches
& Beverages

CHAMPAGNE PUNCH
Yield: 20 servings

1½ quarts ginger ale, chilled
1 12-ounce can frozen orange
   juice concentrate, thawed

1 bottle of dry Champagne,
   chilled
Cherry Ice Ring

Combine ginger ale, orange juice concentrate and Champagne in punch bowl; mix gently. Add Cherry Ice Ring. This is a festive but not a strong alcoholic punch.

Lisa Pruitt

CHERRY ICE RING
Yield: 1 ice ring

1 6-ounce can frozen
   lemonade concentrate,
   thawed
2 cups ginger ale

2 cups water
1 4-ounce jar maraschino
   cherries

Combine lemonade concentrate, ginger ale and water in bowl; mix well. Add undrained cherries; mix well. Pour into ring mold. Freeze until firm. Unmold ice ring. Place in punch bowl.

Lisa Pruitt

CHRISTMAS PUNCH
Yield: 50 servings

1 6-ounce can frozen orange
   juice concentrate, thawed
1 6-ounce can frozen
   lemonade concentrate,
   thawed

1 jar cranberry-raspberry juice
1 28-ounce can pineapple juice
4 cups water
2 quarts ginger ale
Cranberry Ice Ring (page 57)

Combine orange juice and lemonade concentrates, cranberry-raspberry juice, pineapple juice, water and ginger ale in punch bowl. Add Cranberry Ice Ring.

Paige Pruitt

CRANBERRY ICE RING

Yield: 1 ice ring

1 16-ounce jar
cranberry-orange relish

4 cups water

Combine relish and water in bowl; mix well. Pour into ring mold. Freeze until firm. Unmold ice ring. Place in punch bowl.

Paige Pruitt

COFFEE PUNCH

Yield: 1 gallon

1 cup sugar
1 cup water
6 tablespoons instant coffee
3 13-ounce cans evaporated
milk, chilled

1 quart vanilla ice cream,
slightly softened
1 28-ounce bottle of club
soda, chilled

Combine sugar, water and instant coffee in small saucepan. Cook over medium heat until sugar and coffee dissolve, stirring constantly. Chill in refrigerator. Pour coffee mixture into punch bowl. Stir in evaporated milk. Add ice cream. Stir until partially melted. Add club soda; stir gently.

Carol M. Wilson

RICH COFFEE PUNCH

Yield: 15 servings

4 cups strong hot coffee
1/2 cup sugar
1 quart vanilla ice cream

1 cup whipping cream,
whipped

Combine coffee and sugar in bowl; stir until dissolved. Let stand until cool. Combine coffee, ice cream and whipped cream in punch bowl; stir gently. This is a southern favorite.

Nancy Pruitt

HOT CRANBERRY TEA

Yield: 1 gallon

4 cups cranberries	12 to 14 whole cloves
4 cups water	4 cups water
3 cups sugar	Juice of 3 oranges and 3 lemons
1 cup red cinnamon candies	8 cups hot water

Cook cranberries in 4 cups water in saucepan until cranberries pop; strain and set aside. Combine sugar, candies, cloves and 4 cups water in saucepan. Cook until sugar and candy dissolve; strain. Add cranberry liquid; keep warm. Pour into punch bowl. Add orange juice, lemon juice and remaining 8 cups water. Garnish with orange and lemon slices. This is a wonderful, bright red holiday drink given to me by friends in England. Serve in white tea cups.

Mrs. George Forbeck

SIMPLE AND EASY PUNCH

Yield: 30 servings

1 large can cranberry juice cocktail	1 large can apple juice
1 large can Hawaiian punch	1 large can pineapple juice
	1 large bottle of 7-Up

Chill all ingredients in refrigerator. Combine cranberry juice cocktail, Hawaiian punch, apple juice and pineapple juice in punch bowl. Add 7-Up just before serving.

Mae Ola Sanders

TEAHOUSE PUNCH

Yield: 6 servings

4 cups hot tea	1/4 cup lemon juice
1/4 teaspoon nutmeg	Artificial sweetener to equal 1/4
8 whole allspice	cup sugar
1/2 cinnamon stick	1/2 teaspoon orange extract
3 whole cloves	

Combine all ingredients in pitcher. Let steep for 1 hour; strain. Serve over ice.

Maryanne McNeal

WASSAIL BOWL

Yield: 2 gallons

1 tablespoon whole cloves
2 cinnamon sticks
2 quarts apple cider
1 quart cranapple juice
1 large can pineapple juice
1   12-ounce can frozen orange juice concentrate
1   6-ounce can frozen lemonade concentrate
2 cups water
2/3 cup packed brown sugar
1/2 cup sugar
1 cup strong tea

Tie cloves and cinnamon sticks in cheesecloth bag. Combine with cider, juices, juice concentrates, water, sugars and tea in large saucepan. Simmer for 15 minutes. Remove spice bag. Pour into punch bowl. Garnish with orange and lemon slices.

Anne Thomas

CAROL'S DAIQUIRI

Yield: 12 servings

1 quart 7-Up
6 ounces Squirt
1   6-ounce can frozen limeade concentrate
2   6-ounce cans frozen lemonade concentrate
12 ounces white rum

Combine 7-Up, Squirt, limeade and lemonade concentrates in blender container. Process until slushy. Stir in rum. May substitute one 10-ounce package frozen strawberries for limeade concentrate.

Carol Welch

Fluted Fruit Wheels—Cut thin strips of rind evenly from stem end to blossom end of lemons, oranges and limes. Cut fruit into slices of desired thickness. To make twists, cut from 1 side to center and twist. For fans, cut fruit into slices, cutting to but not through bottom side; fan out slices.

EGGNOG

Yield: 12 servings

12 eggs, separated
³/₄ cup sugar

³/₄ cup whiskey
¹/₂ gallon vanilla ice cream

Beat egg whites until stiff peaks form. Beat egg yolks in chilled metal bowl until thick. Add sugar gradually, beating until thick and lemon-colored. Add whiskey; mix well. Fold into egg whites gently. Serve over ice cream in parfait glasses. Do not let ingredients become warm. This is an old south Georgia recipe in which moonshine was once used instead of whiskey.

Connie D. Herrman

HOLIDAY EGGNOG

Yield: 6 servings

6 egg whites
1 cup sugar
2 cups whipping cream
6 egg yolks

6 tablespoons blended
  Canadian whiskey
3 tablespoons dark rum
Nutmeg to taste

Beat egg whites until soft peaks form. Add sugar gradually, beating until very stiff peaks form; set aside. Whip cream in chilled bowl until soft peaks form. Beat egg yolks in mixer bowl until lemon-colored. Add whiskey and rum. Beat at low speed for several minutes. Fold whipped cream gently into egg whites. Fold egg yolk mixture gently into egg white mixture. Serve in small cups with spoon. Sprinkle with nutmeg.

Hugh McElvey, Jr.

MIMOSAS

Yield: 12 servings

4 cups orange juice, chilled
1 bottle of Champagne, chilled

12 whole fresh strawberries

Combine orange juice and Champagne in large pitcher. Pour into stemmed Champagne or wine glasses. Garnish each serving with whole strawberry.

Susan Kesler

ORANGE JULIUS
Yield: 4 servings

1   12-ounce can frozen orange
   juice concentrate
2 cups milk

1 to 2 cups water
1/2 to 1 cup sugar
2 teaspoons vanilla extract

Combine all ingredients in blender container. Process until smooth. May substitute 7-Up for water and sugar.

Sandy Weiters

CAFÉ BRÛLOT
Yield: 12 servings

Zest of 1 orange, cut into thin
   strips
Zest of 1 lemon, cut into thin
   strips
4 cinnamon sticks

1 tablespoon whole cloves
24 sugar cubes
3/4 cup Cognac
6 cups hot fresh coffee

Combine orange and lemon zest, cinnamon and cloves in chafing dish. Add sugar cubes. Pour Cognac over sugar cubes; ignite. Let flames die down. Add coffee gradually. Remove cloves. Ladle into demitasse cups.

Nancy Pruitt

CAFÉ SUISSE MOCHA MIX
Yield: 14 tablespoons mix

1/3 cup sugar
1/4 cup powdered coffee
   creamer

1/4 cup instant coffee
2 tablespoons instant cocoa

Combine sugar, creamer, coffee powder and cocoa in blender container. Process until finely powdered. Store in airtight container. Add 1 tablespoon mix to 6 ounces boiling water in cup for each serving. May use decaffeinated coffee or add dried mint to taste.

Susan Coleman

CAROLINA ICED COFFEE

Yield: 4 servings

4 cups strong cold coffee
1/2 cup half and half
Dash of cinnamon

Sugar to taste
1 cup whipped cream

Combine coffee, half and half, cinnamon and sugar in pitcher. Pour into tall glasses over ice. Garnish with whipped cream.

Mary Inglis

IRISH COFFEE

Yield: 1 serving

2/3 cup hot coffee
1/3 cup Irish whiskey

Whipped cream

Combine coffee and whiskey in Irish coffee cup. Top with whipped cream; do not stir. Sip coffee through cream.

Nancy Pruitt

ITALIAN COFFEE

Yield: 1 serving

1/2 cup hot coffee
1/2 cup hot milk

Cinnamon to taste

Combine coffee and milk in coffee cup. Sprinkle with cinnamon.

Nancy Pruitt

LATIN AMERICAN COFFEE

Yield: 1 serving

1/2 cup hot coffee
1/2 cup hot chocolate

1 cinnamon stick

Combine coffee and hot chocolate in mug. Stir with cinnamon stick.

Nancy Pruitt

MEXICAN COFFEE

Yield: 1 serving

½ cup hot coffee
¼ cup Kahlua

¼ cup rum
Whipped cream

Combine coffee, Kahlua and rum in mug. Top with whipped cream.

Nancy Pruitt

PECAN COFFEE

Yield: 12 servings

1½ cups freshly ground coffee
⅔ cup chopped pecans
15 cups cold water

1 cup praline-flavored liqueur
Half and half to taste
Sugar to taste

Combine coffee and pecans in percolator basket. Add water. Perk using manufacturer's directions. Remove coffee grounds. Stir in liqueur. Serve with half and half and sugar.

Kitty McNeely

DEBUTANTE'S TEA

Yield: 8 cups

4 lemons, thinly sliced
1½ cups sugar

2 dessert spoons loose tea
8 cups boiling water

Place lemons, sugar and tea in deep bowl. Add boiling water; mix well. Steep for 2 hours; strain. Serve hot or cold. This is my grandmother's recipe for debutante tea. It is perfect for summer or winter tea parties, served hot or cold.

Caroline G. McGee

Grape Ice Cubes—Make ice cubes for party beverages using white grape juice and freeze a green grape in each.

FRIENDSHIP TEA MIX

Yield: 12 cups mix

1   18-ounce jar Tang
1 cup instant tea
2 tablespoons cinnamon

1   16-ounce package lemonade
mix
2^1/$_2$ cups sugar

Combine Tang, tea, cinnamon, lemonade mix and sugar in airtight container. Add 2 spoonfuls mix to 1 cup hot water for each serving.

Laura Fifer

INSTANT RUSSIAN TEA MIX

Yield: 4 cups mix

2 cups Tang
^{1}/$_2$ cup sugar
^{1}/$_2$ cup instant tea
1 teaspoon cinnamon

^{1}/$_2$ teaspoon ground cloves
1 envelope instant lemonade
mix

Combine all ingredients in airtight container. Add 2 teaspoons mix to 1 cup boiling water for each serving. Grandmother used to send tins of this to the girls at college, and they loved it.

Paige Pruitt

RUSSIAN TEA

Yield: 6 quarts

4 family-sized tea bags
4 quarts boiling water
1   6-ounce can frozen orange
   juice concentrate
1   6-ounce can frozen
   lemonade concentrate

3 cups sugar
12 whole cloves
2 quarts water

Steep tea in 4 quarts boiling water for 10 to 15 minutes; remove tea bags. Add concentrates, sugar and cloves. Simmer until sugar dissolves; strain. Add remaining 2 quarts water. Heat to serving temperature.

Louise Levzow

SANGRIA TEA
Yield: 3 quarts

1 wine bottle of water
3/4 cup sugar
1 orange, sliced
1 lemon, sliced
1 lime, sliced

2 family-sized tea bags
1 bottle of red wine
1   10-ounce package frozen
    strawberries, puréed
1 quart lemon-lime soda

Bring water and sugar to a boil in saucepan. Add sliced fruit. Cook until sugar dissolves, stirring frequently. Add tea bags; remove from heat. Steep for 3 to 4 minutes; remove tea bags. Let stand until cool. Add wine and puréed strawberries. Chill in pitcher in refrigerator. Add lemon-lime soda just before serving.

Kitty McNeely

SUMMERTIME TEA
Yield: 31 cups

12 tea bags
8 cups boiling water
1   6-ounce can frozen limeade
    concentrate
1   6-ounce can frozen orange
    juice concentrate

2   6-ounce cans frozen
    lemonade concentrate
20 cups water
1 cup sugar

Steep tea in boiling water for 15 minutes; remove tea bags. Add limeade, orange juice and lemonade concentrates; mix well. Add water and sugar. Stir until sugar dissolves. Serve cold.

Louise Baughman

HOT COCOA MIX
Yield: 3 3/4 cups mix

2 cups non-fat dry milk
3/4 cup sugar
1/2 cup instant cocoa

1/2 cup powdered coffee
    creamer
Pinch of salt

Combine all ingredients in airtight container. Combine 1/4 cup mix with 3/4 cup boiling water in mug for each serving.

Jane Kelly

CINNAMON HOT CHOCOLATE MIX   *Yield: 3 cups mix*

1 cup chocolate chips
1/2 cup sugar
1/3 cup water

1/4 teaspoon cinnamon
1 cup whipping cream
Hot milk

Combine chocolate chips, sugar, water and cinnamon in saucepan. Cook over low heat until chocolate melts, stirring constantly. Remove from heat. Let stand until cool. Whip cream until soft peaks form. Fold into chocolate mixture. Store, covered, in refrigerator for several days or drop by heaping tablespoonfuls onto waxed paper-lined tray and freeze. Store frozen chocolate in freezer bag. Combine 1 heaping tablespoon chocolate mixture with 3/4 cup hot milk in mug for each serving. May add 1 teaspoon instant coffee to each serving. using either 3/4 cup hot milk or hot water.

Ellen Garland

INSTANT HOT CHOCOLATE MIX   *Yield: 40 servings*

1 8-quart package non-fat dry milk
1 16-ounce package Nestle's Quick

2 cups confectioners' sugar
1 6-ounce jar powdered coffee creamer
Marshmallows

Combine all ingredients in airtight container. Combine 1/3 cup mix and 3/4 cup boiling water in mug for each serving. Top with marshmallows.

Lynn Clanton

Soups & Stews

POLISH BORSCHT

Yield: 6 to 8 servings

1½ pounds boneless beef
   chuck, cut into 1-inch pieces
3 cups water
3 beef bouillon cubes
2 medium onions, chopped
2 stalks celery, chopped

1 teaspoon salt
¼ teaspoon pepper
1 16-ounce can shoestring beets
Boiled potatoes
Sour cream
Chopped chives

Combine first 7 ingredients in saucepan. Simmer, covered, for 2 hours or until beef is tender. Add undrained beets. Heat to serving temperature. Serve over potatoes. Top with sour cream and chives.

Frances Caldwell

BROCCOLI CHOWDER

Yield: 6 to 8 servings

2 pounds fresh broccoli
2 14-ounce cans chicken broth
3 cups milk
1 cup chopped cooked ham
2 teaspoons salt

¼ teaspoon pepper
1 cup half and half
2 cups shredded Swiss cheese
¼ cup butter

Combine broccoli with 1 can chicken broth in heavy saucepan. Cook, covered, until broccoli is tender-crisp. Remove and chop coarsely. Add remaining can chicken broth to saucepan. Stir in milk, ham and seasonings. Bring to a boil over medium heat, stirring occasionally. Stir in broccoli and remaining ingredients. Heat just to serving temperature.

Ronelle Plocher

CHILLED BROCCOLI SOUP

Yield: 4 to 6 servings

1 package frozen chopped
   broccoli, cooked
2 cans cream of potato soup

2 soup cans milk
1 cup sour cream
2 teaspoons chopped chives

Combine broccoli with soup and milk in saucepan. Cook until heated through. Process with sour cream in small amounts in food precessor until smooth. Chill until serving time. Top servings with chives.

Helen W. Malcolm

CHICKEN AND CORN SOUP

Yield: 6 servings

1 4-pound chicken, cut up
1 medium onion, sliced
4 quarts water
2 cups fresh or frozen corn
1 cup frozen green peas

1 cup uncooked noodles
2 hard-boiled eggs, chopped
2 teaspoons chopped parsley
Salt and pepper to taste

Cook chicken with onion in water in large saucepan until tender. Remove chicken and chop into bite-sized pieces, discarding skin and bones. Return chicken to saucepan. Bring to a boil. Add corn, peas and noodles. Cook for 15 minutes. Add eggs, parsley, salt and pepper. Cook until heated through.

Maggie Bry

QUICK CORN CHOWDER

Yield: 8 servings

2/3 cup chopped onion
1/2 cup chopped green bell
   pepper
1/4 cup margarine
2 cups chicken stock
2 cans cream of chicken soup
2 16-ounce cans white cream-
   style corn

1 cup chopped cooked chicken
2 cups cooked rice
2 potatoes, chopped
5 cups milk
1/4 cup chopped fresh parsley
1/4 teaspoon paprika
1/4 teaspoon salt
Pepper to taste

Sauté onion and green pepper in margarine in large saucepan until onion is golden brown. Add mixture of chicken stock and soup; mix well. Bring to a simmer, stirring constantly. Add corn, chicken, rice, potatoes, milk, parsley and paprika; mix well. Simmer until potatoes are tender, stirring frequently. Stir in salt and pepper.

Janie Wilkerson

CRAB BISQUE
Yield: 4 to 6 servings

4 cups milk
2 cups whipping cream
1 pound fresh or frozen lump
  crab meat
1 medium onion, chopped

2 tablespoons flour
¼ cup melted butter
Salt and cayenne pepper to
  taste

Bring milk and cream to a rolling boil in saucepan. Add crab meat and onion, taking care not to break up crab meat. Stir in mixture of flour and butter gradually. Stir in salt and cayenne pepper. Simmer for 1 hour, stirring occasionally.

Sandy Wieters

SHE-CRAB SOUP
Yield: 20 servings

1 teaspoon fennel seed
1 bay leaf
1 teaspoon peppercorns
1 onion, chopped
2 stalks celery, chopped
Bacon drippings
6 ounces Harvey's Bristol
  Cream
1 pound backfin crab meat

1 pound crab claw meat
8 ounces blue crab roe
8 cups milk
6 cups heavy cream
Mace, salt and white pepper to
  taste
1 cup flour
½ cup melted butter

Tie fennel seed, bay leaf and peppercorns in cheesecloth bag. Sauté onion and celery in bacon drippings in saucepan. Add Harvey's Bristol Cream and crab meat, stirring to deglaze. Stir in roe, milk, cream, mace, salt, white pepper and herbs in cheesecloth bag. Bring to a simmer. Blend flour into butter in skillet. Cook until browned as desired. Stir into soup. Cook until thickened, stirring constantly. Adjust seasonings; remove herb bag. Ladle into serving bowls. This recipe is from the chefs at the Carolina Cafe at the Westin Resort on Hilton Head.

Michael J. Sigler and Craig Priebe

CRAB SOUP
Yield: 4 servings

1 can cream of celery soup
1 can cream of mushroom soup
1 can cream of asparagus soup
1 soup can half and half

1 package fresh or frozen crab
   meat
1 or 2 tablespoons sherry

Combine soups and half and half in saucepan; mix well. Stir in crab meat. Cook just until heated through; do not boil. Stir in sherry. Ladle into serving bowls. This is an easy soup to make from ingredients in the pantry.

Louise S. Hunter

CARL'S CHOWDER
Yield: 10 to 12 servings

3 medium cloves of garlic,
   crushed
2 ounces olive oil
2 ounces onion, finely chopped
3 ounces celery, finely chopped
1   16-ounce can stewed
   tomatoes, chopped
1   6-ounce can tomato paste

6 cups clamato juice
6 cups water
1½ pounds boneless sea trout
   or flounder
Oregano, basil and thyme to
   taste
Salt to taste

Sauté garlic in olive oil in large saucepan until golden brown. Add onion and celery. Sauté until translucent. Add tomatoes, tomato paste, clamato juice, water, fish and herbs. Cook over high heat for 15 minutes. Add salt; reduce heat. Simmer, covered, for 30 minutes. Whisk to break up larger fish pieces. Ladle into serving bowls. Flavor improves overnight.

Carl Gustafson

LOW-CALORIE GAZPACHO

Yield: 6 to 8 servings

2 cups chopped peeled
  cucumbers
1¹/₄ cups chopped green bell
  peppers
1¹/₄ cups chopped onions
1¹/₄ cups chopped peeled
  tomatoes

2 16-ounce cans tomato juice
2 tablespoons chopped garlic
2 tablespoons fresh lemon juice
¹/₃ cup fancy vinegar
¹/₄ teaspoon Tabasco sauce
¹/₂ teaspoon paprika
Chopped chives or onion

Combine cucumbers, green peppers, 1¹/₄ cups onions and tomatoes in large bowl. Add tomato juice, garlic, lemon juice, vinegar, Tabasco sauce and paprika; mix well. Chill overnight or longer. Sprinkle servings with chopped chives or onion. Serve with additional dishes of chopped onion, cucumber and tomato if desired. May chop vegetables coarsely by hand or in food processor.

Abby Dupps

MOM'S ITALIAN SOUP

Yield: 6 to 8 servings

1 stewing chicken
1 pound lean ground beef
2 tablespoons parsley flakes
1 egg
1 teaspoon salt
Bread crumbs
1¹/₂ cups chopped celery

1¹/₂ cups chopped carrots
1 can tomatoes, puréed
1 can chick-peas, drained
3 or 4 potatoes, chopped
3 leaves escarole
1 12-ounce package egg
  noodles

Rinse chicken inside and out. Combine with cold water to cover in saucepan. Bring to a boil; reduce heat. Simmer for 1 hour. Remove chicken; chop into bite-sized pieces, discarding skin and bones. Return chopped chicken to saucepan. Combine ground beef, parsley flakes, egg and salt in bowl. Add enough bread crumbs to bind mixture; mix well. Shape into small meatballs. Add to stock and chicken in saucepan. Add celery, carrots, tomatoes, chick-peas and potatoes. Cook for 1 hour. Steam escarole in a small amount of water in saucepan for 2 to 3 minutes. Add to soup. Stir in noodles. Cook just until noodles are tender. Serve with Italian bread and salad. This recipe has been prepared by my husband's family for generations.

Laurel Clark Rinaldi

CHILLED MUSHROOM VELVET SOUP   *Yield: 4 servings*

8 to 16 ounces mushrooms,
  sliced
1 medium onion, chopped
1/4 cup butter

1 tablespoon (heaping) flour
1 3/4 cups beef broth
1 cup sour cream
1 cup chopped fresh parsley

Sauté mushrooms and onion in butter in saucepan. Stir in flour; remove from heat. Stir in broth gradually. Bring to a boil, stirring constantly. Cool slightly. Combine half the mixture with half the sour cream in blender; process until smooth. Add half the parsley; process until smooth. Repeat process. Chill until serving time.

Helen W. Malcolm

MEXICAN OATMEAL SOUP   *Yield: 6 servings*

1 1/2 cups oats
1 large onion, chopped
3 cloves of garlic, crushed
3 large tomatoes, chopped

1/2 cup butter
6 cups chicken broth
1/2 teaspoon salt

Broil oats on baking sheet until light brown. Sauté onion, garlic and tomatoes in butter in skillet. Add chicken broth and salt. Cook until heated through. Add oats. Cook for 6 minutes. Serve immediately.

Beverly and Caneel Cotton

BLACK OLIVE SOUP   *Yield: 6 to 8 servings*

3 cups chicken stock
1 cup pitted black olives
1 green onion, chopped
1 clove of garlic, chopped
2 eggs

2 teaspoons Worcestershire
  sauce
2 tablespoons chopped parsley
1 cup half and half

Combine first 7 ingredients in blender container. Process for 1 minute. Pour into saucepan. Cook for 2 to 3 minutes or until heated through. Stir in half and half. Serve hot or chilled.

Carolyn Nelson

MOTHER'S PEA SOUP

Yield: 6 servings

1 medium onion, chopped
2 tablespoons butter
1 pound fresh or frozen peas
6 cups water
2 beef bouillon cubes
Salt to taste

1/4 cup chopped parsley
  (optional)
1 egg
2 tablespoons water
1/4 cup flour

Sauté onion in butter in saucepan. Add peas. Simmer for 3 to 4 minutes, stirring occasionally. Add 6 cups water and bouillon cubes. Bring just to the simmering point. Stir in salt and parsley. Beat egg with 2 tablespoons water in small bowl. Beat in flour and salt. Add to soup gradually, stirring as egg cooks. Simmer for 3 to 5 minutes, stirring frequently.

Reni Kuhn

PEANUT SOUP

Yield: 8 servings

1 cup thinly sliced celery
1/2 cup finely chopped onion
1/4 cup butter
2 tablespoons flour
4 14-ounce cans chicken broth

1 1/3 cups creamy peanut butter
1 cup light cream
1/2 teaspoon salt
1/8 teaspoon white pepper
Chopped salted peanuts

Sauté celery and onion in butter in large saucepan over low heat for 10 minutes or until tender but not brown; remove from heat. Stir in flour. Cook until flour is brown. Add chicken broth gradually, stirring constantly. Bring to a boil, stirring constantly. Whisk in peanut butter. Simmer, covered, for 15 minutes. Stir in cream, salt and white pepper. Heat just to serving temperature. Ladle into serving bowls. Top with salted peanuts. This is a classic recipe from south Georgia, where people believe anything can be made with peanuts.

Connie D. Herrman

VEGETABLE SOUP

Yield: 10 servings

1 pound ground beef
1 large can tomatoes
1 can tomato soup
3 soup cans water
1/2 cup butter
Catsup to taste

5 or 6 potatoes, chopped
2 onions, chopped
6 or 7 carrots, sliced
1 can corn, drained
1 can peas, drained
1 bay leaf

Brown ground beef in large saucepan, stirring until crumbly; drain. Add tomatoes, soup, water, butter, catsup, potatoes, onions, carrots, corn, peas and bay leaf. Simmer, covered, for 8 hours or longer. Remove bay leaf; ladle into serving bowls. May vary ingredients to suit individual tastes.

Margie Smith

SHIN BONE VEGETABLE SOUP

Yield: 12 servings

2 to 3 pounds meaty shin bones
5 Italian tomatoes, chopped
2 large onions, chopped
2 stalks celery, chopped
2 carrots, sliced

Salt and pepper to taste
1 pound Portuguese sausage
1 head cabbage, chopped
2 cups uncooked rice

Wash shin bones. Place in saucepan with water to fill halfway. Add tomatoes, onions, celery, carrots, salt and pepper. Simmer, covered, for 1 hour. Add sausage. Simmer for 45 minutes. Add cabbage. Simmer for 45 to 55 minutes or until cabbage is tender. Stir in rice. Simmer for 15 minutes or until rice is tender. Flavor of soup improves with reheating.

Stephen C. DeRiggs

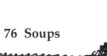

WATERCRESS SOUP
Yield: 6 servings

2 cups chopped onions
  (optional)
1 clove of garlic, minced
1/4 cup butter
4 cups sliced new potatoes
3/4 cup water
1 tablespoon salt

1/4 teaspoon pepper
1 bunch watercress, coarsely
  chopped
11/2 cups milk
11/2 cups water
2 egg yolks
1/2 cup light cream

Sauté onions and garlic in butter in large saucepan. Add potatoes, 3/4 cup water, salt and pepper. Bring to a boil; reduce heat. Simmer until potatoes are tender-crisp. Add watercress, milk and 11/2 cups water. Cook for 15 minutes. Purée in blender. Return to saucepan. Stir in mixture of egg yolks and cream. Cook until thickened to desired consistency, stirring constantly. Ladle into soup bowls.

Ellen Devenere

WATERCRESS-MEATBALL SOUP
Yield: 16 servings

4 ounces transparent noodles
1 pound finely ground pork
1 tablespoon finely chopped
  fresh ginger
2 scallions, finely chopped
8 to 10 water chestnuts, finely
  chopped
2 teaspoons cornstarch

11/2 teaspoons soy sauce
1 teaspoon salt
1/4 teaspoon white pepper
10 cups chicken broth
1 bunch parsley, chopped
2 bunches watercress, chopped
1/8 teaspoon MSG

Soak noodles in hot water to cover in bowl for 30 minutes or until softened. Combine ground pork, ginger, scallions, water chestnuts, cornstarch, soy sauce, salt and white pepper in bowl; mix well. Shape into small balls. Cook in water in saucepan until meatballs float to top. Remove with slotted spoon; drain. Bring chicken broth to a boil in saucepan over low heat. Add meatballs, parsley, watercress and MSG. Cook just until watercress is tender but still green. Serve immediately.

Jill Bradley

Beef Continential

Yield: 6 servings

3 pounds beef, cubed
3/4 cup flour
1/2 cup oil
1 1/2 cups red wine
1 cup sliced mushrooms

Salt and pepper to taste
3 cloves of garlic, minced
2 onions, sliced
3 cups canned beef gravy

Coat beef with flour. Brown in oil in skillet. Add remaining ingredients. Place in baking dish. Bake, uncovered, at 350 degrees for 2 hours, stirring occasionally. Refrigerate overnight. Bake at 350 degrees for 30 minutes.

Lucyle Merriwether

Easy Beef Burgundy

Yield: 8 servings

4 pounds beef sirloin, cut into
   cubes
1 can tomato soup

3 cups Burgundy
4 envelopes dry onion soup mix
3 cans sliced mushrooms

Combine beef, soup, wine and soup mix in deep baking dish; mix well. Bake, covered, at 350 degrees for 2 hours and 45 minutes, stirring occasionally. Add mushrooms. Cook for 15 minutes longer. Serve over noodles or rice.

Ellen Garland

Easy Tender Beef Stew

Yield: 6 servings

3 pounds (about) beef stew
   meat
Oil for browning
1 cup red wine

1 can onion soup
1 can golden mushroom soup
Fresh mushrooms to taste

Brown stew beef on all sides in oil in skillet; drain. Place beef in baking dish. Add wine and soups to skillet, stirring to deglaze. Pour over beef. Add mushrooms. Bake, covered, at 275 degrees for several hours or until done to taste. Serve over rice or noodles.

Mrs. Peter Mortensen

BOEUF BOURGUIGNON

Yield: 6 to 8 servings

3 pounds beef round, cut into
  2-inch cubes
1¹/₂ cups Burgundy
2 tablespoons brandy
2 tablespoons oil
1 teaspoon salt
¹/₂ teaspoon pepper
¹/₂ teaspoon thyme
1 sprig of parsley
1 bay leaf

5 tablespoons butter
2 cloves of garlic, crushed
2 large onions, chopped
1 carrot, chopped
4 tablespoons flour
1 tablespoon tomato paste
1 cup beef broth
1 tablespoon butter
1¹/₂ cups tiny white onions
12 ounces mushroom caps

Marinate beef in mixture of next 8 ingredients in bowl for 2 hours, turning occasionally. Drain, reserving marinade; remove parsley and bay leaf. Pat meat dry. Heat 3 tablespoons butter in heavy skillet. Brown beef quickly on all sides. Remove to casserole. Add 2 tablespoons butter to skillet; stir until melted. Add garlic, chopped onions and carrot. Sauté until lightly browned. Blend in flour and tomato paste. Add reserved marinade and broth. Cook until mixture comes to a boil, stirring constantly. Pour over beef. Bake, covered, at 350 degrees for 2 hours. Let stand until cool. Wrap casserole and freeze. Heat 1 tablespoon butter in skillet. Add tiny onions. Sauté until golden; remove. Add mushroom caps. Sauté for 2 minutes. Place onions and mushrooms in freezer container and freeze. Heat casserole, uncovered, in preheated 350-degree oven for 1 hour. Place onions and mushrooms on top. Bake for 30 minutes longer. Serve with potatoes au gratin.

Anne Bell

Green Onion Frills—Cut off root end and most of stem portion of green onions. Make narrow lengthwise cuts at both ends with sharp knife to produce a fringe. Chill in iced water until ends curl.

THREE-DOG CHILI

Yield: 8 servings

2 pounds lean beef
1 pound smoked Texas Polish
  sausage
Oil for browning
2 cases beer
1 cup chopped onion
1 tablespoon chili powder

¹/₄ teaspoon each salt and
  pepper
¹/₃ cup masa flour
1 cup chopped jalapeño
  peppers or to taste
1 tablespoon cayenne pepper
  or to taste

Cut beef into small cubes; cut sausage into ¹/₈-inch slices. Brown beef on all sides in oil in large cast-iron skillet or stew pot. Add 1 beer, sausage, onion, chili powder, salt and pepper; mix well. Stir in masa flour. Cook for 2 hours, adjusting masa flour or beer as needed for desired consistency. Test consistency by ladling about 3 ounces into dog's bowl. If dog walks away, throw chili away. If dog falls over, throw dog and chili away. If dog likes chili, add enough jalapeño peppers and cayenne pepper to make ears ring, eyes tear and nose bleed. Drink remaining beer as needed. It helps to have a Mexican grandmother to provide the masa flour; otherwise, you can find it at your local market. The name of this chili was applied when the first batch did in 3 dogs.

Jim Robinson

GANG CHILI

Yield: 40 servings

10 pounds ground chuck
2 9-ounce packages Daigo
  taco seasoning
4 #10 cans tomato sauce

2 #10 cans pinto beans or red
  beans
Shredded cheese

Brown ground chuck in large saucepan, stirring until crumbly; drain. Stir in taco seasoning and tomato sauce. Drain and rinse beans. Add to chili. Simmer for 2 hours, stirring occasionally. Sprinkle servings with cheese.

Janice Horton

SOUTHERN CHILI
Yield: 30 to 50 servings

24 ounces dried red kidney beans
Salt to taste
1 pound lean bacon
3 yellow onions, chopped
3 white onions, chopped
2 to 3 pounds ground chuck
4 cloves of garlic, minced
64 ounces whole tomatoes
1   10-ounce can Ro-Tel
   tomatoes with green chilies
1   29-ounce can tomato sauce
1 tomato sauce can water
3 bay leaves
Tony Chachere's Creole
   seasoning
1 cup water
2 packages chili seasoning mix
1½ to 2 pounds Kielbasa
   sausage, sliced

Soak beans in salted water to cover in saucepan for 2 hours. Bring to a boil; turn off heat. Let stand for several hours. Fry bacon in very large saucepan until crisp. Remove bacon with slotted spoon. Add onions to drippings in saucepan. Sauté until brown. Add ground chuck. Cook until medium brown, stirring frequently; drain. Add next 6 ingredients. Bring to a boil; reduce heat. Stir in beans, Tony Chachere's seasoning, 1 cup water and 1 package chili seasoning mix. Cook for 1 hour. Stir in sausage and crumbled bacon. Simmer for several minutes, skimming surface of chili. Stir in remaining package chili mix. Serve with Tabasco sauce, cheese, sour cream, chopped onion and corn bread muffins.

E. G. Robinson, III

FISH STEW
Yield: 8 servings

2 onions, chopped
2 green bell peppers, chopped
5 cloves of garlic, pressed or
   chopped
2 tablespoons olive oil
2 packages frozen fish filets,
   thawed
2 cans tomato soup
1 soup can water
1 can Manhattan clam chowder
2 bay leaves
2 teaspoons cloves
Sugar, salt and pepper to taste
1 pound uncooked shrimp

Sauté onions, green peppers and garlic in olive oil in saucepan. Stir in next 9 ingredients. Simmer for 15 minutes. Stir in shrimp. Simmer for 10 minutes longer. Remove bay leaves; adjust seasonings.

Mrs. Stannard H. McKibben

WILLISTON CATFISH STEW

Yield: 16 servings

5 pounds Irish potatoes	12 hard-boiled eggs, chopped
5 pounds onions	Salt and pepper to taste
5 pounds (or more) catfish	1 can evaporated milk
1 pound fatback, thinly sliced	½ cup butter or margarine

Cut potatoes into 1-inch pieces. Cut onions into 1-inch slices. Cook catfish in water to cover in saucepan until tender; drain, reserving broth. Break catfish into bite-sized pieces, discarding bones. Fry fatback in large saucepan until crisp; remove meat for another use, reserving drippings. Add reserved broth from cooking fish to drippings. Add potatoes and onions. Cook until potatoes are tender. Add eggs, fish, salt and pepper. Bring to the simmering point, adding water as needed for desired consistency. Stir in evaporated milk; remove from heat. Stir in butter. Serve with longhorn cheese, light bread and sweet pickles.

Doc Gilchrist

UNCLE REMUS' FISH STEW

Yield: 12 servings

4 pounds catfish or other fish	2 green bell peppers, chopped
Cornmeal	3 pounds potatoes, peeled,
Salt and pepper to taste	chopped
Oil for deep frying	3 cans stewed tomatoes
2 medium onions, chopped	Tabasco sauce to taste
1 stalk celery, chopped	

Coat fish with mixture of cornmeal, salt and pepper. Deep-fry in hot oil. Remove fish and drain saucepan, reserving a small amount of drippings. Add onions, celery and green peppers to drippings in saucepan. Cook for 5 minutes. Shred fish into saucepan. Cook for 10 minutes, stirring frequently. Add potatoes and tomatoes. Simmer for 30 minutes, stirring frequently. Season with Tabasco sauce and salt. Serve over rice if desired.

Sonny Graham

SHRIMP STEW

Yield: 10 servings

3 tablespoons flour
5 slices streak of lean bacon
3 medium onions, chopped
2¹/₂ cups water
2 tablespoons white wine

1¹/₂ teaspoons Worcestershire
  sauce
Salt and pepper to taste
2 cups small creek shrimp

Sprinkle flour in small skillet or flat pan. Shake over medium heat or place in oven until brown. Fry bacon in saucepan. Stir in onions and browned flour. Stir in water, wine, Worcestershire sauce, salt and pepper. Simmer until thickened, stirring occasionally. Add shrimp and additional water if needed for desired consistency. Cook until shrimp are done to taste. Serve on grits.

John C. West

SHRIMP CREOLE

Yield: 8 servings

1 cup chopped green bell
  pepper
2 cups chopped onions
2 cups chopped celery
4 cloves of garlic, chopped
¹/₄ cup oil

1 6-ounce can tomato paste
1 6-ounce can water
2 large cans tomatoes
1 bay leaf
2¹/₂ pounds peeled fresh shrimp

Sauté green pepper, onions, celery and garlic in oil in stockpot. Add tomato paste and water. Simmer for 5 minutes. Add tomatoes and bay leaf. Simmer for 5 hours. Let stand until cool. Chill in refrigerator. Reheat over low heat. Add shrimp. Cook for 15 minutes or until shrimp turn pink. Remove bay leaf.

Mary Ball

Salads
& Dressings

ANGEL SALAD

Yield: 12 servings

1 16-ounce can pineapple
chunks, drained
1 16-ounce can white sweet
cherries, drained
2 11-ounce cans mandarin
oranges, drained
4 ounces miniature
marshmallows

2 eggs, beaten
3 tablespoons vinegar
3 tablespoons sugar
1 cup whipping cream,
whipped

Combine pineapple, cherries, mandarin oranges and marshmallows in bowl; mix well. Chill in refrigerator. Combine eggs, vinegar and sugar in saucepan. Simmer until thickened, stirring constantly. Add to fruit; mix well. Fold in whipped cream. Chill until serving time. Spoon onto lettuce-lined salad plates.

Jill Trexler

CRAN-ORANGE WREATH SALAD

Yield: 4 servings

1 8-ounce can crushed
pineapple
1/4 cup water
1 3-ounce package raspberry
gelatin

1 jar cranberry-orange relish
1 cup pecan halves
1 cup sliced celery
3 ounces cream cheese, softened
Parsley sprigs

Drain pineapple, reserving juice in saucepan. Add water to juice. Bring to a boil. Dissolve raspberry gelatin in juice mixture. Cool in refrigerator until partially congealed. Stir in pineapple, cranberry-orange relish, pecans and celery; mix well. Pour into individual round molds. Chill until set. Unmold onto salad plates. Decorate as wreaths using cream cheese pressed through pastry tube. Garnish with parsley.

Alanna Stupinsky

EXOTIC SALAD

Yield: 4 servings

4 large naval oranges
2 or 3 cloves of garlic, minced

2 teaspoons oregano
1/2 cup virgin olive oil

Peel oranges; cut into slices crosswise, reserving juice. Combine orange juice, garlic, oregano and olive oil in bowl; mix well. Arrange orange slices in shallow dish; drizzle with orange juice mixture. Marinate in refrigerator for 4 to 5 hours. Arrange on salad plates.

Marguerite Miletic

FRESH FRUIT SALAD

Yield: 4 servings

1 cup sliced strawberries
1 cup sliced bananas
1 cup blueberries
1 cup cantaloupe balls

1 cup raspberries
1 tablespoon brown sugar
1 tablespoon Amaretto

Combine strawberries, bananas, blueberries, cantaloupe and rasp-berries in shallow bowl. Sprinkle with brown sugar; drizzle with Amaretto. Let stand at room temperature for 1 hour for juices to form and to blend flavors. Chill until serving time. Spoon onto salad plates. May be served at room temperature. To serve as a dessert, reduce brown sugar to 1 teaspoon, increase Amaretto to 2 table-spoons and add 1 cup miniature marshmallows. May use any combination of fruit and add others such as peaches, oranges, red or green grapes and honeydew melon.

Sue West

COCONUT FRUIT SALAD

Yield: 8 servings

1 cup drained mandarin orange
  slices
1 cup miniature marshmallows
1 cup coconut
1 8-ounce can crushed
  pineapple, well drained

1 16-ounce can fruit cocktail,
  well drained
1/2 cup chopped maraschino
  cherries
1 cup sour cream
1/2 cup chopped pecans

Combine mandarin orange slices, marshmallows, coconut, pineapple, fruit cocktail, maraschino cherries, sour cream and pecans in bowl; mix well. Chill, covered, in refrigerator overnight. Spoon onto lettuce-lined salad plates.

Mae Ola Sanders

HOLIDAY FRUIT SALAD

Yield: 12 servings

2 eggs
1/4 cup white vinegar
1/4 cup sugar
2 tablespoons butter
2 cups white cherry halves
2 cups chopped pineapple
2 oranges, peeled, chopped

2 bananas, sliced
1/4 cup maraschino cherry
  halves
16 large marshmallows, cut
  into quarters
1 cup whipping cream,
  whipped

Combine eggs, vinegar and sugar in saucepan. Simmer until thickened, stirring constantly. Stir in butter until melted. Add cherry halves, pineapple, oranges, bananas, maraschino cherry halves and marshmallows; mix well. Fold in whipped cream. Chill in refrigerator for 24 hours before serving.

Margaret Prosser

FRUIT STACK SALAD

Yield: 1 serving

1 pineapple slice	1 kiwifruit slice
1 orange slice	1 strawberry half

Layer pineapple slice, orange slice, kiwi slice and strawberry half in a stack on red-tipped lettuce. Serve with poppy seed dressing and a mint leaf on top.

Margaret Wengrow

HOT WINE FRUIT SALAD

Yield: 16 servings

1/2 cup butter	1 16-ounce jar apple rings, drained
1/2 cup sugar	
2 tablespoons flour	1 16-ounce can peaches, drained
1 cup sherry	
1 16-ounce can pears, drained	1 16-ounce can apricots, drained
1 16-ounce can pineapple chunks, drained	

Combine butter, sugar, flour and sherry in saucepan. Simmer until thickened, stirring constantly. Combine pears, pineapple, apples, peaches and apricots in bowl; mix well. Pour in dressing, mixing gently. Chill, covered, in refrigerator overnight. Heat before serving.

Caroline G. McGee

WATERGATE SALAD

Yield: 6 servings

1 16-ounce can crushed pineapple	1 cup miniature marshmallows
	1 cup chopped pecans
1 3-ounce package pistachio instant pudding mix	9 ounces whipped topping

Combine undrained pineapple and pudding mix in bowl; mix well. Stir in marshmallows and pecans. Fold in whipped topping. Chill in refrigerator until serving time.

Lynn Clanton

SEVEN-UP HOLIDAY SALAD

Yield: 12 servings

2 3-ounce packages lemon
   gelatin
2 cups boiling water
2 cups 7-Up
2 cups drained crushed
   pineapple

2 bananas, sliced
2 cups miniature marshmallows
1 cup chopped pecans
Holiday Salad Topping
1 cup shredded sharp Cheddar
   cheese

Dissolve gelatin in boiling water in bowl. Chill until partially congealed. Stir in 7-Up, pineapple, banana slices, marshmallows and pecans. Pour into 9x12-inch dish. Chill until set. Unmold onto serving plate. Spread Holiday Salad Topping over gelatin; sprinkle with cheese. This is excellent with Christmas Dinner.

Vicki Rippeto

HOLIDAY SALAD TOPPING

Yield: 3 cups

2 tablespoons butter
2 tablespoons flour
1 cup pineapple juice
1/2 cup sugar

1 egg, beaten
1 cup whipping cream,
   whipped

Melt butter in saucepan over low heat. Add flour, mixing well. Stir in pineapple juice and sugar. Simmer over medium heat until thickened, stirring constantly. Add a small amount of hot mixture to beaten egg; add egg to hot mixture, stirring until smooth. Chill topping in refrigerator until cool. Fold in whipped cream. Spread on congealed salad.

Vicki Rippeto

STRAWBERRY-BANANA SALAD

Yield: 12 servings

2 6-ounce packages
   strawberry gelatin
1 cup boiling water
1 20-ounce can crushed
   pineapple, drained

2 10-ounce packages frozen
   sliced strawberries, thawed
3 bananas, sliced or mashed
1 cup coarsely chopped walnuts
2 cups sour cream

Dissolve gelatin in boiling water in bowl. Add pineapple, strawberries, bananas and walnuts; mix well. Pour half the mixture into 9x13-inch glass dish. Chill until firm. Spread sour cream over congealed layer. Pour in remaining gelatin mixture. Chill until firm.

Mae Ola Sanders

CORNED BEEF SALAD

Yield: 6 servings

1 3-ounce package lemon
   gelatin
1 cup boiling water
3/4 cup cold water
1 cup mayonnaise
1 12-ounce can corned beef,
   shredded
1 cup chopped celery

3 hard-boiled eggs, finely
   chopped
1 small onion, finely chopped
1 2-ounce jar chopped
   pimento, drained
1/4 cup chopped pickles
Lettuce leaves

Dissolve gelatin in boiling water in bowl. Add cold water; mix well. Chill in refrigerator until partially set. Add mayonnaise, corned beef, celery, eggs, onion, pimento and pickles; mix well. Pour into lightly oiled 8-inch square pan. Chill until firm. Cut into rectangles. Serve on lettuce-lined salad plates. Garnish with sliced boiled egg. Will make 8 to 10 servings if prepared in individual salad molds.

Lorene Cheek

PASTA SALAD

Yield: 8 servings

1 14-ounce can artichoke hearts, drained
1 package sliced smoked sausage
¾ cup pitted black olives
¾ cup sliced fresh mushrooms
½ cup (or more) Italian dressing
1 12-ounce package macaroni
¾ cup diagonally sliced celery
½ cup finely chopped green bell pepper
1 cup cherry tomato halves
Salt and pepper to taste

Combine artichoke hearts, sausage, olives, mushrooms and Italian dressing in bowl; toss lightly. Chill, covered, in refrigerator. Cook macaroni using package directions. Rinse in cold water; drain. Combine macaroni, celery, green pepper, tomatoes, salt, pepper and chilled mixture in large bowl; toss to mix. Garnish with red onion rings and Swiss cheese cubes.

Mrs. Robert Vance Fulkerson

TACO TOSS

Yield: 8 servings

1 pound chopped steak
2 tablespoons chili powder
2 cloves of garlic, minced
1 12-ounce package tacos
1 head lettuce
1 avocodo, sliced
Juice of 1 lemon
1 green bell pepper, sliced
2 red onions, sliced
2 tomatoes, chopped
¼ cup black olives, sliced
1 pound Cheddar cheese, shredded
¼ cup chopped jalapeño pepper
½ cup Italian dressing
2 cups sour cream
1 cup salsa

Brown steak with chili powder and garlic in nonstick skillet, stirring frequently; drain. Break tacos into bite-sized pieces. Tear lettuce into bite-sized pieces. Toss avocado with lemon juice in bowl. Combine steak, tacos, lettuce, green pepper, onions, tomatoes, olives, cheese, avocados, jalapeño pepper and Italian dressing in bowl; mix well. Serve with sour cream and salsa on the side. This is great for a meeting. Have everyone bring 1 ingredient (the portions may vary) and "toss theirs in."

Robert M. Hoffmeier

CHICKEN AND PASTA SALAD
Yield: 4 servings

3 cups julienned cooked
   chicken
1 clove of garlic, minced
1 teaspoon basil
1 tablespoon butter
3 cups cooked fusilli or ziti
   pasta
2 cups fresh basil leaves

³/₄ cup olive oil
2 tablespoons pine nuts
2 cloves of garlic, crushed
1 teaspoon salt
¹/₂ cup freshly grated Parmesan
   cheese
Romaine lettuce leaves
Freshly grated Parmesan cheese

Sauté cooked chicken with garlic and basil in butter in skillet until lightly browned, stirring constantly. Combine basil leaves, olive oil, pine nuts, garlic and salt in food processor container. Process with steel blade until well blended. Pour into bowl. Add Parmesan cheese; mix well. Combine chicken, pasta and enough pesto dressing to coat in bowl; toss well. Line salad bowl with lettuce leaves. Spoon chicken mixture into bowl; sprinkle with Parmesan cheese. Serve with extra dressing on the side. This is best served at room temperature. May store dressing, covered, in refrigerator.

Karen Laughlin

CONGEALED CHICKEN SALAD
Yield: 6 servings

2 envelopes unflavored gelatin
³/₄ cup chicken broth
1 cup mayonnaise
¹/₂ cup pickle relish
2 cups chopped cooked
   chicken breast

1 small jar chopped pimento,
   drained
1 small jar tiny green peas,
   drained

Dissolve gelatin in chicken broth in saucepan over low heat. Add mayonnaise and relish; mix well. Chill until slightly thickened. Add chicken, pimento and peas. Pour into molds. Chill until firm. Unmold onto lettuce-lined salad plates. May mold in cantaloupe halves and slice into quarters when firm.

Jo Gross

CRANBERRY-CHICKEN SALAD

Yield: 12 servings

1 envelope unflavored gelatin
1/4 cup cold water
1   16-ounce can whole
   cranberry sauce
1   8-ounce can crushed
   pineapple
1/2 cup broken walnuts
1 tablespoon lemon juice
1 envelope unflavored gelatin

1/4 cup cold water
1 cup mayonnaise
1/2 cup water
3 tablespoons lemon juice
3/4 teaspoon salt
2 cups chopped cooked chicken
1/2 cup sliced celery
2 tablespoons chopped parsley

Soften gelatin in 1/4 cup cold water in saucepan. Heat until dissolved. Add cranberry sauce, pineapple, walnuts and 1 tablespoon lemon juice; mix well. Pour into 6x10-inch dish or bundt pan. Chill until set. Soften remaining gelatin in 1/4 cup cold water in saucepan. Heat until gelatin is dissolved. Add mayonnaise, 1/2 cup water and 3 tablespoons lemon juice; mix well. Add salt, chicken, celery and parsley; mix well. Pour over congealed layer. Chill until set.

Jo Gross

CHICKEN AND LOBSTER SALAD

Yield: 4 servings

1 whole chicken breast, cooked
1/2 pound lobster meat
1 cup French salad dressing
3 hard-boiled eggs, separated
1 cup finely chopped celery
1 cup mayonnaise

2 tablespoons chili sauce
1 tablespoon chopped chives
Salt to taste
1/2 cup whipping cream,
   whipped
2 cups shredded cabbage

Cut cooked chicken into small strips. Chop lobster. Add salad dressing to chicken and lobster in bowl; mix well. Chop egg whites. Add egg whites and celery to chicken mixture; mix well. Marinate, covered, in refrigerator for 1 hour. Sieve egg yolks. Combine egg yolks, mayonnaise, chili sauce, chives and salt in bowl; mix well. Fold in whipped cream. Add to chicken mixture; mix well. Serve on bed of cabbage or lettuce in salad bowl. This was one of our favorites in Australia. I often serve it now for "company supper" on the island, substituting for lobster the meat from crabs we've caught ourselves that day.

Nancy Stephens

CURRIED CHICKEN-RICE SALAD
Yield: 4 servings

1 tablespoon vinegar
2 tablespoons oil
1/2 teaspoon curry powder
1/4 cup chopped onion
2 cups cooked rice
3/4 cup mayonnaise

2 cups chopped cooked
   chicken breast
1/2 teaspoon salt
1/8 teaspoon pepper
1/2 cup sliced almonds
1 cup chopped celery

Combine first 5 ingredients in bowl. Marinate in refrigerator overnight. Add mayonnaise, chicken, seasonings, almonds and celery; mix well.

Linda Lader

CRAB AND OLIVE SALAD
Yield: 6 servings

2 cups crab meat
2/3 cup chopped olives
Salt and pepper to taste

1²/3 cups chopped celery
1/4 cup mayonnaise
Shredded lettuce

Combine crab meat, olives, salt, pepper, celery and mayonnaise in bowl; mix well. Serve on bed of lettuce in salad bowl.

Elsie A. Crane

MARINATED CRAB SALAD
Yield: 4 servings

1/4 cup olive oil
3 tablespoons white wine
   vinegar
2¹/4 teaspoons pepper
1/4 teaspoon dry mustard
Dash of thyme
1/4 teaspoon basil

1 tablespoon chopped fresh
   parsley
1¹/4 cups sliced onion
2 pinches of sugar
2 tablespoons lime juice
1 pound choice lump crab meat
Red-tipped lettuce leaves

Combine first 10 ingredients in bowl; mix well. Add crab meat; mix well. Marinate, covered, in refrigerator overnight. Serve on bed of lettuce. Garnish with sliced hard-boiled egg and cherry tomatoes.

Cheryl Blair

FISHERMAN'S SALAD

Yield: 8 servings

2 envelopes ranch dressing mix
2 cups buttermilk
2 cups mayonnaise
1 pound broken thin spaghetti,
 cooked
1/2 cup chopped green bell
 pepper
2 cups thinly sliced celery
10 to 12 green onions, thinly
 sliced
3 hard-boiled eggs, chopped

1 2-ounce jar chopped
 pimento, drained
1 1/2 pounds boiled shrimp,
 peeled
1 1/2 pounds crab meat or mock
 crab meat
1 8-ounce can sliced water
 chestnuts, drained
3/4 cup sliced almonds, toasted
3 tablespoons sliced almonds,
 toasted

Combine ranch salad dressing mix, buttermilk and mayonnaise in bowl; mix well. Let stand in refrigerator until thickened. Combine spaghetti, green pepper, celery, green onions, eggs, pimento, shrimp, crab meat, water chestnuts and 3/4 cup almonds in bowl; mix well. Add dressing; toss to mix. Spoon into salad bowl. Garnish with 3 tablespoons almonds.

Mrs. Robert Freeman

SHRIMP REMOULADE

Yield: 6 servings

1 hard-boiled egg, separated
1/2 cup plus 2 tablespoons oil
1/4 cup Creole mustard
3 tablespoons vinegar
1 teaspoon salt
2 tablespoons paprika
1/2 cup minced celery

2 tablespoons grated onion
2 tablespoons minced parsley
2 tablespoons minced green
 bell pepper
2 pounds cooked shrimp,
 peeled

Mash egg yolk in mixer bowl. Add oil slowly, mixing well. Add mustard, vinegar, salt and paprika; beat until thick and well blended. Fold in celery, onion, parsley and green pepper. Chop egg white. Add to mixture; mix well. Stir in shrimp. Chill, covered, in refrigerator for several hours.

Jo Gross Huffman

SEA ISLAND PICKLED SHRIMP

Yield: 12 servings

2 cups pure olive oil
2 cups cider vinegar
½ cup lemon juice
Salt, pepper, garlic salt and
   sugar to taste

Chopped parsley to taste
5 pounds cooked shrimp,
   peeled
8 medium onions, sliced into
   rings

Combine olive oil, vinegar, lemon juice, salt, pepper, garlic salt, sugar and parsley in bowl; mix well. Alternate layers of shrimp and onion rings in large shallow glass dish. Pour marinade over shrimp. Marinate, covered, in refrigerator for 12 hours, stirring occasionally. Let stand at room temperature for 1 hour before serving. Remove from marinade with slotted spoon. Serve on lettuce-lined dish. Garnish with parsley. May store in refrigerator for 2 days.

Lynn Clanton

ARTICHOKE RICE SALAD

Yield: 8 servings

1 package sesame-chicken
   flavored rice mix
4 green onions, thinly sliced
½ green bell pepper, chopped
12 olives, sliced

2 6-ounce jars marinated
   artichoke hearts
⅓ cup mayonnaise
¼ teaspoon curry powder

Cook rice using package directions. Cool to room temperature. Combine rice, green onions, green pepper and olives in bowl; mix well. Drain artichoke hearts, reserving marinade. Cut artichoke hearts into halves. Add to rice mixture. Combine reserved marinade, mayonnaise and curry powder in bowl; mix well. Add to rice mixture; mix well. Chill until serving time.

Nancy Pruitt

PECAN-ASPARAGUS SALAD

Yield: 4 servings

24 fresh asparagus spears
¼ to ⅓ cup coarsely chopped
   pecans

⅓ cup Italian salad dressing
Green leaf lettuce

Cook asparagus in boiling water for 5 minutes or until tender-crisp and bright green; drain. Combine pecans and salad dressing in small saucepan. Heat just to serving temperature. Place asparagus spears on lettuce-lined salad plates. Top with warm pecan dressing.

Sue West

ASPARAGUS VINAIGRETTE

Yield: 8 servings

⅔ cup white vinegar
½ cup sugar
½ teaspoon salt
1 teaspoon whole cloves
3 cinnamon sticks
1 tablespoon celery seed

½ cup water
4 15-ounce cans asparagus,
   drained
1 4-ounce jar chopped
   pimento

Combine first 7 ingredients in saucepan. Bring to a boil. Simmer for 3 to 4 minutes, stirring frequently. Layer asparagus in shallow dish; sprinkle with pimento. Pour hot vinaigrette over asparagus. Marinate, covered, in refrigerator for 24 to 48 hours.

Kitty McNeely

ASPARAGUS SALAD

Yield: 4 servings

24 fresh asparagus spears
Boston or bibb lettuce

Honey mustard salad dressing
⅓ cup chopped mixed nuts

Cook asparagus in boiling water in saucepan until tender-crisp; do not overcook. Drain and cool to room temperature. Place asparagus on lettuce-lined salad plates. Top with salad dressing; sprinkle with chopped nuts.

Sue West

MARINATED BROCCOLI

Yield: 12 servings

1 cup cider vinegar
1 tablespoon sugar
1 tablespoon dillweed
1 tablespoon MSG
1 teaspoon salt

1 teaspoon pepper
1 teaspoon garlic salt
1¹/₂ cups oil
Flowerets of 3 bunches broccoli

Combine vinegar, sugar, dillweed, MSG, salt, pepper, garlic salt and oil in bowl; mix well. Add broccoli; toss to mix. Marinate, covered, in refrigerator for 24 hours.

Barbie Mangum

BROWN DERBY COBB SALAD

Yield: 8 servings

¹/₂ head iceberg lettuce, chopped
¹/₂ bunch watercress
1 small bunch chicory, chopped
¹/₂ head romaine lettuce, chopped
2 medium tomatoes, peeled, cut into quarters
2 cooked chicken breasts, cubed
6 slices crisp-fried bacon, crumbled
1 avocado, diced
3 hard-boiled eggs, chopped
2 tablespoons chopped chives

¹/₂ cup finely crumbled imported Roquefort cheese
1 cup water
1 cup wine vinegar
1 teaspoon sugar
Juice of ¹/₂ lemon
2¹/₂ tablespoons salt
1 tablespoon pepper
1 tablespoon Worcestershire sauce
1 teaspoon English mustard
1 clove of garlic, minced
1 cup olive oil
3 cups vegetable oil

Combine iceberg lettuce, watercress, chicory, romaine lettuce, tomatoes, cubed chicken, crumbled bacon, avocado, eggs, chives and Roquefort cheese in bowl; toss to mix. Combine water, vinegar, sugar, lemon juice, salt, pepper, Worcestershire sauce, mustard and garlic in blender container. Process until well mixed. Add olive oil and vegetable oil, mixing well. Chill in refrigerator. Shake well before serving. Add to salad; toss to coat well.

Chuck Calloway

CAROL'S CAESAR SALAD

Yield: 8 servings

1 large head romaine lettuce, torn
1 large head green or red leaf lettuce, torn
3 cloves of garlic, minced
1 large egg yolk
1 tablespoon Dijon mustard
1 tablespoon anchovy paste

3 tablespoons white vinegar
2½ tablespoons lemon juice
1 cup vegetable oil
½ cup olive oil
2 teaspoons thyme
Freshly ground pepper to taste
1 cup croutons
1 cup grated Parmesan cheese

Combine romaine lettuce and leaf lettuce in large salad bowl. Chill, covered, in refrigerator until serving time. Chop garlic in food processor until very fine. Remove to bowl. Place egg yolk in food processor. Process for 3 to 5 seconds. Add mustard and anchovy paste. Process for 3 to 5 seconds or until smooth. Add vinegar and lemon juice; process until mixed. Add garlic. Process for 3 to 5 seconds. Combine vegetable oil and olive oil in bowl. Add to food processor in a slow steady stream while processor is running. Add thyme and pepper; process until well mixed. Add enough dressing to coat lettuce generously. Add croutons and Parmesan cheese; toss to mix. Serve at once. May prepare croutons by cutting thick slices of oatmeal bread into cubes. Place on baking sheet. Bake at 300 degrees for 20 to 25 minutes or until brown. Cool to room temperature. Store, covered, until needed.

Carol Wilson

CAESAR SALAD

Yield: 6 servings

1 egg
1 tablespoon Worcestershire sauce
3 tablespoons lemon juice
⅛ to ¼ cup vegetable oil
1 clove of garlic

1 head bibb lettuce, torn
1 head iceberg lettuce, torn
¾ cup grated Parmesan cheese
½ cup chopped bleu cheese
3 slices bread, cubed, toasted

Combine first 4 ingredients in bowl; mix well. Cut garlic into halves. Rub large salad bowl with garlic. Combine lettuces, cheeses and dressing in salad bowl; toss to mix. Sprinkle with croutons.

Jeff Wilson

COPPER PENNIES

Yield: 12 servings

1 can cream of tomato soup
1/2 cup vegetable oil
3/4 cup cider vinegar
1 cup sugar
1 1/2 teaspoons Worcestershire
   sauce
1 teaspoon dry mustard

1 tablespoon salt
1/2 tablespoon pepper
1/8 teaspoon red pepper
3 pounds carrots, scraped,
   sliced
1 medium onion, sliced into
   rings

Combine tomato soup, oil, vinegar, sugar, Worcestershire sauce, dry mustard, salt, pepper and red pepper in bowl; mix well. Blanch carrots in boiling water in saucepan for 3 minutes; drain. Add carrots and onion rings to dressing; mix well. Marinate, covered, in refrigerator for several days before serving.

Leigh Glei

HILTON HEAD LAYERED SALAD

Yield: 12 servings

1 head lettuce, shredded
1 cup cauliflowerets
1 cup broccoli flowerets,
   chopped
1/2 cup finely chopped red bell
   pepper
3 green onions, thinly sliced
1   10-ounce package frozen
   tiny peas, thawed

1 1/2 cups mayonnaise
2 tablespoons sugar
4 ounces white Cheddar
   cheese, shredded
6 slices crisp-fried bacon,
   crumbled

Layer lettuce, cauliflowerets, broccoli, red pepper, green onions and peas in 9x13-inch dish. Combine mayonnaise and sugar in bowl; mix well. Spread over layers, sealing to edge. Sprinkle with cheese and bacon. Chill, covered, in refrigerator overnight.

Debbie Fraser

THREE-LETTUCE SALAD

Yield: 12 servings

1 bunch red-tip lettuce
1 bunch spinach
1 bunch green leaf lettuce
1 6-ounce can mandarin
   oranges, drained

¹/₂ cup slivered almonds
1 red onion, sliced into rings
Sweet and Sour Dressing

Wash lettuce, spinach and leaf lettuce; drain. Tear into bite-sized pieces. Combine lettuce, spinach, leaf lettuce, mandarin oranges, almonds and onion rings in bowl; mix well. Add dressing just before serving; toss to mix.

Nancy Pruitt

SWEET AND SOUR DRESSING

Yield: 12 servings

1 16-ounce bottle of sweet
   and sour dressing
1 teaspoon poppy seed

1 teaspoon fresh lemon juice
1 teaspoon blackberry vinegar

Combine sweet and sour dressing, poppy seed, lemon juice and blackberry vinegar in bowl; mix well.

Nancy Pruitt

LOVE THIS SALAD

Yield: 6 servings

1 head iceberg lettuce
¹/₂ red onion, sliced into rings
¹/₄ cup green olives

2 cups marinated artichokes
¹/₄ cup grated Parmesan cheese

Tear lettuce into bite-sized pieces. Combine lettuce, onion, olives and artichokes in bowl; mix well. Add Parmesan cheese; toss to mix.

Hoffmeier House

Pea Salad

Yield: 10 servings

2 10-ounce packages frozen
   tiny peas, thawed
1 cup chopped parsley
1/4 cup chopped green onions
1/2 cup crisp bacon bits
1 cup chopped cashews or
   macadamia nuts
1/2 teaspoon salt
1 teaspoon lemon juice
1/2 cup red wine vinegar

1 1/2 teaspoons salt
1/2 teaspoon finely ground
   pepper
1/2 teaspoon Dijon mustard
1 1/2 teaspoons Worcestershire
   sauce
1 clove of garlic, minced
1/2 teaspoon sugar
1 1/2 cups corn oil
1 cup sour cream

Combine peas, parsley, green onions, bacon bits, cashews and 1/2 teaspoon salt in bowl; mix well. Combine lemon juice, vinegar, 1 1/2 teaspoons salt, pepper, mustard, Worcestershire sauce, garlic and sugar in blender container. Process until smooth adding oil gradually. Mix sour cream and 1/4 cup dressing in bowl. Fold gently into salad. Chill, covered, until serving time. Serve in lettuce-lined salad bowl. Store remaining dressing in refrigerator.

Rob Keith

Layered Potato Salad

Yield: 12 servings

8 baking potatoes
1 medium onion, sliced into
   rings
1/2 cup chopped fresh parsley
2 cups mayonnaise-type salad
   dressing

2 cups sour cream
3 slices crisp-fried bacon,
   crumbled
1 teaspoon horseradish
1 teaspoon celery seed
1/2 teaspoon salt

Boil potatoes in water to cover in saucepan until tender; drain. Cut into 1/8-inch slices. Combine onion rings and parsley in bowl; mix well. Combine salad dressing, sour cream, bacon, horseradish, celery seed and salt in bowl; mix well. Alternate layers of potatoes, dressing and onion mixture in 9x13-inch dish until all ingredients are used, ending with onion mixture. Chill, covered, for 8 hours.

Ellen Garland

RADICCHIO PECAN SALAD
Yield: 6 servings

1 large head red leaf lettuce	5 cloves of garlic, minced
1 medium head romaine lettuce	1 cup olive oil
1 large head radicchio	1¹/₄ cups safflower oil
1 egg	2 ounces bleu cheese, crumbled
2 egg yolks	1 cup finely chopped pecans
¹/₂ cup fresh lemon juice	
Salt and freshly ground pepper to taste	

Tear red leaf lettuce and romaine lettuce into bite-sized pieces. Radicchio leaves may be left whole. Combine in bowl; toss to mix. Combine egg, egg yolks and half the lemon juice in food processor container. Add salt and pepper. Process with steel blade for 1 minute. Add garlic through feed tube. Add olive oil and safflower oil in slow steady stream through feed tube, processing until well blended. Scrape down sides of container; add additional lemon juice, salt and pepper if desired. Pour into bowl. Add bleu cheese; mix well. Chill, covered, in refrigerator. Line salad plates with lettuce mixture. Top with dressing; sprinkle with pecans. Dressing may also be added before greens are tossed.

Christina Richards

WALDORF COLESLAW
Yield: 6 servings

1 cup seedless raisins	1 teaspoon salt
3 cups shredded cabbage	1 tablespoon sugar
1¹/₂ cups chopped apple	1 tablespoon dry mustard
2 tablespoons minced onion	3 tablespoons lemon juice
1 cup mayonnaise	

Plump raisins in boiling water in bowl for several minutes; drain. Combine raisins, cabbage, apple and onion in large bowl; mix well. Combine mayonnaise, salt, sugar, mustard and lemon juice in small bowl; mix well. Add to cabbage mixture; toss to mix. Chill until serving time.

Ronelle Plocher

COLESLAW

Yield: 12 servings

1 large head cabbage, shredded
1 large green bell pepper, cut
   into strips
1 large onion, cut into strips

1 8-ounce can sliced water
   chestnuts
Coleslaw Dressing

Soak cabbage in ice water to cover in bowl for 15 minutes; drain. Layer cabbage, green pepper, onion and water chestnuts in bowl. Add dressing. Chill, covered, for several days before serving. Coleslaw will keep in refrigerator for 2 weeks and remain crisp and crunchy.

Maggie Bry

COLESLAW DRESSING

Yield: 3 cups

1½ cups vinegar
¾ cup oil

1 cup sugar
1 tablespoon mustard

Combine vinegar, oil, sugar and mustard in saucepan; mix well. Bring to a boil.

Maggie Bry

HOT SLAW

Yield: 12 servings

1 head cabbage, finely chopped
¼ cup sugar
Celery seed to taste
1 egg
1 tablespoon prepared mustard

1½ to 2 tablespoons butter
½ cup sugar
¼ cup vinegar
¼ cup water
Salt and pepper to taste

Place cabbage in bowl; sprinkle with sugar and celery seed. Combine egg, mustard, butter, sugar, vinegar, water, salt and pepper in saucepan. Boil for 5 minutes, stirring frequently. Add to slaw; toss to mix. Store dressing in refrigerator.

Opal D. Abbink

SEVEN-DAY SLAW
Yield: 12 servings

1 head cabbage, shredded
1 green bell pepper, chopped
1 onion, sliced into rings
1 4-ounce jar pimento
3 stalks celery, sliced

1/2 cup honey
1 cup vinegar
1 teaspoon salt
2/3 cup oil
2 tablespoons poppy seed

Mix first 5 ingredients in bowl. Bring honey, vinegar, salt, oil and poppy seed to a boil in saucepan, stirring frequently. Pour over salad; do not stir. Chill, covered, for 24 hours to 1 week.

Marilyn McNeely

TABOULI
Yield: 10 servings

1 cup cracked wheat
4 tomatoes, chopped
2 peeled cucumbers, chopped
1 medium onion, chopped

1/3 cup mint flakes
2 teaspoons salt
1/2 cup lemon juice
1 cup olive oil

Soak wheat in warm water until cool; drain, squeezing out moisture. Combine with remaining ingredients in bowl; toss to mix. Chill for 4 hours or longer. May add 1/2 chopped green bell pepper.

Margaret Comstock

TOMATO CREAM CHEESE ASPIC
Yield: 6 servings

1 can tomato soup
8 ounces cream cheese, softened
1 3-ounce package lemon
   gelatin
1/2 cup boiling water

1 cup mayonnaise
Chopped celery and chopped
   green bell pepper to taste
Grated onion to taste

Heat soup and cream cheese in saucepan until cream cheese is melted, stirring constantly. Dissolve gelatin in boiling water. Add to soup mixture; mix well. Add remaining ingredients; mix well. Pour into serving dish. Chill until set. Garnish with sliced hard-boiled eggs. May add shrimp or crab meat to aspic.

Wilma W. Stafford

FRESH TOMATO ASPIC

Yield: 6 servings

2 envelopes unflavored gelatin
1 cups cold water
2 chicken bouillon cubes
1 cup cold water
1 cup vegetable juice cocktail
2 tablespoons lemon juice
2 teaspoons dillweed

1 teaspoon salt
1/4 teaspoon Tabasco sauce
1/4 cup chopped green onions
2 cups chopped peeled
   tomatoes
1 cup chopped peeled, seeded
   cucumbers

Soften gelatin in 1 cup cold water in saucepan. Add bouillon cubes. Heat until gelatin and bouillon are dissolved, stirring frequently. Add remaining cold water, vegetable juice cocktail, lemon juice, dillweed, salt, Tabasco sauce and green onions; mix well. Chill until partially set. Fold in tomatoes and cucumbers. Spoon into greased mold. Chill until firm.

Mary Lea Hamilton

VEGETABLE SALAD

Yield: 8 servings

Flowerets of 1 head broccoli
1 4-ounce jar sliced stuffed
   green olives
2 hard-boiled eggs
1 16-ounce can artichoke
   hearts, drained

1 16-ounce can hearts of palm,
   drained
Ranch salad dressing
Salt and pepper to taste
Bibb lettuce leaves

Cook broccoli in a small amount of water in saucepan until tender-crisp and bright green; drain. Combine broccoli and olives in bowl. Chop eggs into bite-sized chunks. Cut artichokes and hearts of palm into bite-sized pieces. Add egg, artichokes and hearts of palm to broccoli; toss lightly to mix. Stir in enough dressing to moisten. Season with salt and pepper. Serve at room temperature on lettuce-lined salad plates.

Betsy Pratt

MARINATED VEGETABLE SALAD
Yield: 10 servings

1   16-ounce can English peas,
     drained
1   16-ounce can Chinese mixed
     vegetables, drained
1   16-ounce can cut string
     beans, drained
1 cup chopped green bell
     pepper
1 cup chopped celery
1 onion, chopped
1 cup sliced or slivered
     almonds
½ cup vinegar
¼ cup oil
½ cup sugar
Salt and pepper to taste

Combine peas, Chinese vegetables, string beans, green pepper, celery, onion and almonds in bowl; mix well. Mix vinegar, oil, sugar, salt and pepper in bowl. Add to vegetables; mix well. Chill, covered, in refrigerator for 24 hours before serving, stirring once or twice.

Billie Hack

MUSTARD AND CELERY SEED DRESSING *Yield: 3 cups*

2 cups mayonnaise
⅔ cup Dijon mustard
6 tablespoons celery seed
Half and half
Salt and pepper to taste

Combine fist 3 ingredients in bowl; mix well. Add enough half and half to make of desired consistency. Add salt and pepper; mix well.

Deb Drury

SOUR CREAM FRUIT DRESSING
Yield: 3 cups

2 eggs, beaten
¾ cup sugar
½ cup pineapple juice
⅓ cup fresh lemon juice
1 cup sour cream

Combine first 4 ingredients in double boiler. Cook over hot water until mixture thickens, stirring constantly. Cool to room temperature. Fold in sour cream. Chill in refrigerator. Serve on fresh pineapple, watermelon and strawberries or gelatin salads.

Lynn Ruggles

Meat Entrées

BEEF STROGANOFF

Yield: 4 servings

2 medium onions, thinly sliced
1/4 cup butter or margarine
2 1/2 pounds round steak
1 10-ounce can tomato soup
1 6-ounce can mushrooms
1 tablespoon prepared mustard

2 tablespoons brown sugar
Worcestershire sauce to taste
1 cup sour cream
Salt and pepper to taste
Cooked rice or noodles

Sauté onions in butter in skillet; remove to bowl with slotted spoon. Cut steak cross grain into strips. Brown steak in pan drippings, stirring frequently. Add remaining ingredients; mix well. Simmer, covered, for 1 hour, stirring occasionally. Serve over rice or noodles.

Nancy Pruitt

GRAND MARNIER ROAST BEEF

Yield: 6 servings

24 shallots, peeled
2 tablespoons unsalted butter
8 ounces Shitake mushrooms,
   sliced
2 cloves of garlic, minced
1/2 cup dry white wine
1/3 cup Grand Marnier
2 1/2 cups beef broth
1 bay leaf
8 peppercorns
3 whole cloves

2 strips orange rind
1 tablespoon tomato paste
3 tablespoons sugar
3 tablespoons red wine vinegar
1/2 cup orange juice
4 teaspoons arrowroot
2 tablespoons Grand Marnier
Lemon juice to taste
Salt and pepper to taste
1 4-pound filet of beef,
   trimmed, tied

Sauté shallots in butter in skillet. Add mushrooms. Sauté for 5 minutes. Add garlic. Sauté for 1 minute. Add wine and 1/3 cup liqueur. Cook for 1 minute. Add beef broth. Tie bay leaf, peppercorns, whole cloves and orange rind in cheesecloth. Add to mixture. Add tomato paste. Simmer for 30 minutes, stirring frequently. Cook sugar and red wine vinegar in small saucepan until syrupy, stirring frequently. Add orange juice, arrowroot dissolved in 2 tablespoons liqueur and lemon juice; mix well. Stir into Grand Marnier sauce. Place beef in roasting pan. Brown on both sides under broiler. Roast at 450 degrees for 10 to 12 minutes for rare. Cut into slices. Serve with sauce.

Nina Sellew

LOBSTER-STUFFED TENDERLOIN   *Yield: 6 to 8 servings*

2 4-ounce frozen lobster tails	6 slices bacon, partially cooked
1 3 to 4-pound whole beef	1/2 cup chopped green onions
tenderloin, butterflied	1/2 cup margarine
1 tablespoon melted margarine	1/2 cup dry white wine
1 1/2 teaspoons lemon juice	1/8 teaspoon garlic salt

Place frozen lobster tails in boiling salted water in saucepan. Return to a boil. Reduce heat. Simmer for 50 to 60 seconds; drain. Remove lobster from shells. Cut into halves lengthwise. Place lobster meat end to end on beef. Mix melted margarine and lemon juice; drizzle over lobster. Fold beef to enclose lobster; tie securely at intervals. Place on rack in shallow roasting pan. Roast at 425 degrees for 45 to 50 minutes for rare beef. Place partially-cooked bacon on top of beef. Roast for 5 minutes longer. Sauté green onions in remaining 1/2 cup margarine in skillet. Add wine and garlic salt. Cook until heated through. Cut beef into slices; spoon wine sauce over beef.

Phyllis Modell

LONDON BROIL   *Yield: 4 to 6 servings*

2 tablespoons oil	1 teaspoon salt
2 teaspoons chopped parsley	1 teaspoon lemon juice
2 tablespoons Worcestershire	1/2 teaspoon pepper
sauce	1 2-pound London broil
1 clove of garlic, crushed	

Combine oil, parsley, Worcestershire sauce, garlic, salt, lemon juice and pepper in bowl; mix well. Place London broil in shallow glass dish. Pour marinade over beef. Marinate, covered, in refrigerator for 2 hours or longer, turning beef occasionally. Drain beef, reserving marinade. Place on rack in broiler pan. Broil for 5 minutes. Turn beef; brush with reserved marinade. Broil for 5 minutes longer or until done to taste. Cut diagonally into thin slices.

Carolyn Robinson

BARBECUED POT ROAST

Yield: 8 servings

1 bottle of teriyaki sauce
1/4 cup packed brown sugar
1/4 cup whiskey

2 tablespoons vinegar
1 1/2 cups water
1 2 to 3-inch thick chuck roast

Combine teriyaki sauce, brown sugar, whiskey, vinegar and water in bowl; mix well. Place roast in shallow glass dish. Add marinade. Marinate, covered, in refrigerator overnight. Drain, reserving marinade. Broil or grill for 45 minutes, turning and basting with reserved marinade several times. May bake at 500 degrees for 10 minutes, reduce oven temperature to 325 degrees and bake for 1 hour longer or until done to taste, basting with reserved marinade.

Marianne Smith

ROAST ON THE ROCKS

Yield: 10 to 12 servings

1 5 to 6-pound eye of round
    roast
1 onion, cut into small slivers
2 tablespoons salt

1 teaspoon freshly ground
    pepper
1/2 teaspoon ground ginger
Fresh parsley

Select roast for uniformity of shape. Let stand at room temperature for 2 hours before cooking. Cut 16 slits in roast 1 hour before cooking time; place onion slivers in slits. Combine salt, pepper and ginger in bowl; mix well. Rub mixture into surface of beef coating as heavily as possible. Preheat 2 inch deep coals, arranged wide enough to allow placing roast on fresh coals several times during cooking. Brush fine white ash from surface of fire with folded newspaper. Place roast directly on hot coals. Cook for 15 minutes. Turn roast 1/3 turn, placing on fresh hot coals. Cook for 12 minutes. Turn roast, placing uncooked surface on fresh hot coals. Cook for 12 minutes. Roast will be charred on the surface but juicy red inside. Serve on wooden plank. Carve roast diagonally cross grain into 1/8-inch slices. Garnish with parsley.

Tom Whelan

STEAK IN A BAG

Yield: 4 to 6 servings

1/4 cup butter, softened	1 2 to 3-pound top sirloin
1/4 cup oil	steak, 2 1/2 inches thick
1 teaspoon crushed garlic	1 cup bread crumbs
2 teaspoons seasoned salt	1 cup shredded Cheddar cheese
2 1/2 teaspoons pepper	

Combine butter, oil, garlic, salt and pepper in bowl; mix well. Trim steak. Spread with butter mixture. Mix bread crumbs and cheese in shallow dish. Coat surface of steak with crumb mixture. Place steak in oven cooking bag, securing with tie. May refrigerate for several hours. Let steak come to room temperature before cooking. Place cooking bag in roasting pan. Roast, using cooking bag instructions, at 375 degrees for 30 minutes for rare steak or at 425 degrees for 45 minutes for medium rare. Remove to serving plate. Let stand for 5 minutes. Cut into slices.

Virginia Jordan

HAMBURGER QUICHE

Yield: 6 servings

8 ounces ground beef	8 ounces medium Cheddar
1/2 cup mayonnaise	cheese, shredded
1/2 cup milk	1/8 teaspoon oregano
2 eggs	1/8 teaspoon thyme
1 tablespoon cornstarch	Salt and pepper to taste
1/3 cup sliced green onions	1 unbaked 9-inch pie shell

Brown ground beef in skillet, stirring until crumbly; drain. Combine mayonnaise, milk, eggs and cornstarch in bowl; mix until smooth. Stir in ground beef, green onions, cheese, oregano, thyme, salt and pepper. Spoon into pie shell. Bake at 350 degrees for 35 to 40 minutes or until center is firm.

Elaine Boone

BAKED SPAGHETTI

Yield: 6 to 8 servings

1½ pounds ground chuck
2 medium onions, chopped
1 can tomato soup
1 7-ounce bottle of sliced
   olives
1 teaspoon chili powder
1 tablespoon Worcestershire
   sauce

1 clove of garlic
Salt and pepper to taste
1 8-ounce package thin
   spaghetti
1 can mushroom soup
8 ounces medium sharp
   Cheddar cheese, shredded

Brown ground chuck with onion in skillet, stirring frequently; drain. Add tomato soup. Drain olives, reserving liquid. Add olive liquid, chili powder, Worcestershire sauce and garlic to ground beef; mix well. Simmer, covered, for 1 hour, stirring occasionally. Remove garlic. Cook spaghetti using package directions; drain. Add to sauce; mix well. Pour into 3-quart casserole. Spread mushroom soup over top; sprinkle with cheese. Garnish with olives. Bake at 350 to 400 degrees for 30 minutes.

Lynn Clanton

BURRITO PIE

Yield: 6 servings

4 8-inch flour tortillas
¼ cup vegetable oil
8 ounces ground beef
1 small onion, chopped
½ teaspoon garlic salt
1 4-ounce can chopped green
   chilies, drained

1 8-ounce can refried beans
⅓ cup mild taco sauce
2 cups shredded Monterey Jack
   cheese
1 cup shredded Cheddar cheese
1 cup shredded lettuce
1 large tomato, chopped

Brown tortillas 1 at a time in oil in skillet; drain. Brown ground beef with onion in skillet, stirring frequently. Remove from heat. Add garlic salt, green chilies, beans and taco sauce. Layer tortillas, meat sauce and cheese ¼ at a time in greased 9-inch pie plate. Bake at 350 degrees for 30 minutes. Top with lettuce and tomato.

Mary Coleman

SHEPHERD'S PIE

Yield: 6 servings

1 pound ground chuck roast
1 medium onion, chopped
1 10-ounce can tomato soup
1 20-ounce can whole green
   beans

Salt and pepper to taste
5 potatoes, cooked
Butter
Milk

Brown ground beef with onion in skillet, stirring frequently; drain. Add tomato soup and green beans; mix well. Place in casserole. Mash potatoes with butter and milk in bowl. Spread over casserole. Bake at 350 degrees for 30 minutes.

Eola Fienning

THE RECIPE

Yield: 4 to 6 servings

1 cup chopped onion
Butter
1¹/₂ pounds ground beef
1 10-ounce can cream of
   chicken soup
1 10-ounce can cream of
   mushroom soup

1 cup sour cream
Salt and pepper
¹/₄ cup chopped pimento
   (optional)
¹/₂ teaspoon MSG
3 cups cooked noodles
1 cup soft bread crumbs

Sauté onion in butter in skillet until tender. Add ground beef. Cook until ground beef is brown, stirring frequently; drain. Add soups, sour cream, salt, pepper, pimento, MSG and noodles; mix well. Pour into lightly buttered casserole. Sprinkle with bread crumbs; drizzle with melted butter. Bake at 350 degrees for 30 minutes.

Kay Spencer

Herb Bundles—Decorate meat platters with bundles of herbs used in preparing the dish such as watercress, parsley, thyme, rosemary or sage.

THREE-BEAN BEEFY CASSEROLE
Yield: 15 servings

8 ounces bacon
1 large onion, finely chopped
1 pound ground beef
1   16-ounce can white beans
2   16-ounce cans kidney beans
3   16-ounce cans baked beans

⅓ cup packed brown sugar
⅓ cup sugar
¼ cup dark molasses
¼ cup catsup
¼ teaspoon dry mustard

Fry bacon in skillet until crisp. Remove to drain. Add onion to bacon drippings. Cook until tender. Add ground beef. Cook until beef is brown, stirring until crumbly; drain. Combine white beans, kidney beans, baked beans, brown sugar, sugar, molasses, catsup and mustard in bowl; mix well. Add crumbled bacon and ground beef; mix well. Pour into baking dish. Bake at 375 degrees for 1 hour.

Lucille Davis

ISLAND PALMS EN CAUCHETTE
Yield: 8 servings

2   14-ounce cans hearts of palm
16 thin slices baked ham
1 tablespoon water

1 envelope Swiss Béarnaise
   sauce mix

Place 1 stalk of palm on each ham slice; roll to enclose. Place seam side down in 9x13-inch baking dish. Add water. Microwave, covered with plastic wrap, on Medium for 5 minutes or just until heated through. Prepare Béarnaise sauce using package directions. Pour sauce over ham rolls. Serve warm. May cut larger hearts of palm into halves lengthwise. May substitute Belgian endive for hearts of palm.

Ann Scheidle

HERITAGE PEACHY BAKED HAM   *Yield: 8 to 16 servings*

1 ham   **1 16-ounce jar peach preserves**
Whole cloves

Score ham diagonally at 1-inch intervals. Stud with cloves where scores intersect. Place ham in baking pan. Spread peach preserves over ham. Bake, covered with foil, at 325 degrees for 25 minutes per pound. Garnish with cherries and peach slices. Cool before slicing.

Nancy Pruitt

HAM AND TURKEY PIE   *Yield: 6 servings*

1/4 cup butter   **1 small can mushrooms,**
5 tablespoons flour   **   drained**
Pepper to taste   **1/2 cup chopped fresh parsley**
2 cups chicken broth   **1 teaspoon thyme**
1 cup chopped cooked ham   **White wine to taste**
1 cup chopped cooked turkey   **2 unbaked deep-dish pie shells**
1/4 cup chopped green onion

Melt butter in saucepan. Blend in flour and pepper. Add chicken broth; mix well. Simmer over medium heat until thickened, stirring constantly. Remove from heat. Add ham, turkey, green onions, mushrooms, parsley and thyme; mix well. Add white wine if needed for desired consistency. Pour into 1 pie shell; top with remaining pie shell. Seal edges; cut vents. Bake at 350 degrees for 40 minutes or until brown. Let stand for 10 to 15 minutes before serving.

Sue West

LUSCIOUS LAMB

Yield: 6 to 8 servings

1 8-pound leg of lamb
Garlic cloves, cut into slivers
Oregano to taste

Salt and pepper to taste
Onions, carrots and celery

Trim lamb. Make small slits in lamb; place a sliver of garlic into each slit. Season with oregano, salt and pepper. Spread vegetables in roasting pan. Place lamb on vegetables. Roast at 350 degrees for 2 to 2½ hours or until done to taste. Discard vegetables.

Mrs. Patrick L. Baughman

BUTTERFLY LAMB

Yield: 6 servings

2 cups French salad dressing
Rosemary to taste
2 cloves of garlic, minced

1 bay leaf, crushed
1 8-pound leg of lamb, boned

Combine salad dressing, rosemary, garlic and crushed bay leaf in bowl; mix well. Place lamb in shallow dish. Pour marinade over lamb. Marinate, covered, in refrigerator overnight or longer, turning 2 times a day. Drain, reserving marinade. Grill for 45 minutes to 1 hour or until done to taste, basting occasionally with reserved marinade. Slice cross grain.

Allyson Harden

GRILLED LAMB

Yield: 6 servings

1 jar Dijon Poupon mustard
1 mustard jar peanut oil
1 bottle of soy sauce

1 8-pound leg of lamb, boned,
   butterflied

Combine mustard, peanut oil and soy sauce in bowl; mix well. Pour over lamb in shallow dish. Marinate, covered, in refrigerator for several hours, turning lamb occasionally. Grill for 30 to 60 minutes or until done to taste; do not overcook.

Linda Lader

WAUSETTI

Yield: 8 servings

1½ pounds ground pork	8 ounces Old English sharp
2 medium onions, chopped	cheese, cubed
1 10-ounce can tomato soup	1 large can mushrooms
8 ounces uncooked noodles	Cracker crumbs

Brown pork with onions in skillet, stirring frequently; drain. Add soup. Simmer until pork is done to taste, stirring frequently. Cook noodles using package directions. Combine hot noodles and cheese cubes in bowl; mix well. Stir in mushrooms and pork mixture. Pour into 2 buttered 1½-quart casseroles. Top with cracker crumbs. Bake at 350 degrees for 20 minutes. May substitute grapenut flakes for cracker crumbs. This is believed to be derived from an Indian recipe.

Ruth J. Gog

SALTIMBOCCA ALLA ROMANA

Yield: 4 servings

8 slices prosciutto or bacon	7 tablespoons dry white wine
8 3-ounce veal scaloppini	Salt and freshly ground pepper
8 to 12 sage leaves	to taste
¼ cup butter or margarine	1 tablespoon water

Place 1 slice prosciutto on each slice of veal; top with sage leaves. Serve with wooden picks. Melt butter in large skillet. Add veal. Cook until brown on both sides. Add wine, salt and pepper. Simmer for 6 to 8 minutes or until veal is tender. Remove veal to warm serving platter; remoe picks. Add 1 tablespoon water to skillet, stirring to deglaze. Simmer for 1 minute, stirring constantly. Pour over saltimbocca. Garnish with additional sage leaves. Serve immediately.

Franca Lotz

Kumquat Flowers—Cut canned kumquat into 6 wedges to but not through bottom to make petals.

VEAL WITH LEMON AND BRANDY

Yield: 4 servings

³/₄ to 1 pound veal scallops
¹/₂ cup flour
2 tablespoons butter
1 tablespoon lemon juice

2 tablespoons brandy
1 tablespoon chopped parsley
Lemon slices

Flatten veal with meat mallet. Coat with flour. Brown in butter in skillet for 3 minutes on each side. Remove to serving platter. Add lemon juice and brandy to skillet, stirring to deglaze. Simmer for 2 minutes, stirring constantly. Pour over veal. Garnish with parsley and lemon slices. Serve with fettucini.

Gloria Carmines

VERMOUTH VEAL

Yield: 6 servings

6 thin veal slices
Flour
1 egg, beaten
Bread crumbs
3 tablespoons olive oil

3 tablespoons butter
8 ounces dry vermouth
¹/₄ cup butter
Lemon juice to taste
Lemon slices

Coat veal with flour; dip in egg. Coat with bread crumbs. Chill, covered, for 1 hour. Sauté in olive oil and 3 tablespoons butter in skillet. Remove to serving platter; drain skillet. Stir in wine. Simmer until reduced by ²/₃, stirring frequently. Add remaining ¹/₄ cup butter and lemon juice. Heat to serving temperature. Serve with veal. Garnish with lemon slices.

Barbara Morrison

ELEPHANT STEW

Yield: 3800 servings

1 medium elephant

2 rabbits (optional)

Cut elephant into small pieces; allow about 3 months for this step. Combine with water to cover in very large kettle. Cook over fire for 4 weeks. May add rabbits if unexpected guests arrive, but do this only if necessary because most people do not like hare in their stew.

Prep Coach

Chicken Entrées

BIRD OF PARADISE

Yield: 6 servings

6 chicken breasts, boned,
  skinned
1 egg, beaten
1 tablespoon milk

Grated Parmesan cheese
1/4 cup butter or margarine
1/2 cup sherry

Rinse chicken; pat dry. Beat egg with milk in shallow dish. Dip chicken into egg mixture; roll in Parmesan cheese to coat. Brown on all sides in butter in skillet; arrange chicken in baking dish. Add sherry to skillet, stirring to deglaze. Pour over chicken. Bake, covered, at 350 degrees for 35 to 40 minutes or until tender. Serve on bed of wild rice. Garnish with green grapes and toasted pecans. I adapted and simplified this recipe from the version that is the specialty of a well-known restaurant.

Lois B. Borders

CHICKEN IN-A-BLANKET

Yield: 6 servings

1 cup cooking wine
2 cans cream of mushroom soup
2 chicken bouillon cubes

6 chicken breasts, boned,
  skinned
1 pound thinly sliced ham

Combine wine, soup and bouillon cubes in large skillet; mix well. Bring to a simmer in covered skillet, stirring occasionally until bouillon dissolves. Rinse chicken; pat dry. Wrap chicken in ham, securing with toothpick. Arrange in skillet. Simmer, covered, for 30 minutes. Serve on bed of wild rice. Garnish with small bunch of grapes.

Stephen C. De Riggs

Frosted Fruit—Rinse and dry grapes, cranberries or cherries. Dip in egg white beaten until frothy, then in granulated sugar; shake off excess sugar and let dry.

CHICKEN CARUSO WITH RICE
Yield: 6 servings

1½ pounds chicken
Garlic salt and pepper to taste
3 tablespoons butter or
  margarine
1 15-ounce jar spaghetti sauce

1 teaspoon Italian seasoning
2 cups chopped celery
  (optional)
3 cups hot cooked rice

Rinse chicken. Cook as desired; skin, bone and cut into strips. Sprinkle with garlic salt and pepper. Sauté in butter in skillet for 2 minutes. Add spaghetti sauce and Italian seasoning. Simmer, covered, for 10 minutes. Add celery. Cook until tender-crisp. Serve over hot cooked rice. Garnish with sprinkle of Parmesan cheese.

Mary M. Robinson

CHICKEN ELEGANT IN CRUST
Yield: 4 servings

3 chicken breasts, boned,
  skinned
Salt and pepper to taste
¼ cup melted butter
2 tablespoons Dijon mustard

1 cup whipping cream
1 sheet frozen puff pastry
1 egg, beaten
1 teaspoon water

Rinse chicken; pat dry. Cut into 1-inch wide strips. Sprinkle with salt and pepper. Sauté in butter in skillet for 6 to 8 minutes or until no longer pink; do not overcook. Remove chicken to plate. Add mustard to skillet, stirring to deglaze. Whisk in whipping cream gradually. Cook over very low heat for 10 to 15 minutes, stirring frequently. Stir in any juices that have drained from chicken. Add a small amount of sauce to chicken, tossing until coated. Thaw puff pastry for about 20 minutes. Unfold gently. Roll to 13x16-inch rectangle on lightly floured surface. Arrange chicken pieces on pastry to cover lower ⅓ of pastry on long side, leaving 2-inch margin on bottom and sides. Fold sides and bottom over chicken; roll as for jelly roll, sealing edge. Place seam side down on ungreased baking sheet. Beat egg with water in bowl. Brush over dough. Bake at 425 degrees for 30 minutes or until brown. If roll browns too quickly, reduce temperature to 375 degrees. Cut into slices. Serve with remaining sauce.

Robert Vance Fulkerson

APRICOT-GINGER CHICKEN   *Yield: 4 servings*

4 chicken breasts, boned,
  skinned
2 tablespoons butter
2 tablespoons oil
1   3-centimeter piece fresh
  ginger, peeled, shredded

¾ cup apricot nectar
1 tablespoon soy sauce
2 teaspoons cornstarch
1 tablespoon water
1 green onion, chopped

Rinse chicken; pat dry. Heat butter and oil in skillet. Add chicken. Cook for 10 minutes or until tender and golden brown on both sides. Place on serving plate; keep warm. Combine ginger, apricot nectar and soy sauce in glass bowl. Microwave on High for 5 minutes. Stir in cornstarch dissolved in water. Microwave for 2 minutes or until boiling. Stir in green onion. Spoon over chicken.

Doris Gnesin

CHICKEN HAWAIIAN   *Yield: 6 servings*

1   13-ounce can pineapple
  tidbits
1 large green bell pepper, cut
  into strips
1 or 2 cloves of garlic, minced
2 tablespoons oil

2 cans cream of chicken soup
3 cups cubed cooked chicken
2 tablespoons soy sauce
¼ cup slivered almonds,
  toasted

Drain pineapple, reserving juice. Sauté green pepper and garlic in oil in skillet. Stir in soup and reserved pineapple juice. Add chicken, pineapple tidbits and soy sauce. Heat to serving temperature, stirring frequently. Sprinkle with toasted almonds. Serve over hot cooked rice.

Trudy Lynch

CHICKEN MONTEREY

Yield: 4 servings

4 chicken breasts, boned, skinned
4 1/4x3-inch pieces Monterey Jack cheese
Sage to taste
1 tablespoon minced parsley
1/2 cup flour

2 eggs
1 teaspoon grated Parmesan cheese
Salt to taste
1/4 teaspoon pepper
1/4 cup oil

Rinse chicken; pat dry. Pound chicken to flatten. Place 1 piece cheese and sprinkle of sage on each piece chicken; fold chicken to enclose cheese. Mix parsley with flour. Beat eggs with Parmesan cheese, salt and pepper. Coat chicken rolls with flour mixture; dip into egg mixture. Cook in oil in skillet until crisp and golden brown; drain and place in baking dish. Bake at 375 degrees for 20 minutes.

Deborah Yates

CHICKEN SCALLOPINI

Yield: 4 servings

4 chicken breasts, boned, skinned

Caesar salad dressing
Seasoned Italian bread crumbs

Rinse chicken; pat dry. Pound lightly to flatten. Place in shallow dish. Add salad dressing to cover. Marinate in refrigerator for several hours. Drain. Roll chicken in bread crumbs to coat well; place in shallow baking pan. Bake at 375 degrees for 10 to 15 minutes. Turn chicken over. Bake for several minutes longer until golden brown. Garnish with lemon slices.

Nancy Biel

CHICKEN SUPREME

Yield: 10 to 12 servings

3 cups chopped cooked chicken
1 package long grain and wild rice mix
2 cans cream of mushroom soup
1 medium jar chopped pimento, drained
1 can mushroom pieces
1 medium onion, chopped

2 cups French-style green beans or 1 bunch fresh broccoli, chopped, steamed
1 cup mayonnaise
1 cup sliced drained water chestnuts
Salt and pepper to taste

Combine chicken, uncooked rice mix, soup, pimento, undrained mushrooms, onion, green beans, mayonnaise, water chestnuts, salt and pepper in bowl; mix well. Pour into casserole. Bake at 350 degrees for 45 minutes to 1 hour or until rice is tender.

Mike Soper

CHICKEN IN WINE

Yield: 6 servings

6 chicken breasts
3 tablespoons flour
1 cup sour cream
1 can cream of mushroom soup
1/2 cup sauterne

1/2 cup sliced unblanched almonds
1 2-ounce jar chopped pimentos
1 teaspoon paprika

Rinse chicken; pat dry. Arrange chicken in shallow baking dish. Blend flour and a small amount of sour cream in bowl. Blend in remaining sour cream, soup and wine. Pour over chicken. Sprinkle almonds, pimentos and paprika over top. Bake, uncovered, at 325 degrees for 1½ hours or until chicken is tender.

Alice W. Herge

PAN-BARBECUED CHICKEN   *Yield: 4 servings*

3 chicken breasts, boned,
  skinned
2 or 3 cloves of garlic, chopped
3 or 4 scallions, sliced
Olive oil
1   8-ounce can tomato sauce

1 tablespoon Worcestershire
  sauce
3 dashes of dry mustard
3 tablespoons red wine vinegar
Sugar to taste
Salt and pepper to taste

Rinse chicken; pat dry. Cut into chunks or slices. Sauté chicken, garlic and scallions in a small amount of olive oil in skillet over medium heat for 5 minutes. Add tomato sauce, Worcestershire sauce, dry mustard, vinegar, sugar, salt and pepper; mix well. Simmer for 20 minutes, adding a small amount of water if necessary to make of desired consistency. Serve chicken over noodles with fresh green beans and rolls.

Deb Drury

FRIED CHICKEN   *Yield: 4 servings*

1 chicken, cut up
Buttermilk
Flour
Salt and pepper to taste

Oil for deep frying
2 tablespoons flour
1 cup milk

Rinse chicken; pat dry. Place in shallow dish. Add buttermilk to cover. Chill for 1 hour or longer. Mix desired amount of flour with salt and pepper. Drain chicken; coat with seasoned flour. Deep-fry in hot oil in skillet until brown, crispy and fork-tender. Cover during 15 minutes of the cooking time. Drain on brown paper bag. Pour oil from skillet. Blend 2 tablespoons flour into remaining pan drippings in skillet. Add milk gradually, stirring constantly with fork. Bring to a simmer, stirring constantly. May serve chicken hot or cold.

Nancy Pruitt

OVEN-FRIED CHICKEN

Yield: 6 servings

6 chicken breasts, boned,
  skinned
1 egg, beaten

1 cup seasoned bread crumbs
1/4 cup melted butter or
  margarine

Rinse chicken; pat dry. Dip into egg; coat with bread crumbs. Roll in melted butter. Arrange on baking sheet. Drizzle any remaining butter over chicken. Bake at 375 degrees for 15 minutes. Turn chicken over. Bake for 15 minutes or until golden brown. Serve warm or chill and serve with blueberry chutney.

Trisha Hughes

GRILLED CHICKEN

Yield: 4 servings

6 chicken thighs
4 chicken breast quarters
1 8-ounce bottle of Italian
  salad dressing

1 cup white wine
Dillweed and seasoned salt to
  taste

Rinse chicken; pat dry. Place in shallow dish. Pour mixture of salad dressing and white wine over chicken. Sprinkle generously with dillweed and seasoned salt. Marinate in refrigerator for 3 to 4 hours. Drain, reserving marinade. Grill chicken over medium coals on smoker grill for 45 to 55 minutes or until tender, basting frequently with reserved marinade.

Doug West

Citrus Cups—Halve and scoop out oranges, lemons or limes and fill with cranberry relish.

MARINATED CHICKEN BREASTS
Yield: 8 servings

8 chicken breasts
2 cups plain yogurt or sour
    cream
2 teaspoons celery salt
3 cloves of garlic, crushed
1/2 teaspoon salt

1/4 teaspoon pepper
1/4 teaspoon paprika
1/2 cup lemon juice
2 to 2 1/2 tablespoons sugar
Bread crumbs or stuffing mix
    crumbs

Rinse chicken; pat dry. Arrange in shallow dish. Combine yogurt, celery salt, garlic, salt, pepper, paprika, lemon juice and sugar in bowl; mix well. Pour over chicken. Marinate in refrigerator for 24 hours or longer. Place chicken in baking pan. Sprinkle with crumbs. Bake at 350 degrees for 30 to 45 minutes.

Dorothy Lewis

POULET GARNI AUX CHAMPIGNONS
Yield: 8 servings

8 chicken breasts, boned,
    skinned
1/2 cup flour
1 teaspoon salt
1/2 teaspoon paprika
1 teaspoon oregano
1/2 cup butter
2 chicken bouillon cubes

1 cup boiling water
1 cup white wine
1/4 cup butter
1/4 cup flour
1/2 cup sliced onion
8 ounces mushrooms
2 tomatoes, sliced

Rinse chicken; pat dry. Coat with mixture of 1/2 cup flour, salt, paprika and oregano. Melt 1/2 cup butter in 2-quart baking dish. Arrange chicken in baking dish. Bake at 400 degrees for 30 minutes. Dissolve bouillon cubes in boiling water. Add wine. Melt 1/4 cup butter in saucepan. Blend in 1/4 cup flour. Stir in bouillon mixture gradually. Cook until thickened, stirring constantly. Turn chicken over. Add onion, mushrooms and tomatoes. Spoon wine sauce over top. Bake at 350 degrees for 40 minutes.

Joan Sale

OLÉ POULET

Yield: 3 to 4 servings

4 chicken breasts, boned, skinned
Flour
3 tablespoons olive oil
3 green onions, chopped
1 or 2 fresh tomatoes, cut into wedges

1 8-ounce jar pimento-stuffed olives, sliced
1 teaspoon thyme
Pepper to taste
¼ cup pine nuts (optional)

Rinse chicken; pat dry. Cut into strips. Coat strips with flour. Cook in hot olive oil in skillet until brown on all sides. Add green onions, tomatoes and olives. Cook just until tomatoes are heated through. Add thyme, pepper and pine nuts. Serve immediately with yellow rice or couscous and a dry white wine.

Sue and Doug West

LEMON TARRAGON CHICKEN

Yield: 6 servings

1 roasting chicken
2 teaspoons tarragon
½ apple

1 cup beef bouillon
Juice of 1 lemon

Rinse chicken; pat dry. Sprinkle half the tarragon in cavity; add apple. Sprinkle remaining tarragon over outside of chicken. Place in roaster. Roast, covered, at 400 degrees for 1 hour or until tender. Place chicken on serving plate; keep warm. Skim pan juices. Scrape tarragon from chicken into pan juices. Add bouillon. Boil until juices are reduced to ½ cup. Add lemon juice. Heat to serving temperature. Carve chicken. Serve with rice and sauce.

Dianne Light

CHICKEN IN ARTICHOKE SAUCE

Yield: 4 servings

4 chicken breasts, boned,
 skinned
1/4 cup butter or olive oil
3 tablespoons butter
2 tablespoons ranch salad
 dressing

3 tablespoons flour
1/2 cup (or more) milk
2 cans artichoke hearts,
 drained, chopped
Salt and pepper to taste

Rinse chicken; pat dry. Cut chicken into strips. Cook in 1/4 cup butter in skillet until brown on all sides. Melt 3 tablespoons butter in saucepan. Blend in salad dressing and flour. Stir in milk gradually. Cook until thickened, stirring constantly. Add artichoke hearts, salt and pepper. Heat to serving temperature. Ladle sauce into center of serving platter. Arrange chicken strips around sauce. Garnish with parsley sprigs. Serve with wild rice and fresh tomato slices.

Sue and Doug West

SESAME CHICKEN DRUMETTES

Yield: 4 servings

2 pounds chicken drumettes
1/4 cup soy sauce
1/4 cup white wine
1/4 cup teriyaki sauce
1/8 teaspoon garlic juice

1 tablespoon brown sugar
1 teaspoon ground ginger
2 tablespoons sesame seed,
 toasted
Salt and pepper to taste

Rinse chicken; pat dry. Place in 11x13-inch baking dish. Combine soy sauce, wine, teriyaki sauce, garlic juice, brown sugar, ginger, sesame seed, salt and pepper in glass bowl; mix well. Microwave on High for 45 seconds. Cool slightly. Pour over chicken. Marinate in refrigerator for 4 to 6 hours, turning chicken occasionally. Drain, reserving marinade. Arrange chicken in rows on large baking sheet. Brush with reserved marinade. Bake at 375 degrees for 10 minutes. Turn chicken over; brush with reserved marinade. Bake for 10 minutes longer. Serve as main course or as appetizers.

Trisha Hughes

SPICY GINGER CHICKEN

Yield: 6 servings

6 chicken breasts, boned, skinned
Flour
1/4 cup olive oil
1 clove of garlic, minced
2 green onions, chopped
6 fresh mushrooms, sliced
1 package frozen pea pods
1 red bell pepper, cut into strips
1 can sliced water chestnuts, drained
1 package ramen noodles
2 teaspoons cornstarch
1/4 cup white wine
3 tablespoons black bean sauce
2 teaspoons ground ginger
1 teaspoon Tabasco sauce

Rinse chicken; pat dry. Cut into slices; coat lightly with flour. Cook in hot olive oil in skillet until lightly browned. Add garlic and green onions. Cook until chicken is crisp. Add mushrooms, pea pods, red pepper and water chestnuts; mix well. Cook ramen noodles in boiling water for 1 minute; do not use seasoning packet. Stir noodles into chicken mixture. Dissolve cornstarch in wine in bowl. Stir into chicken mixture with remaining ingredients. Serve immediately.

Sheri Burden

SWISS CHICKEN CUTLET

Yield: 5 servings

5 chicken breast filets
Salt to taste
2 eggs, beaten
1 cup fine bread crumbs
1/4 cup oil
3 tablespoons butter
1/4 cup flour
1/2 teaspoon salt
1/8 teaspoon pepper
2 1/2 cups milk
1 cup shredded Swiss cheese
1/2 cup dry white wine

Rinse chicken; pat dry. Pound to 1/4-inch thickness; sprinkle with salt. Dip into beaten eggs; coat with bread crumbs. Heat 2 tablespoons oil in skillet. Cook chicken for 2 minutes on each side, adding oil as necessary. Melt butter in saucepan. Blend in flour, salt and pepper. Stir in milk. Cook until thickened, stirring constantly. Add cheese. Stir until cheese melts; remove from heat. Blend in wine. Pour half the sauce into 9x13-inch baking dish. Arrange cutlets in dish. Pour remaining sauce over top. Chill, covered, in refrigerator. Bake, covered, at 350 degrees for 50 minutes.

Ronelle Plocher

Seafood Entrées

STEAMED FISH WITH VEGETABLES
Yield: 4 servings

4 fish filets
Sliced zucchini
Sliced mushrooms

Sliced red bell pepper
Sliced onion
4 orange slices

Place each fish filet on square of foil. Top with remaining ingredients. Seal tightly; place in baking pan. Bake at 350 degrees for 20 minutes.

Peter Spears

FRESH FISH ORIENTAL
Yield: 2 to 3 servings

1 pound fresh mahi-mahi or
   grouper filets, skinned
Garlic-ginger paste
Juice of 1/2 lime

1/4 cup soy sauce
Dash of white wine (optional)
1/3 cup peanut oil
2 whole green onions, chopped

Spread 1 side of fish filets with garlic-ginger paste. Place spread side in baking dish sprayed with nonstick cooking spray. Squeeze lime juice over fish. Drizzle with soy sauce and wine. Bake at 375 degrees just until fish flakes easily. Heat peanut oil in skillet until very hot. Sprinkle green onions over fish. Pour hot oil gradually over onions and fish. Serve with rice. Garlic-ginger paste can be purchased.

Sue West

GREAT GOBS OF GROUPER
Yield: 4 servings

2 cartons Eggbeaters
1/2 cup milk
Salt and pepper to taste
4 to 6 ounces Special K cereal,
   crushed

1 cup cornflake crumbs
4 1/2-inch thick grouper filets
Canola oil for deep frying

Combine Eggbeaters with milk, salt and pepper in bowl; mix well. Mix cereals in plastic bag. Dip fish filets into Eggbeater mixture; shake in cereal, coating well. Deep-fry in 325 to 350-degree oil for 3 to 4 minutes or until golden brown.

Bobby W. Welch

LEMON BURGER MACKEREL

Yield: 2 or 3 servings

Ground beef
Oil
Soy sauce
1 pound king mackerel or
  dolphin filets

Seasoned salt and pepper to
  taste
Juice of 6 lemons
1/4 cup Worcestershire sauce
1/2 cup melted butter

Shape ground beef into patties. Combine 2 parts oil with 1 part soy sauce in bowl. Dip fish filets into mixture. Place in foil tray. Sprinkle with seasoned salt and pepper. Pour mixture of lemon juice, Worcestershire sauce and butter over fish. Place foil tray on grill. Arrange ground beef patties on grill around foil tray. Grill until fish flakes easily and beef is done to taste.

Jeff, Jonathan and Jay Wilson

SALMON WITH GINGER SAUCE

Yield: 2 to 3 servings

1 pound salmon steaks
Salt and pepper to taste
Melted butter
Lemon juice
3 tablespoons brown sugar

3 tablespoons melted butter
1 teaspoon lemon juice
2 teaspoons water
1/4 teaspoon grated fresh ginger

Season salmon with salt and pepper. Brush with mixture of butter and lemon juice. Place skin side down on grill. Grill for 10 minutes for each inch of thickness, turning once. Combine brown sugar and 3 tablespoons melted butter in saucepan. Cook for 1 to 2 minutes. Add 1 teaspoon lemon juice, water and ginger. Bring to a boil. Simmer for several minutes or until brown sugar is completely dissolved. Serve over salmon. May cook in skillet on top of stove if preferred.

Eileen Albert

SEA PINES SEAFOOD CASSEROLE   *Yield: 12 servings*

8 ounces crab meat
8 ounces lobster meat or
  scallops
1 pound peeled shrimp
½ cup chopped green bell
  pepper
¼ cup minced onion

1½ cups finely chopped celery
1 cup mayonnaise
1 tablespoon Worcestershire
  sauce
½ teaspoon salt
2 cups crushed potato chips
Paprika to taste

Combine seafood, green pepper, onion, celery, mayonnaise, Worcestershire sauce and salt in bowl; mix well. Spoon into large baking dish. Top with potato chips; sprinkle with paprika. Bake at 400 degrees for 20 to 25 minutes or until bubbly. Serve with fruit salad and bread.

Paige Pruitt

PASTA WITH SEAFOOD   *Yield: 8 servings*

1 small onion, chopped
2 stalks celery, chopped
2 cloves of garlic, minced
1 pound mushrooms, sliced
1 red bell pepper, chopped
3 tablespoons olive oil
1 pound peeled shrimp
1 pound scallops
1 pound lump or imitation crab
  meat

4 ounces snow peas
1 cup yogurt
½ cup mayonnaise
½ cup tomato sauce
3 ounces cream cheese
1 package angel hair pasta or
  linguine, cooked
Parmesan cheese to taste

Sauté onion, celery, garlic, mushrooms and bell pepper in olive oil in saucepan. Add shrimp and scallops. Cook for 5 minutes. Add crab meat, snow peas, yogurt, mayonnaise and tomato sauce; mix well. Stir in cream cheese. Serve over pasta. Sprinkle with Parmesan cheese.

Shirley DeVeaux

SEAFOOD KABOBS
Yield: 10 servings

1 pound peeled shrimp	1 pint oysters
1 pound scallops	Teriyaki sauce
2 swordfish or grouper filets, cut up	Onion wedges, green bell pepper strips, mushrooms

Combine seafood with teriyaki sauce in shallow dish. Marinate in refrigerator for 2 hours; drain. Alternate seafood on skewers with onions, bell pepper and mushrooms. Grill or bake at 350 degrees for 20 minutes. Serve with yellow rice.

Nancy Pruitt

CRAB MEAT-STUFFED LOBSTER
Yield: 4 servings

2 cans crab meat	Grated Parmesan cheese
2 cans cream of mushroom soup	4 lobsters, boiled, split
2 egg yolks, beaten	Bread crumbs

Combine crab meat and soup in double boiler; mix well. Cook for 10 minutes. Stir a small of hot mixture into egg yolks; stir egg yolks into hot mixture. Stir in 1/2 cup cheese. Cook until thickened to desired consistency, stirring constantly. Spoon crab meat mixture into lobsters. Sprinkle with additional cheese and bread crumbs. Place on rack in broiler pan. Broil for 5 to 6 minutes or until golden brown.

Phyllis Modell

CRAB CASSEROLE
Yield: 10 servings

1 pound fresh crab meat	8 hard-boiled eggs, chopped
2 cups soft bread crumbs	2 cups mayonnaise
2 tablespoons chopped parsley	1 cup buttered bread crumbs

Combine first 5 ingredients in bowl; mix well. Spoon into 9x13-inch baking dish. Sprinkle with buttered crumbs. Bake at 325 degrees for 1 hour. This recipe is from Mrs. Wallace F. Bennett, wife of the Senator from Utah.

Peggy Morgan

SHERRIED CRAB CASSEROLE   *Yield: 8 servings*

1/2 green bell pepper, chopped	1/2 cup slivered almonds
3 tablespoons butter	1 pound crab meat
Canned or fresh mushrooms	1/2 cup sherry
2 tablespoons flour	Pepper to taste
1 cup milk	2 cups shredded sharp cheese
1 can cream of mushroom soup	Bread crumbs

Sauté green pepper in butter in skillet. Add mushrooms. Sauté until tender. Blend flour and milk in saucepan. Cook until thickened, stirring constantly. Add sautéed vegetables, soup, almonds, crab meat, sherry, pepper and 1³/4 cups cheese; mix well. Spoon into greased baking dish. Top with bread crumbs and remaining 1/4 cup cheese. Bake at 375 degrees for 30 minutes.

Corinne VanLandingham

DAUFUSKIE DEVILED CRABS   *Yield: 4 to 6 servings*

1 cup finely chopped celery	1¹/2 cups bread crumbs
1 large green bell pepper, finely chopped	1/2 cup heavy cream
	1 cup melted butter
1 cup thinly sliced onion	Tabasco sauce to taste
1/2 cup chopped parsley	1¹/2 teaspoons dry mustard
2 pounds crab meat	1 teaspoon salt

Sauté celery, green pepper and onion in nonstick skillet sprayed with nonstick cooking spray. Combine with parsley, crab meat, bread crumbs, cream, butter, Tabasco sauce, dry mustard and salt in large bowl; toss lightly. Spoon into buttered crab shells or baking dish. Bake at 350 degrees for 25 to 30 minutes or until light brown.

Sue Berne

CRAB CHESAPEAKE

Yield: 4 servings

1 pound backfin crab meat
1 cup white sauce
2 hard-boiled eggs, sieved
1 teaspoon dry mustard
1 tablespoon chopped parsley
1 tablespoon lemon juice
1 teaspoon Worcestershire
  sauce
1 teaspoon salt
Cayenne pepper to taste
1/4 cup bread crumbs

Combine first 9 ingredients in bowl; mix lightly. Spoon into baking shells or casserole. Sprinkle with bread crumbs. Bake at 350 degrees for 15 minutes or until heated through.

Elsie L. Brewton

SAUTÉED OYSTERS

Yield: 2 servings

12 large oysters
Flour
1/2 teaspoon basil
1/2 teaspoon tarragon
2 tablespoons melted butter
2 tablespoons dry white wine

Pat oysters dry; coat with flour. Sauté oysters with basil and oregano in butter in skillet; remove to heated platter. Add wine to skillet, stirring to deglaze. Cook until heated through. Spoon over oysters.

Frances Caldwell

MAGGIE'S SCALLOPED OYSTERS

Yield: 8 servings

1 pound butter, softened
4 cups cracker crumbs
1 quart oysters, drained
1 cup heavy cream
Worcestershire sauce, hot sauce
  and pepper to taste

Spread 1/4 of the butter in large baking dish. Layer 1/4 of the cracker crumbs and 1/3 of the oysters in prepared dish. Dot with 1/4 of the butter. Repeat layers until all ingredients are used, ending with cracker crumbs and butter. Combine cream, Worcestershire sauce, hot sauce and pepper in bowl; mix well. Pour over layers. Bake at 425 degrees for 15 to 20 minutes or until oysters curl.

Nancy Stephens

SPINACH AND OYSTER PIE
Yield: 8 servings

2 10-ounce packages frozen chopped spinach, cooked
2 tablespoons sour cream
3 tablespoons grated Parmesan cheese
Garlic salt to taste
1/2 clove of garlic, minced
1 medium onion, chopped
1/2 medium green bell pepper, chopped
1 cup butter
3/4 cup flour
1 1/2 teaspoons paprika
1/2 teaspoon salt
1/4 teaspoon pepper
1 quart fresh oysters
1 tablespoon lemon juice
2 teaspoons Worcestershire sauce
1/4 cup cracker crumbs

Mix drained spinach with sour cream, cheese and garlic salt in bowl. Spread in 10-inch pie plate. Sauté garlic, onion and green pepper in butter in saucepan. Stir in flour, paprika, salt and pepper. Cook for several minutes. Stir in undrained oysters, lemon juice and Worcestershire sauce. Spoon into spinach crust. Sprinkle with cracker crumbs. Bake at 400 degrees for 15 to 20 minutes or until brown.

Nancy H. Roe

SCALLOP-ARTICHOKE CASSEROLE
Yield: 4 servings

8 to 12 ounces scallops
1/2 cup white wine
3 tablespoons flour
Salt and pepper to taste
3 tablespoons melted butter
1/4 cup milk
1/2 cup white wine
1 tablespoon lemon juice
1 tablespoon mayonnaise
1 tablespoon Italian salad dressing
1 can artichoke hearts, drained, chopped
Crumbled crisp-fried bacon
Grated Parmesan cheese

Marinate scallops in 1/2 cup white wine in refrigerator. Blend flour, salt and pepper into butter in saucepan. Cook for several minutes. Add milk, 1/2 cup wine, lemon juice, mayonnaise and salad dressing; mix well. Cook until thickened, stirring constantly. Stir in scallops with wine marinade. Add artichokes. Cook until heated through, stirring constantly. Spoon into 2-quart baking dish. Top with bacon and cheese. Bake at 350 degrees for 20 minutes until brown.

Sue and Doug West

SCALLOPS IN GARLIC SAUCE
Yield: 3 servings

1 clove of garlic, minced
1 tablespoon olive oil
2 tablespoons melted butter
1 tablespoon Italian salad
  dressing
6 to 8 mushrooms, sliced

1 pound fresh scallops
1 teaspoon oregano or *bouquet garni*
Salt and pepper to taste
8 ounces fresh pasta, cooked
Grated Parmesan cheese

Sauté garlic in mixture of next 3 ingredients in skillet. Add mushrooms, scallops, oregano, salt and pepper; mix well. Cook until scallops are tender. Spoon scallops over pasta. Sprinkle with cheese.

Cindy Ware

SCALLOPED SCALLOPS
Yield: 4 servings

1 pound scallops
Buttered crumbs

1 cup heavy cream
1/2 cup sherry

Cut scallops into bite-sized pieces. Arrange in single layer in buttered shallow baking dish. Sprinkle lightly with crumbs; mix gently. Pour mixture of cream and sherry over top. Season with salt and pepper. Top with additional crumbs. Bake at 350 degrees for 30 minutes.

Sally Reeds

BARBECUED SHRIMP
Yield: 6 to 8 servings

1 cup each butter and oil
1 teaspoon lemon juice
2 teaspoons minced garlic
4 bay leaves
2 teaspoons rosemary

1/2 teaspoon each basil, salt, oregano and cayenne pepper
1 tablespoon paprika
3/4 teaspoon pepper
3 to 4 pounds shrimp

Combine first 12 ingredients in saucepan. Cook for 7 to 8 minutes. Let stand for 30 minutes. Add shrimp. Simmer for 6 to 8 minutes. Spread in baking pan. Bake at 450 degrees for 10 minutes. Discard bay leaves. Serve with crusty French bread for dipping up sauce.

Kathy Levinger

SHRIMP AND SAFFRON LINGUINE   *Yield: 2 servings*

2 tablespoons crumbled
  saffron threads
$1/2$ cup dry white wine
3 carrots
Tops of 4 scallions
$51/3$ ounces uncooked linguine
2 teaspoons turmeric
Salt to taste

8 ounces shrimp
2 tablespoons oil
1 teaspoon minced garlic
$1/4$ cup chopped shallots
Pepper to taste
$1/2$ cup canned chicken broth
$3/4$ cup heavy cream

Soak saffron in wine in bowl for 5 minutes. Shred carrots with vegetable peeler, discarding cores. Cut scallion tops lengthwise into very thin strips. Cook pasta with turmeric in salted boiling water in large saucepan for 10 minutes or until *al dente*; drain. Peel shrimp, leaving tails intact. Rinse and pat dry. Sauté in hot oil in large skillet for 1 minute. Add garlic, shallots, salt and pepper. Cook until shrimp are pink; remove to warm plate. Add saffron mixture. Cook until most of liquid has evaporated. Add chicken broth, cream and carrots. Cook until reduced by $1/2$. Add scallion tops, pasta, shrimp and juices from shrimp. Simmer just until heated through.

Vikki Hughes

SAUCY SHRIMP CASSEROLE   *Yield: 6 servings*

$1/4$ cup flour
2 cups milk
1 teaspoon Worcestershire
  sauce
Pepper to taste

8 ounces sharp Cheddar
  cheese, shredded
6 hard-boiled eggs, sliced
1 pound cooked shrimp

Blend flour, milk, Worcestershire sauce and pepper in saucepan. Cook until thickened, stirring constantly. Stir in cheese until melted. Alternate layers of eggs, shrimp and cheese sauce in $11/2$-quart baking dish until all ingredients are used. Bake at 350 degrees for 20 to 25 minutes or until bubbly. Garnish with paprika and parsley.

Corinne VanLandingham

SHRIMP ETOUFFÉE

Yield: 6 servings

3 pounds fresh medium shrimp
2 quarts water
1½ cups chopped onions
1 cup chopped celery
1 cup chopped green bell
  pepper
½ cup melted butter

½ cup melted margarine
3 cloves of garlic, minced
¼ cup flour
¼ to 1 teaspoon Tabasco sauce
½ teaspoon salt
½ to 1 teaspoon pepper
1 cup chopped shallots

Peel shrimp, reserving shells. Combine shells with water in large saucepan. Bring to a boil; reduce heat. Simmer for 30 minutes. Strain and reserve stock. Sauté onions, celery and green pepper in mixture of butter and margarine in large skillet for 10 minutes. Add garlic. Sauté for 2 minutes. Stir in flour gradually. Add reserved shrimp stock 3 to 4 tablespoons at a time, stirring constantly as sauce thickens to desired consistency. Add Tabasco sauce, salt and pepper. Stir in shrimp. Simmer, covered, over medium-low heat for 20 to 30 minutes, stirring occasionally and adding additional shrimp stock as needed for desired consistency. Remove from heat. Stir in shallots. Let stand, covered, for 10 minutes. Serve over hot cooked rice.

Dexter Jeffords

SHRIMP DELIGHT

Yield: 6 servings

1 cup sliced fresh mushrooms
2 tablespoons butter
2 tablespoons flour
½ cup cream
1 can cream of mushroom soup
⅓ cup cooking sherry
¼ cup grated Parmesan cheese

1½ pounds large shrimp,
  cooked
1 15-ounce can artichoke
  hearts, drained, cut into
  halves
½ cup toasted slivered almonds

Sauté mushrooms in butter in skillet; push mushrooms to one side. Stir flour into butter in skillet. Stir in cream gradually. Cook for 1 minute or until thickened, stirring constantly. Add soup, sherry and cheese; mix until cheese melts. Stir in shrimp and artichokes. Cook until heated through, stirring gently. Sprinkle with almonds. Serve over rice.

Peg Bassett

SHRIMP AND RICE ELEGANTE   *Yield: 4 to 6 servings*

Chopped scallions or green
  onions
2 tablespoons butter
1 pound shrimp, cleaned
4 ounces fresh mushrooms, sliced
3 tablespoons chili sauce

1¹/₃ cups instant rice
1²/₃ cups water
1 teaspoon salt
¹/₈ teaspoon pepper
1 cup sour cream
1 tablespoon flour

Sauté scallions in butter in skillet or wok. Add shrimp and mushrooms. Sauté until shrimp are done to taste. Stir in chili sauce, rice, water, salt and pepper. Simmer, covered, for 5 minutes. Stir in mixture of sour cream and flour. Heat just to serving temperature.

Jane W. Kincheloe

SHRIMP AND SPINACH CASSEROLE   *Yield: 6 servings*

3 10-ounce packages frozen
  chopped spinach, thawed,
  drained
Butter
2 pounds uncooked shrimp,
  peeled
Salt and pepper to taste
1 can cream of mushroom soup
1 can Cheddar cheese soup

1 can sliced mushrooms
1 can sliced black olives
1 package mozzarella cheese
  slices
1 package provolone cheese slices
Bread crumbs
Shredded Cheddar cheese
Chopped parsley

Spread spinach in buttered baking dish. Dot with butter. Arrange shrimp over spinach; sprinkle with salt and pepper. Combine soups, mushrooms and olives in bowl; mix well. Spoon over shrimp. Top with cheese slices. Sprinkle with bread crumbs, shredded cheese and parsley. Bake at 325 degrees for 1 hour.

Cheryl Wysocki

Game &
Game Birds

COMPANY VENISON STROGANOFF   *Yield: 10 servings*

2 cups apple cider vinegar
2 cups red wine
1/2 cup olive oil
31/2 cups water
1 lemon, sliced
3 onions, sliced
3/4 cup packed brown sugar
1/2 teaspoon cinnamon
1/2 teaspoon allspice

1/2 teaspoon cloves
1/2 teaspoon (or more) garlic
   powder
1 teaspoon salt
1/2 teaspoon pepper
1   7 to 9-pound venison roast
Oil for browning roast
1/4 cup flour
1 cup sour cream

Combine first 13 ingredients in bowl. Add roast, coating well. Marinate in refrigerator overnight, turning several times. Drain, reserving marinate. Brown roast in a small amount of oil in saucepan. Place in roasting pan. Add 1 cup reserved marinade. Roast at 325 degrees for 3 hours, basting occasionally. Remove roast to serving plate. Blend 1/3 cup pan drippings with flour in saucepan. Stir in remaining marinade and sour cream. Cook until thickened, stirring constantly. Slice venison; serve in gravy.

Trish Highsmith

SMOKED VENISON   *Yield: 6 servings*

1   4-pound venison roast
Dry wine
1/2 cup oil
1/4 cup lemon juice

1 teaspoon pepper
Sour cream
Hot pepper jelly

Marinate venison in wine to cover in bowl in refrigerator for 24 hours or longer. Combine oil, lemon juice and pepper in bowl; mix well. Drain roast, reserving marinade. Place roast on spit on grill over low coals. Grill for about 10 minutes, basting with oil mixture. Add soaked hickory chips to coals. Grill, covered, for 3 hours, basting with oil mixture occasionally and adding briquets as needed to maintain even heat. Remove roast from spit; baste with reserved wine marinade. Wrap with foil; cool to room temperature. Reheat in foil at 250 degrees for 20 minutes. Slice roast. Serve slices topped with sour cream and pepper jelly. May use any cut of venison for this recipe.

Richard Thomas

MARINADE FOR LEG OF VENISON
Yield: 6 cups

2 cups red wine
1/4 cup olive oil
2 small carrots, sliced
2 small onions, sliced
Savory and thyme to taste

2 cloves
2 sprigs of parsley or 1
   teaspoon parsley flakes
2 bay leaves
10 peppercorns

Combine wine, olive oil, carrots, onions, savory, thyme, cloves, parsley, bay leaves and peppercorns in deep bowl; mix well. Marinate venison in refrigerator for 48 hours. Cook as desired. May fill spaces in marinade with apples to conserve wine.

Peggy Carswell

DOVE PIE
Yield: 4 servings

12 whole dove or dove breasts
1 small onion, cut into quarters
1 stalk celery, sliced
1 bay leaf
1 tablespoon salt
3 or 4 peppercorns
1 pint oysters, drained

1 recipe 2-crust pie pastry
Butter, sliced
Salt and pepper to taste
2 tablespoons flour
1/4 cup minced parsley
Paprika to taste

Rinse dove inside and out. Combine with onion, celery, bay leaf, salt, peppercorns and water to cover in saucepan. Simmer, covered, for 45 to 50 minutes or until tender. Let stand in broth until cool. Strain broth, reserving 2 cups. Stuff each dove with 3 to 4 oysters. Line baking dish with half the pastry. Dot with butter. Arrange dove in prepared dish with remaining oysters. Sprinkle with salt and pepper. Blend 2 cups reserved broth with flour in bowl. Spoon over dove. Add parsley. Dot with 1/4 cup butter. Top with remaining pastry. Dot with additional butter; sprinkle with paprika. Bake at 350 degrees for 45 minutes.

Gloria Carmines

SOUTHERN DOVE WITH RICE   *Yield: 8 servings*

8 dove breasts	Salt and pepper to taste
Flour	1/4 cup whipping cream
1/2 cup peanut oil	1 package wild rice mix
2 1/2 cups milk	1/4 cup pine nuts

Rinse dove breasts and pat dry. Coat with flour. Fry in hot peanut oil in skillet until tender and brown on both sides. Remove dove to warm plate. Stir 1/2 cup flour into drippings in skillet. Cook for several minutes. Stir in milk gradually; reduce heat. Simmer for 15 minutes or until thickened, stirring constantly. Stir in salt, pepper and cream. Add dove. Simmer for 15 minutes. Cook wild rice using package directions. Serve dove and gravy over rice. Sprinkle with pine nuts.

Joseph C. Harden

CONNIE'S WILD DUCK SKEWERS   *Yield: 6 to 8 servings*

1/3 cup lime juice	1 tablespoon chili powder
2 tablespoons honey	1 cup chopped onion
1/3 cup olive oil	3 cloves of garlic, minced
2/3 cup soy sauce	1/3 cup olive oil
1 tablespoon curry powder	Boned breasts of 4 mallard
1 teaspoon freshly ground pepper	ducks

Combine lime juice, honey, 1/3 cup olive oil, soy sauce, curry powder, pepper and chili powder in jar; shake well to mix. Sauté onion and garlic in 1/3 cup olive oil in skillet. Add to jar; mix well. Rinse duck breasts and pat dry. Cut each breast half into 2 strips, discarding skin. Combine with marinade in bowl; mix well. Marinate in refrigerator for 3 hours. Soak skewers in water for 1 hour. Drain duck strips, reserving marinade. Thread onto skewers. Grill over hot coals in covered grill for 3 to 4 minutes on each side or until done to taste. Do not overcook; these are best served rare to medium-rare. Heat reserved marinade in saucepan. Serve with duck.

Connie Richards

DUCKS BURGUNDY

Yield: 4 to 6 servings

2 wild ducks, rinsed inside and
   out
Salt to taste
1/4 cup butter
1/4 cup flour
2 cups chicken soup
1 cup Burgundy

1/4 cup chopped onion
2 small bay leaves
1/2 teaspoon salt
Pepper to taste
1   6-ounce can sliced
   mushrooms

Simmer ducks, covered, in a small amount of salted water in saucepan for 30 minutes; drain. Brown in butter in saucepan; remove to plate. Stir flour into drippings in skillet. Stir in soup, wine, onion, bay leaves, 1/2 teaspoon salt and pepper. Cook until thickened, stirring constantly;. Add ducks and mushrooms. Simmer, covered, for 2 hours or until ducks are tender. Remove bay leaves. Serve with hot cooked wild rice.

Gloria Carmines

FRUITED STUFFED WILD GOOSE

Yield: 10 servings

1   6 to 8-pound wild goose
Salt and pepper to taste
1/2 cup chopped onion
1 1/2 cups chopped peeled
   apples
1/2 cup margarine or butter
3 1/2 cups soft bread cubes

1/2 cup raisins
1/4 teaspoon sage
3/4 teaspoon salt
1/8 teaspoon pepper
Bacon slices
2 tablespoons margarine
1 cup orange juice

Rinse goose and pat dry. Sprinkle inside and out with salt and pepper to taste. Sauté onion and apples in 1/2 cup margarine in skillet. Stir in bread cubes, raisins, sage, 3/4 teaspoon salt and 1/8 teaspoon pepper. Spoon into cavity of goose. Arrange bacon slices over breast and legs of goose; place in browning bag. Melt 2 tablespoons margarine with orange juice in saucepan. Spoon into browning bag; secure opening. Roast in moderate oven for 2 hours.

Mary Dawes

MARINATED GOOSE
Yield: 6 servings

1/2 cup oil	1/3 teaspoon thyme
1/2 cup red wine	2 goose breasts, skinned
1/4 cup lime juice	1 cup sour cream
1/2 teaspoon minced garlic	1 tablespoon horseradish
1 tablespoon parsley flakes	Seasoned salt to taste

Combine first 6 ingredients in bowl; mix well. Add goose. Marinate in refrigerator for 12 hours; drain. Grill for 15 to 18 minutes or until medium rare. Serve with mixture of remaining ingredients.

Louise Baughman

ROAST GROUSE WITH SOUR CREAM
Yield: 2 servings

2 grouse, dressed	1/2 teaspoon salt and pepper
Chestnut or corn bread stuffing	1 cup sherry
4 slices bacon	1 cup sour cream

Rinse grouse inside and out. Stuff cavities with chestnut or corn bread stuffing. Truss and place in roasting pan. Layer bacon over breasts of grouse; sprinkle with salt and pepper. Dip 2 heavy paper towels in sherry. Place over grouse. Roast at 350 degrees for 1 hour or until done to taste, basting every 5 minutes. Remove paper towels from grouse. Spoon mixture of sherry and sour cream mixture over grouse.

Tina Bush

QUAIL IN MUSHROOM SAUCE
Yield: 8 servings

8 quail breasts	2 3-ounce cans sliced
Salt and pepper to taste	mushrooms, drained
Flour	1/2 soup can white wine
2 cans cream of mushroom soup	2 cups sour cream

Rinse quail and pat dry. Sprinkle with salt and pepper. Coat with flour. Brown in oil in skillet; drain. Arrange in shallow baking dish. Combine soup, mushrooms, wine and sour cream in bowl; mix well. Spoon over quail. Bake at 350 degrees for 1 hour.

Louise Baughman

Brunch Dishes

BREAKFAST CASSEROLE
Yield: 8 servings

2 5-ounce jars dried beef
12 slices bread
Softened butter
12 slices Old English cheese
1 package little smokies
    sausages, sliced

8 eggs
4 cups milk
Buttered bread crumbs

Rinse dried beef with boiling water. Drain and chop beef. Trim crusts from bread; spread with butter. Arrange 6 slices bread in baking dish. Layer 6 slices cheese, dried beef and sausages over bread. Top with remaining bread slices and cheese. Beat eggs with milk in bowl. Pour over layers. Sprinkle with bread crumbs. Chill overnight. Let stand until room temperature. Bake at 375 degrees for 15 minutes. Reduce oven temperature to 300 degrees. Bake for 40 minutes longer. Serve immediately.

Vicki Rippeto

EGG CASSEROLE FOR BRUNCH
Yield: 8 servings

8 slices Canadian bacon or
    round slices ham
2 cups shredded Cheddar
    cheese
2 cups shredded Swiss cheese
8 eggs

Salt and pepper to taste
8 ounces sour cream
2 tablespoons ranch salad
    dressing
Milk

Arrange Canadian bacon or ham in buttered 9x13-inch baking dish. Sprinkle mixture of cheeses around each slice of bacon, leaving centers uncovered. Break 1 egg into each center; sprinkle with salt and pepper. Combine sour cream and salad dressing in small bowl. Add enough milk to make a smooth sauce. Spoon carefully over eggs. Bake at 350 degrees for 17 minutes or until whites of eggs are set. Garnish with paprika.

Sue and Doug West

BRUNCH EGGS

Yield: 6 to 8 servings

12 slices Canadian bacon
12 1-ounce slices Swiss cheese
12 eggs
1 cup whipping cream

1/3 cup grated Parmesan cheese
Paprika and pepper to taste
Chopped parsley

Arrange Canadian bacon in lightly greased 9x13-inch baking dish. Top with Swiss cheese. Break eggs into dish, spacing evenly. Pour cream over top. Bake at 450 degrees for 10 minutes. Sprinkle with Parmesan cheese, paprika and pepper. Bake for 8 to 10 minutes longer or until set. Sprinkle with parsley. Let stand for 10 minutes before serving.

Pat Campbell

DEVILED EGG CASSEROLE

Yield: 8 to 12 servings

8 to 12 hard-boiled eggs
3 to 4 tablespoons mayonnaise
  or mayonnaise-type salad
  dressing
1 tablespoon finely chopped
  onion
1 tablespoon Worcestershire
  sauce

1/2 teaspoon dry mustard
Salt and pepper to taste
2 cans cream of mushroom soup
16 ounces sour cream or sour
  cream substitute
1 cup shredded Cheddar
  Cheese

Cut eggs into halves lengthwise. Combine yolks with mayonnaise, onion, Worcestershire sauce, dry mustard, salt and pepper in bowl; mix well. Spoon into whites. Combine soup and sour cream in bowl. Spread a thin layer of soup mixture in baking dish. Arrange eggs in dish. Top with remaining soup mixture and cheese. Chill overnight. Bake at 350 degrees for 20 to 30 minutes or until bubbly. Serve on toasted English muffins.

Louise S. Hunter

CRAB MEAT-STUFFED EGGS

Yield: 12 servings

12 hard-boiled eggs
1 cup flaked cooked crab meat
1 cup finely chopped celery
1 cup finely chopped green
   bell pepper
1/3 cup sour cream

1 tablespoon French salad
   dressing
1 teaspoon spicy brown
   mustard
Salt and pepper to taste

Cut eggs into halves lengthwise. Combine yolks with crab meat, celery, green pepper, sour cream, salad dressing, mustard, salt and pepper; mix well. Spoon into egg whites. Chill until serving time.

Sally Byrd

HEAT AND HOLD EGGS

Yield: 6 to 8 servings

12 eggs
1 1/3 cups milk
2 tablespoons flour
1 tablespoon chopped parsley
1 tablespoon chopped pimento

1 tablespoon chopped chives
1/8 teaspoon Tabasco sauce
1 teaspoon salt
1/4 cup butter

Combine eggs, milk, flour, parsley, pimento, chives, Tabasco sauce and salt in bowl; mix well. Melt butter in large skillet. Pour egg mixture into skillet. Cook until soft-set, stirring from outer edge to center. Hold for up to 2 hours in chafing dish, electric skillet or oven set at 200 degrees.

Jo Gross

Tomato Rose—Cut peel gently from firm tomato in a continuous 1/4-inch strip with a sharp knife. Shape peel into rose, starting at base end and placing skin side out. Add fresh herb leaves such as basil to resemble rose leaves.

EGG AND SAUSAGE PUFF　　　*Yield: 6 servings*

1 pound sausage
6 eggs, slightly beaten
1 cup baking mix
1 cup shredded Cheddar cheese

2 cups milk
1 teaspoon dry mustard
1/2 teaspoon oregano

Brown sausage in skillet, stirring until crumbly; drain. Combine with remaining ingredients in bowl; mix well. Chill in refrigerator. Spoon into greased 2-quart baking dish. Bake at 350 degrees for 1 hour or until set. May vary by using hot or mild sausage, turkey sausage, egg substitue or skim milk.

Gloria J. Underwood

CALIBOGUE SHRIMP AND GRITS　　　*Yield: 10 servings*

1 onion, finely chopped
1 pound unsalted butter
2 pounds shrimp, peeled
1 teaspoon paprika
1 teaspoon *fines herbs*

1 teaspoon Old Bay seasoning
Salt and pepper to taste
1 pound bacon, crisp-fried,
　crumbled
2 cups grits, cooked

Sauté onion in 1/2 cup butter in saucepan over low heat. Add remaining butter. Cook until butter melts. Add shrimp. Cook until shrimp begins to turn pink, stirring frequently. Stir in seasonings. Cook until shrimp are done to taste. Stir in bacon; adjust seasonings. Spoon 1/2 cup grits onto each serving plate. Ladle shrimp and sauce onto grits.

Cindy Branning

CAROLINA CHEESE GRITS　　　*Yield: 6 servings*

1 cup grits, cooked
1/2 cup butter
8 ounces sharp cheese, chopped

2 eggs, beaten
1/4 cup milk

Combine first 3 ingredients in baking dish. Add mixture of eggs and milk. Let stand for 1 hour. Bake at 425 degrees for 45 minutes.

Janie Wilkerson

CHEESE GRITS-SAUSAGE CASSEROLE *Yield: 8 servings*

1 pound mild sausage
Tabasco sauce to taste
1/3 clove of garlic, minced
1/2 teaspoon salt (optional)
1/8 teaspoon pepper
1 cup uncooked instant grits
2 cups boiling water

1 cup shredded extra-sharp
  Cheddar cheese
1/4 cup melted butter
2 eggs, beaten
1 4-ounce can chopped mild
  green chilies

Brown sausage in skillet, stirring until crumbly; drain. Stir in Tabasco sauce, garlic, salt and pepper. Cook grits in water using package directions. Add sausage mixture, cheese, butter, eggs and green chilies; mix well. Spoon into greased 9x13-inch baking dish. Bake at 350 degrees for 1 hour.

Carol Wilson

SUPER BREAKFAST PIZZA *Yield: 8 servings*

1 can crescent rolls
1 pound bacon
1 cup frozen hashed brown
  potatoes, thawed
1 cup shredded cheese

5 eggs
1/4 cup milk
1/2 teaspoon salt
1/4 teaspoon pepper
2 tablespoons Parmesan cheese

Separate roll dough into triangles. Arrange in ungreased 12-inch pizza pan, pressing edges to seal. Cook bacon in skillet until crisp. Crumble over crust. Layer potatoes and shredded cheese over bacon. Beat eggs with milk, salt and pepper in bowl. Pour over layers. Sprinkle with Parmesan cheese. Bake at 375 degrees for 25 to 30 minutes or until filling is set and crust is brown.

Paige Pruitt

BREAKFAST QUICHES

Yield: 12 servings

12 ounces sausage
2 unbaked 9-inch pie shells
8 ounces mozzarella cheese,
   shredded

8 eggs, beaten
1½ cups milk
1 teaspoon salt
½ teaspoon pepper

Brown sausage in skillet, stirring until crumbly; drain. Spread in pie shells; sprinkle with cheese. Combine eggs, milk, salt and pepper in bowl; mix well. Pour over cheese. Bake at 375 degrees for 30 minutes.

Lisa Pruitt

CRAB QUICHE

Yield: 6 servings

1 unbaked 9-inch pie shell
3 eggs, slightly beaten
½ teaspoon Worcestershire
   sauce
1 cup coarsely shredded Swiss
   cheese

1 cup sour cream
7½ ounces lump crab meat
1 3-ounce can French-fried
   onions
¾ teaspoon salt

Bake pie shell partially at 300 degrees. Increase oven temperature to 350 degrees. Combine remaining ingredients in bowl; mix well. Spoon into pie shell. Bake at 350 degrees for 50 to 55 minutes or until set. May bake and freeze this quiche, allowing 3 to 4 hours thawing time in refrigerator. Reheat at 300 degrees for 30 minutes, covering loosely with foil if necessary to prevent overbrowning.

Elsie L. Brewton

SAUSAGE QUICHE

Yield: 6 servings

1 pound sausage
3 eggs
1 teaspoon salt
8 ounces cream cheese, softened

1 cup shredded sharp Cheddar
   cheese
1 unbaked pie shell

Brown sausage in skillet, stirring until crumbly. Drain and rinse sausage. Beat eggs with salt in bowl. Add sausage, cream cheese and Cheddar cheese; mix well. Spoon into pie shell. Bake at 475 degrees for 10 minutes. Reduce oven temperature to 375 degrees. Bake for 30 to 40 minutes longer or until set.

Lynn Clanton

BREAKFAST SOUFFLÉ

Yield: 4 servings

2 eggs, beaten
3/4 cup flour

3/4 cup milk
1/4 cup melted butter

Beat eggs with flour and milk in bowl. Add butter; mix well. Pour into cold small baking dish. Place in cold oven. Set oven temperature at 400 degrees. Bake soufflé for 20 minutes.

Bob Kay

SIMPLE CHEESE SOUFFLÉ

Yield: 4 servings

1/4 cup butter
1/4 cup flour
1 teaspoon salt

1 cup milk
1 cup shredded Cheddar cheese
4 eggs, separated

Melt butter in saucepan. Stir in flour and salt. Cook for several minutes. Stir in milk. Cook until thickened, stirring constantly. Stir in cheese until melted. Add a small amount of hot mixture to beaten egg yolks; add egg yolks to hot mixture. Cook until thickened, stirring constantly. Beat egg whites in glass mixer bowl for 1 minute. Fold gently into hot mixture. Spoon into greased soufflé dish. Bake at 325 degrees for 45 minutes.

Valerie Curry

SAUSAGE CASSEROLE

Yield: 8 to 10 servings

1 package wild rice mix with
  herbs and seasonings
2 pounds sausage
1 large green bell pepper,
  chopped
2 stalks celery with leaves,
  chopped

1 large onion, chopped
2 envelopes chicken noodle
  soup mix
4 cups water
1 can water chestnuts, sliced or
  chopped

Cook rice using package directions. Brown sausage in skillet, stirring until crumbly; drain. Add green pepper, celery with leaves and onion; mix well. Cook over low heat for 10 minutes. Stir in soup mix, water, rice and water chestnuts. Simmer for 3 minutes. Spoon into large baking dish. Bake, covered, at 350 degrees for 2 hours.

Katie Robertson

SAUSAGE-EGG CASSEROLE

Yield: 6 to 8 servings

1 pound lean sausage
6 to 8 slices white or whole
  wheat bread
1 cup shredded Cheddar cheese
4 eggs, slightly beaten

2 cups milk
1/2 teaspoon salt
1/2 teaspoon dry mustard
1/4 teaspoon pepper

Brown sausage, stirring until crumbly; drain. Trim crusts from bread; cut bread into cubes. Sprinkle into greased 2-quart baking dish. Layer sausage and cheese over bread. Combine eggs, milk, dry mustard, salt and pepper in bowl; mix well. Pour over layers. Chill overnight. Bake at 350 degrees for 30 to 40 minutes or until set.

Claudia Ware

SAUSAGE AND WILD RICE
Yield: 6 to 8 servings

1 package wild rice mix
1 pound lean sausage
1 can mushroom soup

1 small jar chopped pimento
1 to 1½ cups shredded cheese
(optional)

Cook rice using package directions. Brown sausage in skillet, stirring until crumbly; drain. Combine rice, sausage, soup and pimento in casserole. Bake at 325 degrees for 20 minutes. Top with cheese. Bake for 5 to 10 minutes or until cheese melts. Serve with baked or stewed apples or curried or fresh fruit and muffins.

Louise S. Hunter

STRAWBERRY CHEESE RING
Yield: 16 servings

1 pound sharp cheese, shredded
1 cup finely chopped nuts
1 small onion, finely grated

1 cup mayonnaise
¼ teaspoon pepper
1 jar strawberry preserves

Combine first 5 ingredients in bowl; mix well. Pack into ring mold. Chill until firm. Unmold. Fill with preserves. Serve with Triscuits.

Paige Pruitt

SPICY WELSH RAREBIT
Yield: 4 servings

1 teaspoon flour
1 teaspoon dry mustard
1 tablespoon catsup
1 teaspoon Worcestershire
   sauce

1 egg
Milk
8 ounces sharp Cheddar cheese
¼ cup butter or margarine

Blend flour and dry mustard with a small amount of water in bowl. Stir in next 3 ingredients. Add ½ cup milk; mix well. Melt cheese with butter in 2-quart saucepan. Add egg mixture gradually, stirring constantly. Stir in enough milk to make of desired consistency. Cook until thickened, stirring constantly. Serve over toast.

Edna B. Roth

Vegetables
& Side Dishes

ASPARAGUS PUFF CASSEROLE

Yield: 6 servings

2 cans cut asparagus
1 cup mayonnaise
1 can cream of celery, chicken
  or mushroom soup

2 eggs, beaten
1 cup shredded medium sharp
  cheese
Butter

Drain asparagus, reserving 2 tablespoons liquid. Combine asparagus and reserved juice in blender container. Process for 1 to 2 minutes or until smooth. Combine with mayonnaise, soup, eggs and cheese in bowl; mix well. Spoon into baking dish. Dot with butter. Bake at 350 degrees for 40 to 45 minutes or until set.

Nancy Pruitt

CHEESY GREEN BEAN CASSEROLE

Yield: 6 servings

2 cans green beans, drained
2 or 3 cans mushrooms
2 tablespoons flour
1 teaspoon sugar
1/2 teaspoon salt
5 1/3 tablespoons melted
  margarine

1 onion, grated
2 cups sour cream
1 1/2 cups shredded Cheddar
  cheese

Place green beans in baking dish. Drain mushrooms, reserving liquid of 1 can. Blend flour, sugar and salt into margarine in saucepan. Add onion and mushrooms. Cook for several minutes. Stir in reserved mushroom liquid. Cook until thickened, stirring constantly. Stir in sour cream. Spoon over beans; top with cheese. Bake at 375 degrees until bubbly. May substitute 3 packages frozen French-style green beans for canned or Swiss cheese for Cheddar.

Mrs. Oswald Lightsey

GREEN BEAN CASSEROLE
Yield: 6 servings

4 cups cut green beans
8 slices bacon, crisp-fried
1 medium onion, chopped

1/2 cup sugar
1/2 cup vinegar
1 tablespoon bacon drippings

Cook beans in water in saucepan until tender-crisp; drain. Layer beans, crumbled bacon and onion 1/2 at a time in baking dish. Stir sugar and vinegar into bacon drippings in skillet. Cook for 1 minute. Pour over layers. Bake at 325 degrees for 2 hours.

Kaye Black

CREOLE LIMA BEANS
Yield: 5 servings

3 slices bacon
1 large onion, chopped
1/2 cup chopped green bell
  pepper

2 cups canned tomato wedges
1 teaspoon sugar
2 cups cooked baby lima beans
Salt and freshly ground pepper

Brown bacon in skillet; remove and crumble bacon. Add onion and green pepper to drippings in skillet. Sauté until vegetables are tender but not brown. Add tomatoes and sugar. Cook for 15 minutes, stirring occasionally. Add undrained beans, salt and pepper. Simmer until heated through. Serve sprinkled with bacon.

Tom E. Newell and Keith A. Gallion

BROCCOLI CASSEROLE
Yield: 8 servings

2 packages frozen chopped
  broccoli
1 cup mayonnaise
2 eggs, beaten

2 tablespoons chopped onion
1 can cream of celery soup
1 cup shredded sharp cheese
10 butter crackers, crushed

Cook broccoli using package directions for 5 minutes; drain. Combine with mayonnaise, eggs, onion, soup and half the cheese in bowl; mix well. Spoon into baking dish. Sprinkle with remaining cheese and cracker crumbs. Bake at 350 degrees for 45 minutes.

Nancy Easterlin

CARROT CASSEROLE

Yield: 6 servings

6 large carrots, sliced
2 tablespoons horseradish
2 tablespoons grated onion
2 tablespoons margarine
1/2 cup mayonnaise

1/2 teaspoon salt
Pepper to taste
Bread crumbs or cracker
  crumbs
Grated Parmesan cheese

Cook carrots in a small amount of water in saucepan until tender-crisp. Drain, reserving 1/4 of the cooking liquid. Combine reserved liquid with horseradish, onion, margarine, mayonnaise, salt and pepper in bowl; mix well. Pour over carrots in small baking dish. Top with crumbs and cheese. Bake at 350 degrees for 20 minutes or until heated through.

Kaye Black

GLAZED CARROTS AND GRAPES

Yield: 8 servings

3 10-ounce packages frozen
  carrots, cooked, drained
1 tablespoon brown sugar
3 tablespoons vodka

1 1/2 teaspoons cornstarch
2 teaspoons water
1 1/2 cups green grapes

Combine carrots with brown sugar and vodka in saucepan. Blend cornstarch with water in small bowl. Stir into carrots. Cook until thickened, stirring constantly. Add grapes. Serve immediately.

Virginia Jordan

Radish Accordion—Select long narrow radishes. Cut thin slice from each end. Cut crosswise into slices, leaving bottom intact. Chill in iced water until slices open.

Sea Pines Corn Pudding

Yield: 8 servings

10 ears of corn	5 or 6 dashes of Tabasco sauce
3 eggs, beaten	1/2 teaspoon salt
1 cup milk	1 teaspoon freshly ground pepper
1/2 cup cream	8 fresh tomatoes
1 tablespoon melted butter	1 tablespoon butter

Cut corn from cobs, scraping well to remove pulp. Combine corn with eggs, milk, cream, 1 tablespoon melted butter, Tabasco sauce, salt and pepper in bowl; mix well. Spoon into 1½-quart baking dish. Bake at 350 degrees for 45 to 50 minutes or just until firm to the touch. Cool to room temperature. Cut tops from tomatoes. Scoop out pulp and reserve for another use; invert to drain. Spoon corn pudding into tomatoes; dot with 1 tablespoon butter. Place in oiled or foil-lined baking pan. Bake at 350 degrees for 15 to 20 minutes or until heated through.

Sherry Halloran

Eggplant Parmesan

Yield: 6 to 8 servings

3 eggs	Oil for deep frying
1/2 cup milk	3 to 4 cups spaghetti sauce
2 large eggplant, peeled, thinly sliced	2 to 3 cups shredded mozzarella cheese
3 to 4 cups Italian bread crumbs	Grated Parmesan cheese

Beat eggs with milk in mixer bowl. Dip eggplant slices into egg mixture; coat with bread crumbs. Deep-fry in 375-degree oil until light brown on both sides. Drain on paper towels. Spread thin layer of spaghetti sauce in 9x13-inch baking dish. Alternate layers of eggplant, mozzarella cheese and remaining spaghetti sauce in prepared dish until all ingredients are used. Top with Parmesan cheese. Bake, covered with foil, at 350 degrees for 45 minutes or until heated through. Serve with tossed salad and Italian bread. May substitute zucchini, shrimp or flounder for eggplant, using marinara sauce for seafood dishes.

Robert Savarese, D.M.D.

BAKED OKRA

Yield: 4 servings

1 pound whole fresh okra
Bacon slices

Freshly ground pepper to taste

Cut tops from okra. Arrange in single layer in baking dish. Layer bacon generously over okra. Sprinkle with pepper. Bake at 375 degrees for 20 minutes or until bacon is crisp.

Lois R. West

FRIED OKRA

Yield: 8 servings

2 pounds okra
1/2 cup cornmeal
1/2 cup flour

Oil for deep frying
Salt to taste

Wash okra; okra should be wet. Mix cornmeal and flour in bowl. Coat okra with flour and cornmeal mixture. Deep-fry in hot oil until crisp and brown. Drain on brown paper bag. Season with salt

Nancy Pruitt

FRIED ONION RINGS

Yield: 6 to 8 servings

3 or 4 large Vidalia or Bermuda
  onions
2 to 3 cups buttermilk
1 egg, beaten
1 1/2 teaspoons baking powder
2/3 cup water

1 cup flour
1 tablespoon oil
1 teaspoon lemon juice
1 teaspoon salt
1/4 teaspoon cayenne pepper
Oil for deep frying

Slice onions 3/8 inch thick; separate into rings. Soak in buttermilk in shallow dish for 30 minutes. Combine egg, baking powder, water, flour, 1 tablespoon oil, lemon juice, salt and cayenne pepper in bowl; mix well. Drain onion rings. Dip into batter. Deep-fry in hot oil until golden brown. Drain on paper towels.

Elsie L. Brewton

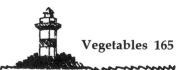

SAUTÉED PEAS
Yield: 2 servings

12 ounces fresh snow peas
1/2 can chicken broth

Juice of 1/2 lemon
Sesame seed

Combine pea pods with chicken broth and lemon juice in saucepan. Bring to a boil. Cook for 3 to 4 minutes or until peapods are tender-crisp and bright green. Sprinkle with sesame seed. May add 1 to 2 chopped green onions, 1 clove of garlic or 1 teaspoon ginger-garlic paste; may sprinkle with cashews.

Sue West

NEW POTATOES AND CARROTS
Yield: 4 servings

12 new potatoes, unpeeled, cut
   into halves
3 tablespoons butter
1/3 cup water

1/2 teaspoon salt
2 cups 1/4-inch carrot slices
1 tablespoon dillweed

Brown potatoes in butter in skillet. Add water and salt. Cook over low heat for 10 minutes. Add carrots. Cook for 10 minutes longer. Stir in dillweed. Serve hot.

Caneel Cotton

POTATO PUFF CASSEROLE
Yield: 8 servings

8 to 10 medium potatoes,
   peeled
8 ounces cream cheese
1 cup sour cream
1/4 cup butter

1/3 cup chopped chives
Salt and pepper to taste
Butter
Paprika to taste

Cook potatoes in water to cover until tender; drain. Combine with cream cheese, sour cream, 1/4 cup butter, chives, salt and pepper in bowl; beat until smooth. Spoon into greased 2-quart baking dish. Dot with additional butter; sprinkle with paprika. Bake at 350 degrees for 25 minutes.

Louise S. Hunter

TWICE-BAKED POTATOES

Yield: 6 servings

6 potatoes
1/2 cup butter
1/2 cup sour cream
1/4 cup bacon bits or chives

1 teaspoon salt
1/2 teaspoon pepper
1 cup shredded cheese

Grease potatoes. Bake in moderate oven just until tender. Cut into halves lengthwise. Scoop pulp into bowl, reserving shells. Add butter to pulp; mash until smooth. Add sour cream, bacon bits, salt and pepper; mix well. Spoon into reserved shells. Sprinkle with cheese. Place on baking sheet. Bake at 400 degrees for 10 to 15 minutes or until cheese melts. May store, tightly wrapped, in refrigerator for up to 5 days. May freeze and bake for 25 minutes.

Nancy Pruitt

RATATOUILLE

Yield: 6 servings

1 medium eggplant
Salt to taste
2 large onions, sliced
2 green or red bell peppers,
  chopped
1/2 cup olive oil
4 ripe tomatoes, peeled,
  seeded, coarsely chopped

2 zucchini, sliced 1/2-inch thick
1 tablespoon finely chopped
  parsley
Marjoram and basil to taste
Pepper to taste
1 small clove of garlic, minced

Peel eggplant and cut into 1/2-inch slices. Sprinkle with salt; place in bowl. Place weight on eggplant. Let stand for 30 minutes. Drain and chop eggplant. Sauté onions and bell peppers in olive oil in large saucepan. Add tomatoes, eggplant, zucchini, parsley, marjoram, basil, salt and pepper. Simmer for 30 minutes. Add garlic. Cook for 15 minutes or until vegetables are tender and liquid is reduced to desired consistency. Serve hot or cold.

Nancy Stephens

SPINACH CHAUSSON   *Yield: 6 servings*

3/4 cup unsalted butter, chilled
2 cups flour
1 egg
3 tablespoons ice water
1 teaspoon chopped fresh
  tarragon or 1/2 teaspoon dried
  tarragon
1 teaspoon chopped fresh
  oregano or 1/2 teaspoon dried
  oregano
1 teaspoon chopped fresh
  chives or 1/2 teaspoon dried
  chives
1/4 teaspoon salt
1 pound fresh spinach
2 cups thinly sliced leek
2 tablespoons unsalted butter

4 ounces fresh mushrooms,
  thinly sliced
1 can artichoke hearts, drained,
  chopped
2 ounces cream cheese
1/4 cup whipping cream
1 small clove of garlic, minced
1 1/2 teaspoons fresh lemon juice
1/2 teaspoon chopped fresh
  chives
1/4 teaspoon tarragon
Freshly grated nutmeg to taste
Salt and pepper to taste
Grated Parmesan cheese to
  taste
1 egg, beaten

Cut 3/4 cup butter into flour in large bowl until mixture resembles coarse cornmeal; make well in center. Add 1 egg, ice water, 1 teaspoon tarragon, oregano, 1 teaspoon chives and 1/4 teaspoon salt to well. Mix with fork, mixing in flour to form dough. Shape into disc on floured surface. Chill, wrapped in plastic wrap, for 1 hour. Cook spinach in heavy saucepan over medium-high heat for 2 minutes or until wilted. Cool to room temperature. Squeeze to remove moisture; chop coarsely. Cook leek, covered, in 2 tablespoons butter in same saucepan for 15 minutes. Add mushrooms. Cook until mushrooms are tender and liquid has evaporated. Stir in artichoke hearts, spinach, cream cheese, whipping cream and garlic. Cook for 3 minutes or until cream cheese is melted and cream is absorbed; remove from heat. Stir in lemon juice, 1/2 teaspoon chives, 1/4 teaspoon tarragon, nutmeg, salt and pepper. Cool completely. Stir in Parmesan cheese. Roll chilled pastry into 15-inch circle on lightly floured surface. Roll around rolling pin; transfer to greased baking sheet. Spoon filling onto half the circle, leaving 1/2-inch border. Brush border with beaten egg. Fold pastry over filling. Seal edge with fork. Decorate as desired. Brush top with beaten egg. Chill for 30 minutes. Brush with remaining egg. Bake at 375 degrees for 30 minutes. Let stand for 5 minutes or longer. Serve hot or warm as main dish or appetizer.

Catherine Smith

CREAMY RANCH SPINACH SOUFFLÉ   *Yield: 4 servings*

2 packages frozen spinach
  soufflé, thawed
1/2 cup sour cream

1 tablespoon ranch salad
  dressing mix

Spread 1 package soufflé in ungreased 1 1/2 or 2-quart baking dish. Spread with mixture of sour cream and salad dressing mix. Top with remaining package soufflé. Bake at 350 degrees for 50 to 60 minutes or until set and brown. Serve immediately.

Sue West

CREAMED SPINACH CASSEROLE   *Yield: 6 servings*

3 packages frozen chopped
  spinach
Salt to taste
8 ounces cream cheese

6 tablespoons margarine or
  butter
Grated Parmesan cheese to
  taste

Cook spinach in salted water using package directions; drain. Stir in cream cheese and margarine. Spoon into baking dish; sprinkle with Parmesan cheese. Bake at 300 degrees for 30 minutes.

Lynn Baughman Asnip

SPINACH CASSEROLE   *Yield: 12 servings*

8 ounces uncooked noodles
3 packages chopped spinach,
  thawed, drained
1 cup sour cream

1 can cream of mushroom soup
1 envelope onion soup mix
Bread crumbs or cheese slices

Cook noodles using package directions. Combine with spinach, sour cream, mushroom soup and soup mix in bowl; mix well. Spoon into baking dish. Top with bread crumbs or cheese slices. Bake at 350 degrees for 45 minutes.

Janet P. Kissling

SOUR CREAM SQUASH
Yield: 8 servings

2 pounds yellow squash,
  chopped
Salt to taste
1 large onion, chopped
1/4 cup butter
1 teaspoon sugar
Pepper to taste

1 tablespoon flour
1 1/2 cups sour cream
1/2 cup chopped green bell
  pepper
1/4 cup toasted slivered almonds
Oregano to taste

Cook squash in salted water in saucepan just until tender; drain. Sauté onion in butter in skillet. Add onion, sugar, salt and pepper to squash in bowl; mix well. Blend flour with a small amount of sour cream in saucepan. Add remaining sour cream and green pepper. Cook until thickened, stirring constantly. Stir in almonds. Add to squash mixture; mix well. Stir in oregano. Spoon into baking dish. Bake at 350 degrees for 30 to 45 minutes or until bubbly and brown.

J. W. Bird

SQUASH AND CORN SOUFFLÉ
Yield: 4 to 6 servings

4 yellow summer squash,
  chopped
2 packages frozen corn soufflé,
  thawed

1 cup shredded Cheddar cheese

Cook squash in water in saucepan for 5 minutes or just until tender; drain. Mash larger pieces. Add 1 package corn soufflé; mix well. Spoon into soufflé or baking dish. Sprinkle with half the cheese. Stir remaining package corn soufflé in bowl; spread over casserole. Top with remaining cheese. Bake at 375 degrees for 45 minutes or until brown and bubbly. May steam squash if preferred.

Sue West

HONEY CRANBERRY SQUASH

Yield: 4 servings

2 acorn squash
Honey

1 can whole cranberry sauce

Cut squash into halves; discard seed. Microwave, covered with plastic wrap, on High for 5 minutes. Fill centers with mixture of honey and cranberry sauce. Microwave, covered, for 2 minutes longer.

Barbara Lee Keeney

SQUASH SUPREME

Yield: 6 servings

2 cups chopped yellow squash
1¹/₂ carrots, grated
¹/₂ cup chopped onion
1 can cream of chicken soup
1 cup sour cream

Salt and pepper to taste
1 package herb-seasoned
  stuffing mix
¹/₄ cup butter

Cook squash in water in saucepan until tender; drain and mash. Add carrots, onion, soup, sour cream, salt and pepper; mix well. Layer half the stuffing mix, squash mixture and remaining stuffing mix in baking dish sprayed with nonstick cooking spray. Dot with butter. Bake at 350 degrees for 30 minutes.

Jo Hagan Proffitt

SWEET POTATO SUPREME

Yield: 8 servings

3 cups mashed cooked sweet
  potatoes
¹/₄ cup packed brown sugar
¹/₂ teaspoon each coconut,
  almond and orange extracts

¹/₂ cup melted butter
¹/₂ cup self-rising flour
¹/₂ cup packed brown sugar
¹/₂ cup melted butter
1 cup finely chopped pecans

Combine sweet potatoes, ¹/₄ cup brown sugar, ¹/₂ cup butter and flavorings in bowl; mix well. Spoon into 2-quart baking dish. Mix flour, ¹/₂ cup brown sugar, ¹/₂ cup butter and pecans in bowl. Sprinkle over casserole. Bake at 350 degrees for 30 minutes or until golden.

Pat Lusk

SOUTHERN SWEET POTATOES

Yield: 6 servings

2 (or more) sweet potatoes
³/₄ cup milk
¹/₂ cup pineapple juice
1 cup chopped pineapple

2 tablespoons melted butter
¹/₂ teaspoon cinnamon
Marshmallows

Bake sweet potatoes until tender. Mash enough to measure 2 cups. Combine with milk, pineapple juice, pineapple, butter and cinnamon in bowl; beat until light, adding additional milk or juice if needed for desired consistency. Spoon into buttered baking dish. Top with marshmallows. Bake until marshmallows are brown. Serve with poultry or ham.

Barb Fuller

SWEET POTATO CASSEROLE

Yield: 8 to 10 servings

2 cans sweet potatoes or yams
2 tablespoons melted butter
¹/₂ cup milk, scalded
3 tablespoons brown sugar
1 teaspoon cinnamon

¹/₂ teaspoon nutmeg
¹/₄ teaspoon paprika
¹/₂ teaspoon salt
1 cup chopped walnuts
10 large marshmallows

Drain sweet potatoes, reserving liquid. Mash sweet potatoes in bowl. Add butter, milk, brown sugar, cinnamon, nutmeg, paprika and salt; beat until smooth. Add a small amount of reserved sweet potato liquid if needed for desired consistency. Fold in walnuts. Spoon into buttered 1¹/₂ or 2-quart baking dish. Top with marshmallows, pressing until tops of marshmallows are level with top of sweet potato mixture. Bake at 350 degrees for 40 minutes.

Ann Scheidle

Cooked Vegetable Garnishes—Decorate large platters with bundles of julienne carrots and celery tied with chives, slices of baked sweet potato or thin wedges of baked acorn squash.

FRESH TOMATO TART
Yield: 12 servings

4 cups flour
1 tablespoon sugar
3 tablespoons baking powder
1 teaspoon salt
3/4 cup margarine
1 1/4 cups buttermilk
12 medium tomatoes, chopped

2 cups chopped fresh basil or 1
  cup prepared pesto
1 teaspoon salt
4 cups shredded Cheddar
  cheese
4 cups shredded Swiss cheese
1 1/2 cups mayonnaise

Mix flour, sugar, baking powder and salt in bowl. Cut in margarine with pastry blender. Add buttermilk; mix to form dough. Roll between waxed paper to fit shallow 3-quart baking dish. Place in baking dish; flute edges. Bake at 400 degrees for 15 minutes or until puffed and golden. Reduce oven temperature to 375 degrees. Combine tomatoes, basil and salt in bowl; mix well. Spread evenly in crust. Spoon mixture of cheeses and mayonnaise over top. Bake for 20 to 25 minutes or until heated through. Serve immediately. This is best with homemade mayonnaise.

Catherine Smith

TOMATO CASSEROLE
Yield: 4 to 6 servings

8 fresh tomatoes, sliced
1/2 cup bread crumbs
1/2 cup shredded Cheddar
  cheese

Sugar, garlic salt, salt and
  pepper to taste
Butter

Alternate layers of tomatoes, bread crumbs and cheese in 2 or 2 1/2-quart baking dish until all ingredients are used, sprinkling tomatoes with sugar and seasonings to taste. Dot with butter. Bake at 350 degrees for 50 minutes. Serve with grilled steaks, chicken or pork chops.

Betty Letson

TONY'S TOMATOES ROCKEFELLER *Yield: 12 servings*

12 thick tomato slices	6 eggs, slightly beaten
2 10-ounce packages frozen chopped spinach	3/4 cup melted butter or margarine
1 cup soft bread crumbs or stuffing mix	1/2 teaspoon minced garlic
1 cup seasoned bread crumbs	1/2 cup grated Parmesan cheese
1 to 11/2 cups finely chopped green onions	1 teaspoon thyme
	Hot sauce to taste
	1 teaspoon salt

Arrange tomato slices in lightly greased 9x13-inch baking dish. Cook spinach using package directions; drain well. Combine with soft bread crumbs, seasoned bread crumbs, green onions, eggs, butter, garlic, cheese, thyme, hot sauce and salt in bowl; mix well. Mound mixture onto tomato slices. Bake at 350 degrees for 15 minutes or until spinach mixture is set.

Mrs. Marc A. Puntereri

PEPPERONI AND CHEESE ZUCCHINI *Yield: 4 servings*

4 cups sliced zucchini	1 teaspoon oregano
2 medium onions, sliced	8 ounces American cheese, sliced
Salt and pepper to taste	16 slices 1 inch pepperoni
2 tablespoons olive oil	1/4 cup grated Parmesan cheese
1 6-ounce can tomato paste	

Cook zucchini and onions with salt and pepper in olive oil in large heavy skillet over medium heat for 15 minutes. Stir in tomato paste and oregano. Alternate layers of zucchini mixture, American cheese and pepperoni in 2-quart baking dish until all ingredients are used. Sprinkle with Parmesan cheese. Bake at 350 degrees for 20 to 25 minutes or until heated through.

Karen Laughlin

MONTEREY ZUCCHINI

Yield: 8 servings

4 medium-large zucchini
4 slices white bread, cubed
1 cup grated Parmesan cheese
1/2 cup melted butter

1/4 teaspoon garlic powder
1/4 teaspoon oregano
1 teaspoon salt
1/4 teaspoon pepper

Cook zucchini in salted water to cover in saucepan for 10 minutes. Drain and cool. Cut into halves lengthwise. Scoop out and chop pulp, reserving shells. Combine pulp with bread cubes, cheese, butter, garlic powder, oregano, salt and pepper in bowl; mix well. Spoon into reserved shells; place on baking sheet. Bake at 350 degrees until golden brown.

Margaret D. Jones

ZUCCHINI FRITTERS

Yield: 2 dozen

1 large or 2 medium zucchini,
  coarsely grated
1 large onion, finely grated
1 egg, beaten

Salt and pepper to taste
1/2 cup (about) flour
Oil for frying

Drain zucchini and onion in colander for 1 hour or longer, pressing occasionally to remove excess liquid. Combine with egg, salt, pepper and enough flour to make a stiff batter. Drop by spoonfuls into hot oil in skillet. Fry until brown on both sides; drain on paper towels. Serve hot with sour cream.

Nancy Biel

ZUCCHINI AND TOMATO BAKE

Yield: 8 servings

3 medium zucchini
1 large tomato
2 tablespoons minced onion
1/2 teaspoon oregano
1/2 teaspoon basil

Salt and pepper to taste
1/2 cup herb-seasoned stuffing mix
3/4 cup shrdded Cheddar cheese

Slice zucchini 1/2 inch thick; arrange in shallow baking dish. Slice tomato 1/4 inch thick; cut slices into quarters. Spread over zucchini. Sprinkle with onion, oregano, basil, salt and pepper. Bake, covered, at 350 degrees for 15 minutes. Sprinkle with stuffing mix and cheese. Bake, uncovered, for 5 minutes longer.

Gene Ann Ellison

VEGETABLE CASSEROLE

Yield: 6 servings

1   16-ounce can French-style green beans, drained
1   12-ounce can Shoe Peg corn, drained
1/2 cup chopped celery
1/2 cup chopped onion
1   2-ounce jar chopped pimento

1/2 cup sour cream
1 can cream of celery soup
1/2 cup shredded sharp cheese
1 teaspoon salt
1/2 teaspoon pepper
1 cup butter cracker crumbs
1/4 cup melted margarine
1/2 cup slivered almonds

Combine beans, corn, celery, onion, pimento, sour cream, soup, cheese, salt and pepper in bowl; mix well. Spoon into baking dish. Mix cracker crumbs, melted margarine and almonds in bowl. Sprinkle over casserole. Bake at 350 degrees for 45 minutes.

Margie Dawson

TOSSED VEGETABLES

Yield: 15 servings

1 onion or green onions to taste
4 carrots
2 stalks celery
3 medium potatoes, unpeeled
1 small bunch broccoli
1 small head cauliflower
8 ounces green beans
4 tablespoons oil

1/2 cup water
3 tablespoons butter
2 tablespoons lemon juice
1 teaspoon prepared mustard
1/8 teaspoon basil
1/8 teaspoon oregano
Salt and pepper to taste
Grated Parmesan cheese

Chop onion, carrots, celery, potatoes, broccoli, cauliflower and green beans into bite-sized pieces. Sauté onion, carrots and celery in 2 tablespoons oil in heavy 8-quart saucepan over medium-high heat for 10 minutes or until tender-crisp, stirring frequently. Remove with slotted spoon. Add 1/2 cup water, 1 tablespoon oil, beans, cauliflower and broccoli. Cook until tender-crisp; remove with slotted spoon. Add remaining 1 tablespoon oil and potatoes. Cook for 10 minutes or until tender and brown. Return cooked vegetables to saucepan. Add butter, lemon juice, mustard, basil, oregano, salt and pepper; mix well. Sprinkle with cheese. Simmer for 5 minutes or just until heated through; do not overcook.

Dale Bradley

MIXED VEGETABLE CASSEROLE

Yield: 6 servings

2 16-ounce cans mixed
    vegetables, drained
1 8-ounce can water
    chestnuts, drained, chopped
3/4 cup mayonnaise

1 onion, chopped
1 cup shredded cheese
1 stack Ritz crackers, crushed
6 tablespoons melted butter

Combine vegetables, water chestnuts, mayonnaise, onion and cheese in bowl; mix well. Spoon into casserole. Sprinkle with cracker crumbs. Drizzle with butter. Bake at 375 degrees for 30 minutes.

Louise L. Baughman

KAYE'S MACARONI AND CHEESE

Yield: 12 servings

1 package macaroni, cooked
1 pound sharp cheese, chopped
1 onion, finely chopped
1 cup mayonnaise
1 small jar chopped pimento

1 can cream of mushroom soup
1 small package cheese tidbits, crushed
2 tablespoons melted margarine or butter

Combine macaroni with cheese, onion, mayonnaise, pimento and soup in bowl; mix well. Spoon into greased 2 or 3-quart baking dish. Mix cheese tidbit crumbs with butter in bowl. Sprinkle over casserole. Bake at 325 degrees for 25 minutes.

Nancy W. Pruitt

PASTA PRIMAVERA

Yield: 6 to 8 servings

1 medium onion, minced
1 large clove of garlic, minced
1/2 cup unsalted butter
1 pound thin asparagus, sliced diagonally into 1/4-inch pieces
8 ounces mushrooms, thinly sliced
6 ounces cauliflowerets
1 medium zucchini, sliced 1/4-inch thick
1 small carrot, cut into halves lengthwise, sliced diagonally 1/8-inch thick

1 cup whipping cream
1/2 cup chicken stock
2 tablespoons chopped fresh basil or 2 teaspoons dried basil
1 cup tiny peas
2 ounces prosciutto or cooked ham, chopped
5 green onions, chopped
Salt and freshly ground pepper
1 pound fettucini or linguine, cooked *al dente*, drained
1 cup freshly grated Parmesan cheese

Sauté onion and garlic in butter in large deep skillet or wok over medium-high heat for 2 minutes. Add asparagus, mushrooms, cauliflower, zucchini and carrot. Sauté for 2 minutes. Reserve several asparagus tips, mushrooms and zucchini pieces for garnish. Increase heat to high. Stir in cream, stock and basil. Cook for 3 minutes. Stir in peas, prosciutto and green onions. Cook for 1 minute. Season with salt and pepper. Add pasta and cheese; toss to mix well. Cook just until heated through. Garnish with reserved vegetables.

Phyllis Modell

NOODLE PUDDING

Yield: 8 servings

1 package egg noodles, cooked
½ cup butter
3 eggs
1 cup cottage cheese
1 cup sour cream

¾ cup sugar
¼ teaspoon cinnamon
1 teaspoon salt
½ cup grated apple
½ cup raisins

Combine first 8 ingredients in bowl; mix well. Add apple and raisins if desired. Spoon into baking dish. Bake at 350 degrees for 1 hour.

Sue Ansel

ROLLED LASAGNA

Yield: 18 to 20 servings

2 cups ricotta cheese
½ cup shredded provolone
  cheese
1 cup shredded mozzarella
  cheese
½ cup grated Parmesan cheese
4 egg yolks
2 tablespoons chopped green
  onions
1 tablespoon chopped parsley
1 clove of garlic, minced
½ teaspoon salt

¼ teaspoon pepper
18 to 20 lasagna noodles,
  cooked
3 tablespoons flour
¼ teaspoon nutmeg
¼ teaspoon cayenne pepper
½ teaspoon salt
3 tablespoons melted butter
½ cup milk
½ cup heavy cream
Marinara Sauce (page 179)
2 teaspoons chopped parsley

Combine ricotta cheese with half the provolone, mozzarella and Parmesan cheeses in bowl. Add egg yolks, green onions, 1 tablespoon parsley, garlic, ½ teaspoon salt and ¼ teaspoon pepper; mix well. Rinse noodles under cold water; pat dry. Blend flour, nutmeg, cayenne pepper and ½ teaspoon salt into butter in 1-quart saucepan. Cook for several minutes; remove from heat. Stir in milk and cream. Cook until thickened, stirring constantly. Spread ¼ cup white sauce in each of two 9x11-inch baking dishes. Spread about 2 tablespoons prepared cheese filling on each noodle; roll to enclose filling. Arrange noodle rolls in prepared baking dishes. Spoon Marinara Sauce over tops. Spread with remaining white sauce. Sprinkle with remaining cheeses and 2 teaspoons parsley. Bake at 375 degrees for 30 to 35 minutes or until bubbly.

Maggie Kern

MARINARA SAUCE

Yield: 18 to 20 servings

1 cup chopped onion
1/2 cup shredded carrot
1 clove of garlic, minced
1/4 cup butter
2 large cans tomato sauce
2 large cans tomato paste
6 tomato paste cans water
2 tablespoons chopped parsley
3 tablespoons sugar
1 tablespoon basil
1 teaspoon oregano
1/2 teaspoon salt
Pepper to taste
2 pounds ground chuck
4 ounces mushrooms
1 to 2 pounds Sa-Zi-Sa Italian
  sausage
1 thin rib pork chop

Sauté onion, carrot and garlic in butter in 5-quart saucepan until tender. Stir in tomato sauce, tomato paste, water, parsley, sugar, basil, oregano, salt and pepper. Simmer for 1 1/2 hours or until thickened to desired consistency. Brown ground chuck with mushrooms in skillet, stirring frequently; remove from heat. Add sausage and pork chop. Simmer for 15 minutes longer; drain. Add to sauce. Simmer, covered, for 30 minutes. Simmer, uncovered, for 30 minutes longer. Chill for 24 hours. May omit sugar and increase carrot to 1 cup.

Maggie Kern

SPINACH PESTO

Yield: 8 to 10 servings

5 ounces fresh spinach, torn
6 cloves of garlic, crushed
1 cup fresh parsley
2/3 cup grated Parmesan cheese
1/2 cup finely chopped walnuts
  (optional)
1 tablespoon anchovy paste
  (optional)
1 tablespoon minced basil
3 tablespoons minced fresh
  tarragon or 1 tablespoon
  dried tarragon
1/2 teaspoon salt
1/2 teaspoon pepper
3/4 cup olive oil
16 ounces uncooked spinach
  fettucini or spaghetti

Combine spinach, garlic, parsley, cheese, walnuts, anchovy paste, basil, tarragon, salt and pepper in food processor container; process until smooth. Add olive oil in fine stream, processing constantly until smooth. Cook pasta using package directions; drain well. Toss with pesto in serving bowl. Garnish with pimento and basil leaves.

Carol M. Wilson

BROWN RICE

Yield: 6 servings

1 cup uncooked rice
1 cup beef broth
1 cup consommé

1 small onion, chopped
1 small can mushrooms
Butter or margarine

Combine rice with beef broth, consommé, onion and mushrooms in baking dish; mix well. Dot with butter. Bake, covered, at 325 degrees for 1 hour. May top with 6 pork chops for a 1-dish meal.

Lynn Clanton

CHINESE-STYLE RICE

Yield: 6 servings

1 cup uncooked rice
1 small onion, chopped
Butter or margarine

2 eggs, beaten
Salt and pepper to taste
Soy sauce to taste

Cook rice using package directions. Sauté onion in a small amount of butter in skillet. Stir in eggs. Cook until eggs are soft-set, stirring constantly. Stir in rice, salt, pepper and soy sauce. Cook until heated through and browned to taste.

Lois Seifried

GREEN RICE

Yield: 12 servings

1½ cups rice, cooked
4 or 5 green onions, chopped
½ cup oil
½ cup milk
1 cup chopped parsley
1 pound Velveeta cheese, shredded

½ cup chopped green bell pepper
2 eggs, beaten
½ teaspoon thyme
1 tablespoon sweet basil
Paprika, salt and pepper to taste

Combine rice with green onions, oil, milk, parsley, cheese, green pepper, eggs, thyme, basil, paprika, salt and pepper in bowl; mix well. Spoon into baking dish. Bake at 325 degrees for 1 hour, adding a small amount of milk if needed for desired consistency.

Maurine Louise Holmes

CRUNCHY SWEET AND SOUR RICE   *Yield: 8 servings*

4 cups cooked brown rice
1 small red bell pepper,
   chopped
2 green onions, chopped
1/3 cup sliced water chestnuts
1 tablespoon cornstarch

1/2 cup chicken stock
1/2 cup pineapple juice
1 1/2 tablespoons white vinegar
2 teaspoons sugar
1 tablespoon peanut butter

Combine rice, bell pepper, green onions and water chestnuts in bowl; mix well. Blend cornstarch with chicken stock in saucepan. Stir in pineapple juice, vinegar, sugar and peanut butter. Cook until thickened, stirring constantly. Simmer for 1 minute. Add to rice mixture.

Doris Gnesin

RAVISHING RICE   *Yield: 6 servings*

1/2 cup uncooked rice
2 envelopes chicken noodle
   soup mix
4 1/2 cups water
1 pound hot sausage

1 cup chopped celery
1 large Spanish onion, chopped
1 large green bell pepper,
   chopped
Slivered almonds

Combine rice, soup mix and water in saucepan. Cook for 7 minutes; do not drain. Brown sausage in skillet, stirring until crumbly; drain. Add sausage, celery, onion and green pepper to rice mixture; mix well. Spoon into baking dish. Top with almonds. Bake at 350 degrees for 1 to 1 1/2 hours or until rice is tender.

Kaye Black

Bell Pepper Garnish—Accent rice dishes with sautéed julienned red, yellow and green bell peppers.

BAKED WILD RICE

Yield: 4 to 6 servings

1 small to medium onion,
  chopped
9 fresh mushrooms, sliced
2 tablespoons Italian salad
  dressing

1 package long grain and wild
  rice mix
1 can consommé
1/2 soup can water
1 tablespoon sherry (optional)

Sauté onion and mushrooms in salad dressing in medium saucepan. Combine with rice and contents of seasoning packet in baking dish. Stir in consommé, water and sherry; mix well. Bake, covered, at 375 degrees for 45 minutes or until liquid is absorbed.

Sue West

WILD RICE WITH WINE

Yield: 6 servings

1 package wild rice
1/2 cup chopped celery
1/2 cup chopped onion
1/4 cup butter

1 can sliced water chestnuts
1/4 to 1/2 cup dry white wine
Toasted almonds

Cook rice using package directions. Sauté celery and onion in butter in skillet. Add water chestnuts. Add to rice. Stir in wine. Spoon into 2-quart baking dish. Bake, covered, at 325 degrees for 20 minutes. Sprinkle with almonds. Bake, uncovered, for 5 to 10 minutes longer.

Louise L. Baughman

BARBECUE SAUCE

Yield: 3 cups

1 small jar mustard
1/2 cup sugar
1/4 cup packed brown sugar
1/2 cup margarine

1/2 cup apple cider vinegar
1/3 cup catsup
Salt and pepper to taste

Combine mustard, sugar, brown sugar, margarine, vinegar, catsup, salt and pepper in saucepan. Simmer for 30 minutes. Use with chicken or pork.

Louise L. Baughman

ANOTHER BARBECUE SAUCE

Yield: 6 cups

½ cup lime juice
1 can tomato soup
½ cup butter
½ cup water
1 teaspoon Worcestershire
  sauce
3 tablespoons sugar
3 tablespoons chili powder

2 tablespoons prepared
  mustard
1½ teaspoons salt
3 tablespoons minced garlic
1 large onion, chopped
1 lemon, sliced
1 apple, chopped

Combine first 9 ingredients in saucepan. Add garlic, onion, lemon and apple; mix well. Bring to a boil; reduce heat. Simmer for 15 minutes. Store in refrigerator. Use with ribs or pork chops.

Louise Levzow

BÉARNAISE SAUCE

Yield: 4 servings

2 egg yolks
¼ teaspoon salt
Cayenne pepper to taste
½ cup melted butter

1 tablespoon lemon juice
1 teaspoon minced onion
1 teaspoon minced parsley
1½ teaspoons tarragon vinegar

Beat egg yolks in mixer bowl until thick and lemon-colored. Add salt and cayenne pepper. Add melted butter and lemon juice 1 teaspoon at a time, beating constantly. Stir in remaining ingredients.

Lisa Pruitt

CURRY SAUCE

Yield: 3 cups

1 can cream of mushroom soup
1 cup sour cream
⅔ cup mayonnaise

¼ cup sliced fresh mushrooms
1 teaspoon curry powder

Heat soup in saucepan. Stir in sour cream, mayonnaise, mushrooms and curry powder; mix well. Heat to serving temperature. Serve over vegetables or chicken.

Nancy Pruitt

CURRANT JELLY SAUCE

Yield: 12 servings

1 egg, beaten
1 teaspoon dry mustard
1 teaspoon flour
3 tablespoons vinegar

1 tablespoon water
1 small jar currant jelly
1½ tablespoons butter

Combine egg, dry mustard, flour, vinegar and water in bowl; mix until smooth. Melt jelly with butter in double boiler, stirring frequently until well blended. Add egg mixture. Cook until thickened, stirring constantly. Serve with tongue or ham.

Fran Gurganus

HOLLANDAISE SAUCE

Yield: 6 to 8 servings

3 tablespoons dry coffee
   creamer
4 egg yolks
¼ cup fresh lemon juice

¼ cup water
½ teaspoon salt
½ cup butter

Combine creamer with egg yolks, lemon juice, water and salt in bowl; beat until smooth. Melt butter in double boiler over hot water. Add egg yolk mixture. Cook until thickened, whisking constantly. Store in refrigerator; reheat over hot water. Serve over asparagus, broccoli or Eggs Benedict.

Sis Ward

EASY HOLLANDAISE SAUCE

Yield: 3 servings

1 egg yolk
Juice of 1 lemon

¼ cup butter

Beat egg yolk with lemon juice in double boiler. Place over hot water. Cook over hot water until smooth, stirring in butter 1 tablespoon at a time.

Anna Hall

MUSHROOM ASPARAGUS SAUCE *Yield: 4 cups*

1 cup sliced fresh mushrooms
1/4 cup butter
1 can cream of asparagus soup
1/2 cup half and half

1 can sliced water chestnuts,
  drained, chopped
1/2 teaspoon curry powder

Sauté mushrooms in butter in skillet until brown. Stir in soup, half and half, water chestnuts and curry powder; mix well. Heat to serving temperature. Serve with fish.

Jeff Fuller

SWEET AND HOT MUSTARD *Yield: 2 cups*

2 cans dry mustard
1 cup wine or tarragon vinegar

1/2 cup packed brown sugar
2 eggs, beaten

Blend dry mustard with vinegar in bowl. Let stand overnight. Combine with brown sugar and eggs in double boiler. Cook over hot water until thickened, stirring constantly. Store in airtight containers in refrigerator.

Sandy Wieters

THE SAUCE *Yield: 10 to 12 servings*

1 1/2 cups mayonnaise
2 tablespoons (heaping)
  horseradish
1 small onion, grated

1/2 teaspoon prepared mustard
1/4 teaspoon salt
1/4 teaspoon pepper
1/2 cup melted butter

Combine mayonnaise, horseradish, onion, mustard, salt and pepper in bowl; mix well. Add butter; mix well. Chill overnight. Serve on steak, broccoli or asparagus or as dip with carrot sticks.

Linda Jenkins McConnell

RAISIN SAUCE

Yield: 2 cups

1/2 cup packed brown sugar
1 teaspoon dry mustard
2 teaspoons cornstarch
2 tablespoons vinegar

2 tablespoons lemon juice
1 1/2 cups water
1/4 teaspoon grated lemon rind
1/2 cup raisins

Mix brown sugar, dry mustard and cornstarch in saucepan. Add vinegar, lemon juice and water; blend well. Stir in lemon rind and raisins. Cook over low heat until thickened, stirring constantly. Serve with baked ham.

Louise Levzow

TINGLE'S RED SAUCE FOR FISH

Yield: 8 servings

1 can tomatoes
1 onion, chopped
2 tablespoons lemon juice

1/2 teaspoon oregano
1/4 teaspoon rosemary
1/4 teaspoon garlic powder

Process tomatoes in blender until smooth. Combine with onion, lemon juice, oregano, rosemary and garlic powder in saucepan. Simmer for 25 minutes. Serve hot over fish.

William Tingle

TERIYAKI MARINADE

Yield: 1 cup

1/2 cup soy sauce
1/3 cup sake, white wine or
    sherry
3 tablespoons brown sugar

1 clove of garlic, crushed
1/2 teaspoon dry mustard
1 tablespoon shredded
    gingerroot

Combine soy sauce, wine, brown sugar, garlic, dry mustard and gingerroot in bowl; mix well. Use with stir-fry recipes, and as marinade for grilled chicken or sirloin tip. May add onion, pineapple juice and a small amount of oil if desired.

Nancy Hollingsworth

DIET-CONSCIOUS TERIYAKI MARINADE *Yield: 1¹/4 cups*

1/3 cup low-sodium soy sauce
2 tablespoons frozen apple
  juice concentrate

2/3 cup water
3 tablespoons minced garlic
1¹/2 teaspoons grated ginger

Combine soy sauce, apple juice concentrate, water, garlic and ginger in bowl; mix well. Store in airtight container in refrigerator.

Francie Hall

BASIC WHITE SAUCE   *Yield: 1¹/4 cups*

2 tablespoons butter
2 tablespoons flour
1 cup milk or half and half

1/4 teaspoon salt
1/8 teaspoon white pepper

Melt butter in double boiler or saucepan over low heat. Blend in flour gradually. Stir in milk gradually. Cook until thickened, stirring constantly. Season with salt and white pepper. Decrease butter and flour to 1 tablespoon each for thinner white sauce. Increase butter and flour to 3 tablespoons each for thicker white sauce.

Lisa Pruitt

CHEESED APPLES   *Yield: 6 to 8 servings*

1/2 cup butter, softened
1 cup sugar
8 ounces Velveeta cheese,
  shredded

3/4 cup flour
1 can apples

Cream butter and sugar in mixer bowl until light. Add cheese; mix well. Stir in flour and apples. Spoon into 2-quart baking dish. Bake at 350 degrees for 30 minutes. Serve hot. May serve as dessert with ice cream or whipped cream.

Sherrie Morrison

SCALLOPED APPLES
Yield: 6 servings

1 can sliced apples
6 tablespoons melted margarine
1 tablespoon lemon juice
20 butter crackers, crushed

1/4 cup sugar
1/4 cup packed brown sugar
1 teaspoon pumpkin pie spice
2 tablespoons butter

Drain apples. Combine with margarine and lemon juice in bowl; mix well. Stir in 1/4 of the cracker crumbs. Spoon into baking dish. Mix sugar, brown sugar and pumpkin pie spice in bowl. Sprinkle over casserole. Top with remaining cracker crumbs. Dot with butter. Bake at 350 degrees for 45 to 60 minutes or until brown.

Lynn Clanton

SPICED FRUIT
Yield: 12 servings

1 20-ounce can sliced peaches
1 20-ounce can sliced pears
1 medium can pineapple chunks
8 ounces candied cherries
Apple rings

6 tablespoons melted margarine
1 cup packed light brown sugar
1 teaspoon (heaping) curry
   powder
Nutmeg and cinnamon to taste

Drain peaches, pears and pineapple. Combine with cherries and apple rings in bowl. Add mixture of remaining ingredients; mix well. Spoon into baking dish. Bake at 325 degrees for 30 minutes.

Wendy Hack

BAKED PINEAPPLE
Yield: 6 servings

1 can pineapple tidbits
8 day-old biscuits
1 cup sugar

2 eggs, slightly beaten
1/2 cup melted butter

Drain pineapple, reserving juice. Combine reserved juice with biscuits in bowl. Let stand for biscuits to absorb juice. Add pineapple, sugar, eggs and butter; mix well. Spoon into baking dish. Bake at 350 degrees for 45 minutes.

Ina Carpenter

CRANBERRIES AND RICE

Yield: 8 servings

3 or 4 cups hot cooked rice
1   16-ounce can whole
    cranberry sauce

1 teaspoon curry powder

Pack hot rice into 3 or 4-cup ring mold. Heat cranberry sauce with curry powder in double boiler until bubbly; mix well. Unmold rice ring onto serving plate or chafing dish. Spoon cranberry mixture into center. Cranberries will shade rice ring from crimson to pale pink.

Nancy Pruitt

CRANBERRY SAUCE

Yield: 4 cups

2 cups water
2 cups sugar

4 cups cranberries

Combine water and sugar in large saucepan. Bring to a boil. Cook for 5 minutes. Stir in cranberries. Bring to a boil. Boil for 5 minutes, stirring down foam. Cool to room temperature. Spoon into airtight containers. Chill for 8 hours before serving. Store in refrigerator.

Carol Welch

MELROSE CONSERVE

Yield: 3 cups

1 pound red rose petals
3 cups spring water

1 pound very fine sugar

Combine rose petals with water in saucepan. Cook, covered, for 30 minutes or until color has been drawn from petals. Strain gently, reserving petals. Stir sugar into rose water. Bring to a boil, stirring occasionally. Cook until syrupy, stirring occasionally. Mix in reserved petals. Cool to room temperature. Rose petals and syrup will be beautifully red. This is an old English recipe.

Vivian Butler

PICKLED PEACHES

Yield: 8 pints

5 quarts peaches
Whole cloves
3 cups honey
3 cups vinegar

2 cups water
1 teaspoon salt
2 cinnamon sticks

Scald peaches. Stud each with 3 or 4 cloves. Bring next 4 ingredients to a boil in saucepan. Add cinnamon sticks. Add peaches a few at a time. Cook until peaches are tender and slightly transparent. Pack into hot sterilized jars; fill with syrup, leaving ½-inch headspace. Seal with 2-piece lids.

Lucy Crowley

PEAR RELISH

Yield: 6 pints

1 gallon chopped peeled pears
2 red bell peppers
3 medium onions
2½ cups vinegar

2 cups sugar
1½ teaspoons mixed spices
1½ teaspoons salt

Grind pears with bell peppers and onions. Combine with vinegar, sugar, mixed spices and salt in saucepan. Cook for 30 minutes, stirring frequently. Spoon into hot sterilized jars, leaving ½ inch headspace. Seal with 2-piece lids.

Janie Wilkerson

Breads &
Coffee Cakes

ONION CRESCENT CRUNCH STICKS   *Yield: 32 servings*

2 eggs, beaten
2 tablespoons melted butter
1 teaspoon flour
1 teaspoon parsley flakes
1/2 teaspoon garlic salt

1/4 teaspoon onion salt
1 8-count can crescent rolls
2 3-ounce cans French-fried
   onions, crushed

Combine eggs, butter, flour, parsley flakes, garlic salt and onion salt in bowl; mix well. Separate roll dough into 4 rectangles, pressing diagonal perforations to seal. Cut each rectangle into 8 strips. Dip each strip into egg mixture; coat with crushed onions. Place on un-greased baking sheet. Bake at 375 degrees for 12 to 15 minutes or until brown. May serve as appetizer.

Susan Kesler

JIFFY BISCUITS   *Yield: 9 servings*

2 tablespoons mayonnaise
1 cup self-rising flour

2/3 cup milk

Combine mayonnaise, flour and milk in small bowl; mix well. Spoon into 9 greased muffin cups. Bake at 425 degrees for 10 minutes or until brown. May drop onto hot baking sheet if preferred.

Kitty McNeely

LOW COUNTRY BISCUITS   *Yield: 18 servings*

3/4 cup shortening
2 cups self-rising flour

1/4 cup sugar
3/4 cup milk

Cut shortening into mixture of flour and sugar in bowl. Add milk; mix just until moistened. Knead lightly on floured surface. Roll or press 1/4 inch thick. Cut as desired; place on baking sheet. Bake at 400 degrees for 12 to 15 minutes or until light brown.

Louise L. Baughman

Sour Cream Biscuits
Yield: 12 servings

2 cups self-rising flour   1 cup sour cream

Combine flour and sour cream in bowl; mix well. Roll ½ inch thick on floured surface; cut with biscuit cutter. Place on baking sheet. Bake at 425 degrees for 10 minutes. May cut very small and fill with ham for hors d'oeuvres. May add chopped parsley, onion or herbs.

Pam Smith

Scones
Yield: 16 servings

2 cups self-rising flour
½ teaspoon baking powder
2 teaspoons baking soda
1 tablespoon sugar

½ teaspoon cream of tartar
½ teaspoon salt
½ cup shortening
⅔ cup milk

Mix flour, baking powder, baking soda, sugar, cream of tartar and salt in bowl. Cut in shortening. Add milk; mixing just until moistened. Press lightly into ½-inch thick circle on floured surface; cut into rounds. Place on greased baking sheet. Bake at 425 degrees for 15 to 20 minutes or until light brown. Serve with tea.

Bill Ward

Carolina Corn Bread
Yield: 8 servings

2 eggs
1 cup buttermilk

2 cups self-rising cornmeal

Beat eggs with buttermilk in mixer bowl. Stir in cornmeal. Heat a small amount of oil in cast-iron skillet, muffin cups or cornstick pan. Add batter. Bake at 400 degrees for 25 to 30 minutes or until brown.

Dorsey Yount

CORN BREAD CASSEROLE

Yield: 16 servings

2 large onions, chopped
6 tablespoons butter or
  margarine
2 eggs
2 tablespoons milk
2 17-ounce cans cream-style
  corn

1 16-ounce package corn
  bread mix
1 cup sour cream
2 cups shredded sharp
  Cheddar cheese

Sauté onions in butter in medium skillet until golden brown. Blend eggs and milk in medium bowl. Add corn and corn bread mix; mix well. Spoon into greased 9x13-inch baking dish. Layer onions, sour cream and cheese over batter. Bake at 425 degrees for 35 minutes or until golden brown. Let stand for 10 minutes before serving.

Lois H. Richardson

MEXICAN CORN BREAD

Yield: 8 servings

1 cup cornmeal
2 teaspoons baking powder
1/2 teaspoon salt
1 8-ounce can cream-style corn
1/2 cup sour cream
1/4 cup corn oil

2 eggs
4 green chili peppers, rinsed,
  chopped
2 cups shredded Cheddar
  cheese

Combine cornmeal, baking powder, salt, corn, sour cream, oil, eggs and chili peppers in bowl; mix well. Stir in 1 1/2 cups cheese. Spoon into greased 8 or 9-inch baking pan. Sprinkle with remaining 1/2 cup cheese. Bake at 350 degrees for 1 hour. Cool slightly before serving.

Lisa Pruitt

CORN BREAD

Yield: 8 servings

1 package jiffy corn bread mix
3 eggs, beaten
3/4 cup oil

1 small can cream-style corn
8 ounces sour cream

Combine corn bread mix, eggs, oil, corn and sour cream in large bowl; mix well. Spoon into greased baking pan. Bake at 350 degrees for 25 minutes.

Barbara Leonard

SPINACH SPOON BREAD

Yield: 8 servings

1 10-ounce package frozen onions in cream or cheese sauce
1 10-ounce package frozen chopped spinach
2 eggs, slightly beaten
1 cup sour cream

1/2 cup melted butter or margarine
1/4 teaspoon salt
1 8-ounce package corn muffin mix
1/2 cup shredded Swiss or Cheddar cheese

Cook onions and spinach separately, using package directions; drain spinach well. Combine onions, spinach, eggs, sour cream, butter and salt in bowl; mix well. Stir in corn muffin mix. Spoon into 1 1/2-quart baking dish. Bake at 350 degrees for 30 to 35 minutes or until wooden pick inserted in center comes out clean. Sprinkle with cheese. Bake for 2 minutes longer or until cheese melts.

Lynn Clanton

DOUGHNUT HOLES

Yield: 2 dozen

2 eggs
1 cup sugar
2 tablespoons melted butter
3/4 cup sour milk
3 cups flour
1 teaspoon baking powder

1 teaspoon baking soda
1/2 teaspoon nutmeg
1 teaspoon salt
Oil for deep frying
Cinnamon-sugar

Beat eggs in mixer bowl. Add sugar and melted butter; mix well. Add sour milk, flour, baking powder, baking soda, nutmeg and salt; mix well. Drop by teaspoonfuls into deep hot shortening in saucepan. Deep-fry until brown; drain on paper towels. Coat with cinnamon-sugar.

Kay Spencer

APPLESAUCE RAISIN BREAD

Yield: 10 servings

1 1/2 cups flour
1 teaspoon baking powder
1 teaspoon baking soda
1 cup quick-cooking oats
1/2 cup packed brown sugar
1 teaspoon cinnamon

1/2 teaspoon nutmeg
1 teaspoon salt
2 eggs
1/3 cup oil
1 cup applesauce
1 cup raisins

Mix flour, baking powder, baking soda, oats, brown sugar, cinnamon, nutmeg and salt in bowl. Add eggs, oil and applesauce; stir to mix well. Stir in raisins. Spoon into greased 5x9-inch loaf pan. Bake at 350 degrees for 1 hour; top will crack. Cool in pan for 10 minutes. Remove to wire rack to cool completely.

Frances Caldwell

FOOL-PROOF BANANA BREAD
Yield: 10 servings

3 very ripe bananas
1 teaspoon baking soda
2 eggs, beaten
1/2 cup butter or margarine,
   softened

1 cup sugar
2 cups flour
1 teaspoon baking powder
1 1/2 teaspoons vanilla extract
1 teaspoon salt

Mash bananas with baking soda in bowl; set aside. Beat eggs with butter in bowl until smooth. Add sugar, flour, baking powder, vanilla and salt; mix well. Add banana mixture; mix well. Spoon into greased loaf pan. Bake at 350 degrees for 1 hour or just until bread tests done; do not overbake. Cool in pan for 10 minutes; remove to wire rack to cool completely. May make into muffins or prepare in food processor for a more cake-like consistency.

Ellery Inglesby

BANANA-BLUEBERRY BREAD
Yield: 10 servings

1/2 cup shortening
1 cup sugar
2 eggs
1 cup mashed banana
1/2 cup quick-cooking oats
1 1/2 cups flour

1 teaspoon baking soda
1/4 teaspoon salt
1/2 cup chopped pecans or
   walnuts
1/2 cup fresh blueberries

Cream shortening in mixer bowl until light. Add sugar gradually, beating until fluffy. Beat in eggs 1 at a time. Stir in banana. Mix oats, flour, baking soda, salt, pecans and blueberries in bowl. Add to batter; mix just until moistened. Spoon into greased and floured 5x9-inch loaf pan. Bake at 350 degrees for 50 to 55 minutes or until wooden pick inserted in center comes out clean. Cool in pan for 10 minutes. Remove to wire rack to cool completely.

Barbara DeLoach

BANANA-STRAWBERRY BREAD   *Yield: 10 servings*

2 cups self-rising flour
1 cup sugar
1 teaspoon cinnamon
1/2 teaspoon cloves
2 eggs

1 1/3 cups mashed bananas
3/4 cup mashed strawberries,
   sweetened to taste
1/2 cup oil
1/3 cup chopped nuts

Mix flour, sugar, cinnamon and cloves in bowl. Add eggs, bananas, strawberries and oil; mix just until moistened. Stir in nuts. Spoon into greased and floured loaf pan. Bake at 325 degrees for 1 hour to 1 hour and 5 minutes or until loaf tests done. Cool in pan for 10 minutes. Remove to wire rack to cool completely. May add red food coloring if desired.

Kitty McNeely

BUTTERED BEER LOAVES   *Yield: 20 servings*

6 cups self-rising flour
6 tablespoons sugar

2   12-ounce cans cold beer
1 cup melted butter

Combine flour, sugar and beer in bowl; mix well. Spoon into 2 greased 5x9-inch loaf pans. Bake at 350 degrees for 30 minutes. Pour butter over tops. Bake for 10 minutes longer or until light brown. Serve warm.

Mrs. John Gathings

GARLIC-CHEESE SOURDOUGH BREAD *Yield: 10 servings*

1 loaf sourdough bread
1/2 cup melted butter or
   margarine

1 envelope garlic-cheese salad
   dressing mix

Cut sourdough bread into slices. Combine butter with salad dressing mix in bowl; mix well. Brush on bread slices. Wrap bread in foil. Bake at 350 degrees for 20 to 25 minutes or until heated through. Serve immediately.

Sue West

Bishop's Bread

Yield: 50 servings

1¹/₂ cups sifted flour
1¹/₂ teaspoons baking powder
¹/₄ teaspoon salt
³/₄ cup semisweet chocolate
   chips

2 cups chopped pecans
1 cup raisins
1 cup glacéed cherry halves
3 eggs
1 cup sugar

Line bottoms of 5 small loaf pans with waxed paper; grease pans and paper. Sift flour, baking powder and salt into bowl. Stir in chocolate chips, pecans, raisins and cherries; toss to coat well. Beat eggs in bowl until foamy. Add sugar gradually, beating constantly. Fold in fruit mixture. Spoon into prepared pans. Bake at 325 degrees for 1¹/₂ hours. Cool in pans for 10 minutes. Remove to wire rack to cool completely. Cut into thin slices; this is more like a cookie than a bread.

Nancy W. Richardson

Golden Cheese Bread

Yield: 10 servings

1¹/₄ cups sifted flour
2 tablespoons sugar
1 tablespoon baking powder
¹/₂ teaspoon salt
1 cup shredded Cheddar cheese

³/₄ cup uncooked instant whole
   wheat cereal
1 egg
³/₄ cup milk
¹/₄ cup oil

Sift flour, sugar, baking powder and salt into medium bowl. Stir in cheese and cereal. Beat egg with milk and oil in small bowl. Add to flour mixture, mixing just until moistened. Spoon into greased loaf pan. Bake at 400 degrees for 30 minutes or until wooden pick inserted in center comes out clean. Cool in pan on wire rack for 5 minutes. Remove to serving plate. Serve warm. Toast leftovers for breakfast.

Ellen Garland

ONION-CHEESE SUPPER BREAD

Yield: 6 to 8 servings

1/2 cup chopped onion
1 tablespoon margarine
1 egg, beaten
1/2 cup milk
1 1/2 cups baking mix

1 cup shredded Cheddar cheese
1 tablespoon poppy seed
2 tablespoons melted butter or
    margarine

Sauté onion in margarine in skillet until golden brown. Combine egg and milk in bowl; mix well. Stir in baking mix just until moistened. Stir in onion and half the cheese. Spoon into greased 8-inch baking pan. Sprinkle with remaining cheese and poppy seed. Drizzle with melted butter. Bake at 400 degrees for 20 to 25 minutes or until golden brown. Serve hot.

Margaret D. Jones

POPPY SEED BREAD

Yield: 40 servings

3 eggs
2 1/4 cups sugar
1 1/2 cups oil
1 1/2 cups milk
3 cups flour
1 1/2 teaspoons baking powder
1 1/2 teaspoons salt

1 1/2 teaspoons each vanilla,
    butter and almond extracts
1 1/2 tablespoons poppy seed
1/4 cup orange juice
1 cup sugar
1/2 teaspoon each vanilla,
    butter and almond extracts

Beat eggs with 2 1/4 cups sugar in mixer bowl. Add oil, milk, flour, baking powder, salt and 1 1/2 teaspoons of each of the flavorings; mix well. Stir in poppy seed. Spoon into 4 greased and floured small loaf pans. Bake at 350 degrees for 1 hour. Combine orange juice, 1 cup sugar and 1/2 teaspoon of each of the flavorings in bowl; mix well. Punch holes in warm loaves. Pour glaze over loaves.

Paige Pruitt

IRISH SODA BREAD

Yield: 10 servings

3 cups sifted flour
3 tablespoons sugar
1 tablespoon baking powder
1/2 teaspoon baking soda
1 cup dried currants or raisins

1/2 teaspoon salt
11/3 cups buttermilk
2 tablespoons sugar
2 tablespoons hot water

Mix flour, 3 tablespoons sugar, baking powder, baking soda, currants and salt in bowl. Add buttermilk; stir to mix well. Knead on floured surface 10 times. Shape into 1 large round loaf or 3 small loaves. Place on ungreased baking sheet. Cut cross in top of loaf. Bake at 375 degrees for 35 minutes or until light brown. Drizzle with mixture of 2 tablespoons sugar and hot water. Serve hot with butter. It is a favorite for St. Patrick's Day.

Dorothy Cullings

SWISS BRAIDED BREAD

Yield: 20 servings

1 envelope dry yeast
11/2 cups 110-degree milk
1/2 cup sugar

11/2 teaspoons salt
1/4 cup oil
41/2 cups flour

Sprinkle yeast on warm milk in bowl. Add sugar and salt; stir to mix well. Add oil and half the flour; mix well. Add remaining flour; mix well. Knead on floured surface for 10 minutes or until smooth and elastic, kneading in additional flour if needed. Place in greased bowl, turning to grease surface. Let rise, covered with warm damp cloth, in warm place for 11/2 hours or until doubled in bulk. Divide into 2 portions. Divide each portion into 3 equal parts. Roll into 6 ropes. Braid 3 ropes together to form 2 loaves; do not stretch ropes. Place on greased baking sheet. Grease tops. Let rise for 45 to 60 minutes or until doubled in bulk. Bake at 350 degrees for 30 minutes. Brush with melted butter.

Nancy C. Miller

Sally Lunn Bread

Yield: 12 servings

1 cake or envelope yeast	2 eggs
1 cup warm milk	3¹/₂ cups flour
3 tablespoons shortening	1¹/₄ teaspoons salt
3 tablespoons sugar	

Dissolve yeast in warm milk. Cream shortening and sugar in mixer bowl until light and fluffy. Beat in eggs. Add sifted mixture of flour and salt alternately with yeast mixture, mixing well after each addition. Let rise in warm place until doubled in bulk. Knead lightly on floured surface. Place into greased 10-inch Sally Lunn ring mold or tube pan. Let rise until doubled in bulk. Bake at 300 degrees for 1 hour. Cool on wire rack.

Katie Robertson

Sourdough Bread

Yield: 20 servings

1 cup sourdough starter	¹/₄ cup sugar
1 cup warm water	2 tablespoons oil
¹/₂ cup sugar	1 tablespoon salt
3 tablespoons potato flakes	6 cups flour
1¹/₂ cups warm water	Melted margarine

Combine first 4 ingredients in bowl; mix well. Let stand, covered with cheesecloth, at room temperature for 24 hours. Chill, covered, until needed, removing 1 cup to use or discard and feeding as above every 5 days. Remove 1 cup starter from refrigerator. Let stand at room temperature for 8 hours or longer. Combine with 1¹/₂ cups warm water, ¹/₄ cup sugar, oil, salt and flour in bowl; mix well. Knead on lightly floured surface until smooth and elastic. Place in greased bowl, turning to grease surface. Let rise, covered with damp cloth, for 8 to 12 hours. Knead on floured surface 10 times. Divide into 2 portions; shape into loaves. Place in 2 greased loaf pans. Let rise for 8 to 12 hours. Bake at 350 degrees for just 25 to 30 minutes; top may not brown. Broil for 1 minute if necessary to brown tops. Remove to wire rack to cool. Brush tops with melted margarine.

Gloria Freer

WHOLE WHEAT BREAD

Yield: 20 servings

1 envelope dry yeast
1/4 cup 110-degree water
3 tablespoons oil
1/2 cup honey

1/4 cup molasses
2 cups water
2 teaspoons salt
6 1/2 cups whole wheat flour

Dissolve yeast in 1/4 cup warm water in large bowl. Cool to 85 degrees. Combine oil, honey, molasses, 2 cups water and salt in bowl; mix well. Add 2 cups whole wheat flour; mix well. Add to yeast; mix well. Mix in enough remaining flour to form a stiff dough. Knead on floured surface for 8 to 10 minutes or until smooth and elastic. Let rise for 1 1/2 hours or until doubled in bulk. Shape into 2 loaves; place in 2 greased 4x8-inch loaf pans. Bake at 375 degrees for 45 minutes. Remove to wire rack to cool.

Nancy C. Miller

BANANA MUFFINS

Yield: 1 dozen

3 large ripe bananas
3/4 cup sugar
1 egg, slightly beaten
1/3 cup melted butter

1 1/2 cups flour
1 teaspoon baking powder
1 teaspoon baking soda
1/2 teaspoon salt

Mash bananas in bowl. Add sugar, egg and butter; mix well. Add mixture of flour, baking powder, baking soda and salt; mix just until moistened. Spoon into paper-lined muffin cups. Bake at 375 degrees for 20 minutes. Remove to wire rack to cool.

Elaine Boone

Butter Curls—Dip blade of vegetable peeler into hot water and pull firmly over slightly softened stick of butter. Chill curls in ice water.

YOGURT BRAN MUFFINS

Yield: 4 dozen

2 cups unbleached flour
1¹/₂ cups bran
1¹/₂ teaspoons baking soda
1¹/₂ teaspoons salt
2 cups plain yogurt

¹/₂ cup safflower or vegetable
  oil
¹/₂ cup dark molasses
³/₄ cup raisins

Mix flour, bran, baking soda and salt in bowl; make well in center. Combine yogurt, oil, molasses and raisins in small bowl; mix well. Spoon into well in dry ingredients; mix just until moistened. Spoon into greased muffin cups. Bake at 350 degrees for 35 minutes. Remove to wire rack to cool.

Dorothy Collins

PINEAPPLE MUFFINS

Yield: 36 to 40 miniature muffins

¹/₂ cup butter or margarine,
  softened
1 cup sugar
1 egg
2 cups flour
1 teaspoon baking soda

1 teaspoon cinnamon
1 teaspoon allspice
¹/₂ teaspoon cloves
1 8-ounce can crushed
  pineapple

Cream butter and sugar in mixer bowl until light and fluffy. Add egg and flour; mix well. Add baking soda, cinnamon, allspice, cloves and pineapple; mix just until moistened. Spoon into greased miniature muffin cups. Bake at 350 degrees for 12 minutes. Remove to wire rack to cool.

Nancy Pruitt

APPLESAUCE PANCAKES

Yield: 4 servings

4 eggs
1 cup milk
2 tablespoons melted butter

³/₄ cup applesauce
1¹/₂ cups flour
¹/₄ teaspoon salt

Combine eggs, milk, butter, applesauce, flour and salt in bowl; beat until very smooth. Spoon onto heated buttered griddle. Bake until light brown on both sides. Serve with butter and confectioners' sugar. These pancakes are very thin and moist.

Clare Fisher

YUMMY PANCAKES

Yield: 6 servings

2 cups self-rising flour
2 teaspoons baking powder
1 tablespoon sugar
¹/₃ cup oil
1 egg

Milk
2 cups sugar
1 cup water
¹/₂ teaspoon mapleine flavoring

Mix flour, baking powder and 1 tablespoon sugar in bowl. Measure oil in 2-cup measure. Add egg and enough milk to fill measure; mix well. Add to dry ingredients; mix well. Spoon onto hot griddle. Bake until brown on both sides. Combine 2 cups sugar, water and flavoring in saucepan. Bring to a boil. Cook until sugar dissolves. Serve hot over pancakes.

Louise S. Hunter

BLENDER CROISSANTS
Yield: 32 servings

1 cup warm water
2 envelopes dry yeast
1 5-ounce can evaporated milk
1 egg
1/3 cup sugar
1/4 cup melted butter

5 cups flour
1 cup chilled butter, coarsely
  chopped
1 egg, beaten
1 tablespoon water

Combine warm water, yeast, evaporated milk, 1 egg, sugar and melted butter in blender container; process until smooth. Add 1 cup flour gradually, processing until smooth. Place remaining 4 cups flour in large bowl. Add 1 cup chopped butter and yeast mixture; mix gently until moistened. Chill, covered, for 4 hours or longer. Divide dough into 4 portions. Remove 1 portion at a time from refrigerator. Roll into 16-inch circle on floured surface. Cut into 8 wedges. Roll up from wide ends; shape into crescents. Place point side down 2 inches apart on nonstick baking pan. Let rise, covered, for 3 to 4 hours or until doubled in bulk. Brush with mixture of 1 egg and water. Bake at 400 degrees for 12 to 15 minutes or until golden brown. Serve warm with softened butter. The secret of flaky croissants is to keep the dough cold.

Al Seine

POTATO ROLLS
Yield: 5 dozen

1 cup shortening
1/4 cup sugar
2 eggs
1 cup mashed cooked potatoes
1 1/2 teaspoons salt

1 envelope dry yeast
1/2 cup lukewarm water
1 1/2 cups milk, scalded, cooled
  to lukewarm
7 cups enriched flour

Combine shortening, sugar, eggs, potatoes and salt in bowl; mix well. Dissolve yeast in 1/2 cup lukewarm water in bowl. Add to potato mixture with milk; mix well. Sift in flour. Knead until smooth. Place in greased bowl, turning to grease surface. Let rise in warm place for 1 1/2 hours or until doubled in bulk. Shape into rolls; place in baking pan. Bake at 400 degrees for 15 to 20 minutes or until light brown. May store in refrigerator until needed.

Rhetta Andreas

REFRIGERATOR YEAST ROLLS

Yield: 4 dozen

1 envelope dry yeast	7 cups flour
1/2 cup warm water	1/2 cup sugar
2 eggs	1 cup shortening
1 teaspoon sugar	2 cups water
1 teaspoon salt	

Combine dry yeast, 1/2 cup warm water, eggs, 1 teaspoon sugar and salt in mixer bowl; mix at low speed for 2 minutes. Set aside. Mix flour, 1/2 cup sugar, shortening and 2 cups water in mixer bowl; mix at medium speed for 3 minutes. Add yeast mixture; mix at medium speed for 3 minutes. Let rise, covered, in warm place for 3 hours or until doubled in bulk. Punch down dough. Chill, covered, for 3 hours to 4 days. Shape into 1 1/2-inch balls. Arrange in 3 greased 9-inch baking pans. Let rise in warm place for 2 hours or until doubled in bulk. Bake at 400 degrees for 10 to 12 minutes or until golden brown.

Mrs. Robert H. Stafford

REFRIGERATOR ROLLS

Yield: 3 dozen

1 1/2 cups boiling water	2 envelopes dry yeast
1 cup shortening	1/2 cup warm water
3/4 cup sugar	5 cups flour
1 teaspoon salt	Melted butter
2 eggs, beaten	

Pour boiling water over mixture of shortening, sugar and salt in bowl. Add eggs. Cool to lukewarm. Dissolve yeast in warm water in small bowl. Add to shortening mixture. Stir in flour. Place in greased bowl, turning to grease surface. Chill, covered, in refrigerator overnight. Knead desired amount of dough on floured surface. Roll into circle; cut with cutter. Dip into melted butter; fold into halves. Place in baking pan. Let rise for 2 hours or until doubled in bulk. Bake at 375 degrees for 15 to 20 minutes or until golden brown. May bake just until set, freeze and bake until brown when needed.

Louise S. Hunter

COFFEE CAKES

Yield: 16 servings

2¹/₂ cups flour
1 cup packed dark brown sugar
1 cup packed light brown sugar
¹/₂ cup butter

2 eggs
1 cup buttermilk
1 teaspoon baking soda
Cinnamon to taste

Combine flour, brown sugars and butter in bowl; mix until crumbly. Reserve 1 cup of the mixture. Combine remaining crumb mixture with eggs, buttermilk and baking soda in bowl; mix well. Spoon into 2 greased pie plates. Sprinkle with reserved crumbs and cinnamon. Bake at 350 degrees for 45 minutes.

Liz Rinaldi

POPPY SEED COFFEE CAKE

Yield: 16 servings

1 2-layer package yellow cake
   mix
1 4-ounce package coconut
   instant pudding mix
4 eggs

¹/₂ cup oil
1 cup warm water
¹/₄ cup poppy seed
1 teaspoon coconut extract

Combine cake mix, pudding mix, eggs, oil, water, poppy seed and coconut extract in mixer bowl; beat for 4 minutes. Spoon into greased and floured tube pan. Bake at 350 degrees for 50 minutes. Cool in pan for 10 minutes. Remove to serving plate.

Laurel Sonfield

QUICK CARAMEL COFFEE RING
Yield: 16 servings

½ cup chopped nuts	2 tablespoons water
½ cup melted margarine	2 10-ounce cans flaky biscuits
1 cup packed brown sugar	

Sprinkle 3 tablespoons nuts into 12-cup bundt pan coated with 2 tablespoons butter. Combine remaining nuts, remaining butter, brown sugar and water in saucepan. Bring to a boil. Separate biscuits; cut each into halves. Shape into balls. Layer biscuits and hot syrup ½ at a time in prepared pan. Bake at 375 degrees for 20 to 25 minutes or until golden brown. Invert immediately onto serving plate.

Carol Lewis

TENNIS BALL BREAD
Yield: 16 servings

½ cup sugar	½ cup butter
1 tablespoon cinnamon	1 cup packed brown sugar
3 cans biscuits	2 teaspoons water

Mix sugar and cinnamon in bowl. Cut biscuits into quarters. Coat with cinnamon-sugar. Place in greased bundt pan. Combine butter, brown sugar and water in saucepan. Cook until butter melts and brown sugar dissolves. Boil for 2 minutes. Pour over biscuits. Bake at 350 degrees for 25 minutes. Invert immediately onto serving plate. Cool for several minutes. Pull apart to serve.

Paige Pruitt

GINGERBREAD SQUARES

Yield: 12 servings

3/4 cup packed brown sugar
3/4 cup melted shortening
3/4 cup molasses
2 eggs
2 1/4 cups flour
2 1/2 teaspoons baking powder
2 teaspoons ginger

1 1/2 teaspoons cinnamon
3/4 teaspoon baking soda
1/2 teaspoon nutmeg
1/2 teaspoon ground cloves
3/4 cup chopped pecans
1 cup boiling water

Combine brown sugar, shortening and molasses in large mixer bowl; mix well. Add eggs; beat well. Combine dry ingredients and pecans in bowl; mix well. Add to molasses mixture; mix well. Stir in boiling water. Pour into greased 9x13-inch baking pan. Bake in preheated 350-degree oven for 40 minutes. Cut into squares. May be frozen.

Andy Rose

YULETIDE COFFEE CAKE

Yield: 8 servings

1 cup packed light brown sugar
1/2 cup flaked coconut
1/2 cup chopped pecans
1 teaspoon cinnamon
2 cups flour
1 cup sugar
2 teaspoons baking powder

1 teaspoon salt
2   4-ounce packages vanilla
    instant pudding mix
1 cup water
3/4 cup vegetable oil
1 teaspoon vanilla extract
4 eggs

Mix brown sugar, coconut, pecans and cinnamon in bowl; set aside. Combine flour, sugar, baking powder, salt and pudding mix in mixer bowl. Add water, oil, vanilla and eggs; mix well. Beat at low speed for 30 seconds. Beat at medium speed for 2 minutes. Layer batter and coconut mixture 1/2 at a time in greased and floured 9x13-inch baking pan. Chill overnight if desired. Bake coffee cake in preheated 325-degree oven for 40 to 60 minutes or until coffee cake tests done.

Fran Marriott

Just Desserts

FRESH APPLE CRUMBLE

Yield: 6 servings

4¹/₂ cups sliced peeled apples
¹/₂ cup sugar
¹/₂ teaspoon cinnamon
¹/₂ cup flour
¹/₈ teaspoon salt

¹/₄ cup packed dark brown
  sugar
¹/₄ cup butter
¹/₃ cup chopped pecans

Combine apples, sugar and cinnamon in bowl; toss to mix. Spoon into buttered baking dish. Combine flour, salt and brown sugar in bowl. Cut in butter until mixture is crumbly. Stir in pecans. Sprinkle over apples. Bake, covered, at 375 degrees for 15 minutes. Remove cover. Bake for 30 minutes longer.

Gene Ann Ellison

APRICOT AFTER ALL DESSERT

Yield: 6 servings

1 pound wafer-type crackers,
  crumbled
¹/₂ cup butter, softened
¹/₂ cup confectioners' sugar
2 eggs

³/₄ cup chopped pecans
1 16-ounce can apricot halves
2 cups whipping cream,
  whipped, sweetened

Spread ²/₃ of the cracker crumbs in serving dish. Cream butter and confectioners' sugar in mixer bowl until light and fluffy. Add eggs; beat well. Spread over cracker crumb layer. Sprinkle with half the pecans. Mash apricots. Spread over layers. Sprinkle with remaining pecans and cracker crumbs. Chill in refrigerator overnight. Spread sweetened whipped cream over dessert.

Janie Wilkerson

BANANAS FOSTER

Yield: 4 servings

2 tablespoons butter
¼ cup packed brown sugar
2 bananas, cut into thirds
Cinnamon to taste

½ lemon
1 ounce banana liqueur
2 ounces dark rum
Vanilla ice cream

Melt butter in chafing dish over hot flame. Add brown sugar, stirring until well blended and sizzling. Add bananas; sprinkle with cinnamon and lemon juice. Sauté until bananas are soft and glazed. Stir in banana liqueur and rum. Ignite immediately. Stir until flame dies out. Spoon over ice cream.

Dick Patrick

BISCUIT TORTONI

Yield: 8 servings

1 cup whipping cream,
  whipped
2 egg whites, stiffly beaten
2 egg yolks

⅓ cup sugar
1 teaspoon vanilla extract
1 cup Amaretto cookie crumbs

Blend whipped cream and egg whites together in bowl; set aside. Combine egg yolks and sugar in small bowl; beat well. Add vanilla; mix well. Fold into whipped cream mixture. Spoon into soufflé cups; sprinkle with cookie crumbs. Freeze until firm.

Karen Basirico

CARAMEL CUSTARD

Yield: 6 servings

16 tablespoons sugar
8 egg yolks

3 cups whipping cream
2 teaspoons vanilla extract

Sprinkle 8 tablespoons sugar into saucepan. Cover with enough water to make thin layer; sugar will sink. Boil until sugar caramelizes or is golden brown, stirring constantly. This is a slow process and must be watched carefully; approximate time is 20 minutes. Pour into 2-quart ovenproof casserole or 6 individual ramekins. Let stand at room temperature. Beat remaining 8 tablespoons sugar and egg yolks in mixer bowl until thick and lemon-colored. Add cream and vanilla; mix well (do not whip). Pour over caramelized sugar. Place casserole or ramekins in large pan half-filled with water. Bake at 325 degrees for 45 minutes or until top is brown and custard is set. Invert onto serving dish or serve from baking dish.

Lois R. West
Adapted by Sue West

CHEESE FLAN

Yield: 6 servings

1 cup sugar
1/3 cup water
8 ounces cream cheese, softened
1   14-ounce can sweetened
   condensed milk

1 can water
6 eggs, beaten
1 teaspoon vanilla extract
1/2 teaspoon grated lemon rind
1/2 teaspoon salt

Combine sugar and 1/3 cup water in saucepan. Heat over medium-low heat until mixture caramelizes or is golden brown, shaking pan at intervals. Pour into flan mold immediately, tilting mold to coat sides. Combine cream cheese, sweetened condensed milk, water, eggs, vanilla, lemon rind and salt in bowl; mix well. Pour into prepared mold. Bake at 350 degrees for 1 hour or until custard tests done. Chill before serving. Store in refrigerator.

Marilyn Fraser

EASY AND ELEGANT CREAM
Yield: 6 servings

3/4 cup sugar
1 envelope unflavored gelatin
1/4 cup water
1/2 cup half and half

1 teaspoon vanilla extract
1 1/2 cups sour cream
1   10-ounce package frozen
    strawberries, thawed

Combine sugar, gelatin and water in saucepan. Let stand for 5 minutes or until gelatin is softened. Cook until sugar and gelatin are dissolved, stirring frequently. Remove from heat. Stir in half and half. Mix vanilla with sour cream. Add to gelatin mixture gradually. Pour into individual dessert glasses. Chill in refrigerator overnight. Spoon strawberries over cream just before serving. Garnish with pirouette cookies.

June A. Scibelli

CHOCOLATE CHIP EGGNOG BALL
Yield: 6 servings

6 ounces cream cheese,
   softened
4 cups sifted confectioners'
   sugar
1 or 2 tablespoons whipping
   cream
1 teaspoon brandy extract

1/2 teaspoon salt
1/4 teaspoon cinnamon
1/8 teaspoon nutmeg
1/4   12-ounce package Nestle
    little bits, crushed
1 1/4 cups finely chopped pecans

Combine cream cheese, confectioners' sugar and cream in mixer bowl; beat well. Add brandy extract, salt, cinnamon and nutmeg; mix well. Stir in cookie crumbs. Shape into ball. Roll in chopped pecans. Chill in refrigerator until serving time.

Lisa Pruitt

CATERPILLAR
Yield: 6 servings

1 box thin chocolate wafers	4 cups whipping cream, whipped

Place wafers on edge in a row on chilled platter with whipped cream between wafers. Cover top and side with remaining whipped cream. May add bits of wafers for eyes, nose and mouth. Chill for 8 hours to overnight. Cut into diagonal slices.

Mary Coleman

CHOCOLATE MOUSSE CAKE
Yield: 8 servings

2 cups semisweet chocolate chips	2 24-count packages double ladyfingers
2 teaspoons vanilla extract	1 cup whipping cream
2 tablespoons sugar	2 tablespoons confectioners' sugar
1 cup scalded whipping cream	2 tablespoons baking cocoa
4 eggs	1 tablespoon rum
6 tablespoons strong brewed coffee	1 teaspoon vanilla extract
2 tablespoons rum	

Line 4x8-inch loaf pan with plastic wrap or foil with ends extending over ends of pan. Combine chocolate chips, 2 teaspoons vanilla and sugar in blender container. Pour hot cream into container. Process for 1 minute or until chocolate is melted. Add eggs. Process for 20 seconds longer. Stir coffee and 2 tablespoons rum together in bowl. Separate ladyfinger halves. Dip each ladyfinger into coffee mixture; arrange with rounded side against sides of prepared loaf pan. Spoon half the chocolate mousse into pan. Top with layer of ladyfingers. Spoon in remaining mousse; top with remaining ladyfingers, rounded side up. Sprinkle with remaining coffee mixture. Chill, covered, in refrigerator for several hours to overnight. Beat remaining 1 cup cream, confectioners' sugar, cocoa, 1 tablespoon rum and 1 teaspoon vanilla in bowl until stiff. Invert cake onto serving plate. Frost with whipped cream frosting. Chill for 1 hour or until serving time.

Phyllis Modell

WENDY'S CHOCOLATE LUSH PIE

Yield: 12 servings

1 cup flour
1/2 cup melted margarine
1/2 cup chopped pecans
8 ounces cream cheese,
  softened
1 teaspoon vanilla extract

1 cup confectioners' sugar
12 ounces whipped topping
1 6-ounce package chocolate
  instant pudding mix
2²/₃ cups milk

Combine flour and margarine in bowl; mix well. Stir in pecans. Press mixture into greased 9x13-inch baking pan. Bake at 350 degrees for 20 minutes or until brown. Cool to room temperature. Combine cream cheese, vanilla, confectioners' sugar and 1 cup whipped topping in bowl; mix well. Spread over cooled crust. Prepare pudding using package directions with 2²/₃ cups milk. Spread over cream cheese mixture; top with remaining whipped topping. Garnish with graham cracker crumbs or chocolate shavings.

Marge Weaver

LUSCIOUS CHOCOLATE SQUARES

Yield: 10 servings

1/2 cup melted margarine
1 cup flour
1 cup finely chopped pecans
8 ounces cream cheese, softened
1 cup confectioners' sugar

1 cup whipped topping
2 3-ounce packages chocolate
  instant pudding mix
3 cups milk
9 ounces whipped topping

Combine melted margarine, flour and pecans in bowl; mix well. Pat into 8x13-inch baking pan. Bake at 300 degrees for 25 minutes. Let stand until completely cooled. Spread mixture of cream cheese, confectioners' sugar and 1 cup whipped topping over baked layer. Combine pudding mix and milk in mixer bowl. Beat at low speed for 2 minutes. Let stand for 2 minutes. Spread over cream cheese layer. Top with remaining 9 ounces whipped topping. Chill in refrigerator overnight.

Jane Dawes

FRUIT PIZZA

Yield: 8 servings

1 package refrigerator sugar
  cookie dough
8 to 12 ounces cream cheese,
  softened
1/2 cup sugar
1 1/2 teaspoons vanilla extract
1   11-ounce can mandarin
  oranges, drained

3/4   8-ounce can pineapple
  chunks, drained
1 large banana, sliced
1 pint fresh strawberries
1/2   8-ounce jar orange
  marmalade
1 teaspoon (or less) water

Cut cookie dough into slices. Arrange to cover pizza pan, pressing slices to spread out. Bake using package directions. Combine cream cheese, sugar and vanilla in bowl; mix well. Spread over baked cookie crust. Arrange mandarin oranges, pineapple chunks, banana slices and strawberries to cover cream cheese layer, pressing lightly into cream cheese. Mix orange marmalade with water. Spread over top of pizza. Chill in refrigerator for 2 hours before serving.

Jill Fuller

CRÊPES IN FRUIT SAUCE

Yield: 24 servings

1/4 cup butter
2 sugar cubes
1 orange
1 cup orange juice
1 cup plain yogurt

Grated rind of 1 orange
1 to 2 ounces Cointreau
24 Orange Dessert Crêpes
  (page 219)

Melt butter in flambé pan. Rub sugar cubes over orange skin to pick up orange zest. Add to butter, stirring until melted. Add orange juice, yogurt and orange rind. Cook until heated through. Add Cointreau; flame. Fold Orange Dessert Crêpes. Soak in hot mixture.

Anne Hack

ORANGE DESSERT CRÊPES
Yield: 20 to 24 crêpes

3 eggs
2 egg yolks
1/4 teaspoon salt
1 cup flour
1 tablespoon sugar

1/2 cup orange juice
1/2 cup milk
2 tablespoons oil
1 teaspoon grated orange rind

Combine eggs, egg yolks, salt, flour, sugar, orange juice, milk, oil and orange rind in blender container. Process for 1 minute. Scrape down sides. Process for 15 seconds or until smooth. Chill in refrigerator for 1 hour. Stir before using. Ladle onto crêpe griddle or into traditional crêpe pan. Cook until light brown on both sides.

Christina Young

CHRISTMAS GRAPE DESSERT
Yield: 12 servings

2 pounds seedless purple
   grape halves, peeled
1   8-ounce can crushed
   pineapple, drained
1   8-ounce jar maraschino
   cherries, drained

2 cups chopped pecans
3 egg yolks
3 tablespoons sugar
3 tablespoons butter
Juice of 1 lemon
1 cup whipped cream

Combine grapes, pineapple, cherries and pecans in bowl; mix well. Chill, covered, in refrigerator. Combine egg yolks, sugar and butter in double boiler. Cook over hot water until thick, stirring frequently. Remove from heat. Add lemon juice; mix well. Chill, covered, in refrigerator until cold. Fold in whipped cream. Drain grape mixture. Fold whipped cream mixture into grape mixture. Serve in parfait glasses. Christmas was not Christmas at my grandmother's house without Grape Dessert. It was always served along with ambrosia, pecan pie, fruitcake and German Chocolate Cake.

Connie D. Herrman

Baked Grapefruit Alaska

Yield: 4 servings

2 medium grapefruit
1 pint vanilla ice cream,
   slightly softened
3/4 cup orange-flavored liqueur,
   chilled

4 egg whites
1/2 teaspoon cream of tartar
1/2 cup sugar

Cut grapefruit crosswise into halves. Trim a small slice from bottom of each half to stay level on plate. Cut around sections, removing grapefruit and cutting into small pieces. Chill, covered, in refrigerator. Remove membrane from grapefruit shells. Chill shells, covered, in refrigerator. Combine softened ice cream and orange liqueur in bowl; mix well. Freeze for 2 to 3 hours or until firm. Scoop ice cream into grapefruit shells. Freeze, covered, for up to 24 hours or until very firm. Beat egg whites in mixer bowl until frothy. Add cream of tartar and sugar gradually, beating until stiff peaks form. Place chilled grapefruit over ice cream in shells. Spread meringue over top quickly, sealing to edge. Place on baking sheet. Bake at 475 degrees until light brown. I make meringue before guests arrive. It holds until ready to cover shells and bake. This is a spectacular dessert, as good as it is pretty.

Helen W. Malcolm

Churned Peachy Ice Cream

Yield: 16 servings

5 eggs
2 cups sugar
1/2 gallon milk
2 13-ounce cans evaporated
   milk

2 14-ounce cans sweetened
   condensed milk
1/4 cup vanilla extract
1/4 cup peach schnapps
1 quart sliced peaches

Combine eggs, sugar and milk in saucepan. Cook over low heat until custard coats a spoon, stirring constantly. Remove from heat. Cool to room temperature. Add evaporated milk, sweetened condensed milk, vanilla and peach schnapps; mix well. Stir in peaches. Pour into ice cream freezer container. Freeze using manufacturer's directions.

Lee Ware

ICE CREAM LIQUEUR DESSERT

Yield: 4 servings

1 quart vanilla ice cream,
   softened

¹/₄ cup brandy
¹/₄ cup Crème de Cacao

Combine ice cream, brandy and Crème de Cacao in blender container. Process until well blended. Pour into brandy snifters.

Mary Ball

APRICOTS AND SHERBET

Yield: 4 servings

1 16-ounce can apricots,
   drained
2 tablespoons light rum

Juice of 1 lemon
1 quart pineapple sherbet

Purée apricots in blender. Add rum and lemon juice. Process until mixed. Spoon sherbet into glasses; top with apricot mixture. Garnish with whipped cream.

Lil Sneddon

HOMEMADE SHERBET

Yield: 4 servings

Juice of 3 or 4 lemons
1¹/₄ cups sugar
3 bananas, mashed

1 6-ounce can frozen orange
   juice concentrate
3 juice cans water

Combine lemon juice, sugar, bananas, orange juice concentrate and water in bowl; mix well. Pour into shallow freezer container. Freeze until firm, stirring several times as it freezes.

Ellen Garland

FROZEN PINEAPPLE DESSERT   *Yield: 6 to 8 servings*

2 cups buttermilk
1 cup sugar

1 6-ounce can crushed
   pineapple

Combine buttermilk and sugar in mixer bowl; beat until sugar is dissolved. Stir in crushed pineapple. Pour into freezer container. Freeze until firm. Let stand at room temperature for 15 minutes before serving. This dessert tastes like pineapple sherbet and is great to have on hand for unexpected guests.

Jo Anne Conner

FROZEN GRAND MARNIER MOUSSE   *Yield: 12 servings*

6 tablespoons Grand Marnier
   liqueur
2 tablespoons orange juice
1¼ cups almond macaroon
   cookie crumbs
5 egg yolks
½ cup sugar

1 tablespoon grated orange rind
5 egg whites
Pinch of salt
3 tablespoons sugar
2 cups whipping cream,
   whipped

Combine half the liqueur and orange juice in bowl; mix well. Stir in cookie crumbs. Beat egg yolks in mixer bowl. Add ½ cup sugar; beat for 5 minutes or until mixture is pale and thick. Mix orange rind with remaining 3 tablespoons liqueur. Add to egg yolk mixture; mix well. Beat egg whites with salt until soft peaks form. Add remaining 3 tablespoons sugar gradually, beating until stiff peaks form. Fold in egg yolk mixture and whipped cream. Alternate layers of whipped cream mixture and crumb mixture in twelve 6-ounce glass parfait or wine glasses, ending with crumbs. Freeze for 1 hour. Cover loosely, but airtight, with plastic wrap. Freeze for 3 hours to 4 weeks. Serve directly from freezer.

Anne Halloran

FROZEN LEMON MOUSSE
Yield: 8 servings

30 (about) lemon or vanilla
  wafers
4 egg yolks
1/2 cup fresh lemon juice
1/4 cup sugar
2 tablespoons grated lemon
  rind

4 egg whites
1/8 teaspoon cream of tartar
1/8 teaspoon salt
3/4 cup sugar
1 1/2 cups whipping cream

Line bottom and side of buttered 9-inch springform pan with wafers. Combine egg yolks, lemon juice, 1/4 cup sugar and lemon rind in bowl; mix well. Beat egg whites in mixer bowl until foamy. Add cream of tartar, salt and remaining 3/4 cup sugar gradually, beating until stiff peaks form. Fold egg whites and whipping cream into egg yolk mixture. Spoon into prepared pan. Freeze until firm. Cover with foil. Freeze for 8 hours to 2 weeks. Soften in refrigerator for 1 hour before serving. Garnish with fresh strawberries.

Helen W. Malcolm

ORANGE ICEBOX CAKE
Yield: 8 servings

1 tablespoon unflavored gelatin
1/4 cup cold water
1/2 cup boiling water
1 cup sugar
Pinch of salt
1 cup orange juice

2 tablespoons lemon juice
48 ladyfingers
3 egg whites, stiffly beaten
1 cup whipping cream,
  whipped

Soften gelatin in cold water in bowl for several minutes. Add boiling water, stirring until gelatin is dissolved. Add sugar, salt, orange juice and lemon juice; mix well. Chill in refrigerator until partially set. Beat with wire whisk. Fold egg whites into mixture. Line bottom and side of buttered springform pan with ladyfingers. Alternate layers of gelatin mixture and ladyfingers in springform pan. Chill until set. Unmold onto serving plate. Garnish with whipped cream just before serving. This is a terrific light summer dessert.

Abbie Kelly

PEACHY DESSERT

Yield: 8 servings

3 cups graham cracker crumbs
3/4 cup melted margarine
2 envelopes whipped topping
  mix
1 cup cold milk
3/4 cup sugar
8 ounces cream cheese, softened

1/4 teaspoon almond extract
6 to 8 peaches, peeled, sliced
1 teaspoon Fruit Fresh
2 peaches, chopped
1/2 to 3/4 cup sugar
2 tablespoons cornstarch

Combine graham cracker crumbs and margarine in bowl; mix well. Press half the mixture into trifle dish. Combine whipped topping mix and milk in mixer bowl; beat well. Add 3/4 cup sugar, cream cheese and flavoring; mix well. Spoon half the mixture over crumb layer. Combine sliced peaches and Fruit Fresh in bowl; mix well. Purée chopped peaches in blender. Combine puréed peaches, remaining sugar and cornstarch in saucepan; mix well. Cook for 2 to 3 minutes or until liquid is clear, stirring constantly. Stir in sliced peaches. Spoon over cream cheese layer. Add remaining cream cheese mixture; top with remaining crumbs. Chill in refrigerator.

Mrs. William Lewis

GREAT GRANDMA'S PUDDING

Yield: 6 servings

2 ounces unsweetened
  chocolate
2 cups milk
1/2 cup flour

1 cup sugar
Dash of salt
1/2 cup milk
2 egg yolks, beaten

Combine chocolate and 2 cups milk in saucepan. Cook over low heat until chocolate is melted, stirring frequently. Combine flour, sugar, salt and remaining 1/2 cup milk in bowl; mix well. Add to chocolate mixture. Bring to a boil, stirring constantly. Add a small amount of hot mixture to eggs; stir eggs into hot mixture. Simmer until thickened, stirring constantly. Pour into individual serving dishes. Chill in refrigerator.

Elizabeth Ware

BREAD PUDDING

Yield: 12 servings

3 cups scalded milk, cooled
1   24-inch loaf day-old French
    bread, cubed
1   29-ounce can sliced peaches,
    drained, mashed
1   12-ounce can peaches,
    drained, thinly sliced
¼ cup melted salted butter

4 large eggs
1 cup sugar
½ teaspoon vanilla extract
1 teaspoon cinnamon
¾ teaspoon nutmeg
¼ teaspoon allspice
½ teaspoon salt
Brandy Sauce

Combine milk, bread cubes, peaches and butter in bowl; mix well. Beat eggs in mixer bowl until frothy. Add sugar, vanilla, spices and salt; mix well. Pour into bread mixture; mix well. Spoon into buttered 4-quart casserole. Place in larger shallow pan half-filled with water. Bake at 350 degrees for 1 hour or until brown. Serve with Brandy Sauce.

Bill Dalton

BRANDY SAUCE

Yield: 12 servings

3 large eggs, beaten
¼ cup sugar
¼ teaspoon vanilla extract
¼ cup melted salted butter

¼ cup brandy or cognac
⅛ teaspoon ground cloves
½ cup milk

Combine eggs, sugar, vanilla and butter in small saucepan; beat well. Cook over low heat until mixture thickens, stirring constantly. Pour into blender container. Add brandy, cloves and milk. Process at high speed for 1 to 1½ minutes or until sauce has consistency of heavy cream.

Bill Dalton

STRAWBERRY DELIGHT

Yield: 8 to 10 servings

1 cup flour
1/2 cup chopped pecans
1/2 cup melted butter
1/4 cup packed brown sugar
1 10-ounce package frozen
    strawberries, thawed

1 cup sugar
2 teaspoons fresh lemon juice
2 egg whites
1 cup whipping cream,
    whipped
Sliced fresh strawberries

Combine flour, pecans, butter and brown sugar in bowl; mix well. Pour into 8-inch square baking pan. Bake at 350 degrees for 20 minutes, stirring occasionally. Cool to room temperature. Combine thawed strawberries, sugar, lemon juice and egg whites in mixer bowl. Beat at high speed for 10 to 12 minutes or until stiff peaks form. Fold in whipped cream. Press 2/3 of the baked crumb mixture into 9-inch springform pan. Spoon strawberry mixture into pan; sprinkle with remaining crumbs. Freeze, covered, until firm. Remove sides of springform pan. Garnish with sliced strawberries.

Mary Ann Hall

TRIFLE

Yield: 6 to 8 servings

1 4-ounce package vanilla
    pudding and pie filling mix
1/2 yellow cake or 1 pound cake
4 teaspoons sherry

1 16-ounce package frozen
    strawberries, thawed
12 ounces whipped topping
2 tablespoons slivered almonds

Prepare pudding mix using package directions. Cool to room temperature. Cut cake into bite-sized pieces. Alternate layers of half the cake, half the sherry, half the strawberries and half the pudding in 2-quart glass serving bowl; repeat layers. Top with whipped topping; sprinkle with almonds. Chill, covered, in refrigerator for 1 hour or longer.

Emily Smith

Cakes & Cheesecakes

APPLE DRABBLE CAKE

Yield: 16 servings

3 cups flour
1 teaspoon salt
1 teaspoon baking soda
1½ cups oil
2 cups sugar
2 teaspoons vanilla extract

3 eggs
3 cups chopped apples
1½ cups chopped pecans
1 cup packed brown sugar
½ cup margarine
¼ cup milk

Sift flour, salt and baking soda together. Combine oil, sugar and vanilla in bowl; mix well. Add flour mixture and eggs alternately to sugar mixture, mixing well after each addition; batter will be thick. Stir in apples and pecans. Spoon into greased and floured bundt pan. Bake at 350 degrees for 1 to 1¼ hours. Combine brown sugar, margarine and milk in small saucepan. Cook for 2½ minutes, stirring frequently. Pour over hot cake. Cool in pan.

Nancy Biel

GERMAN APPLE CAKE

Yield: 16 servings

½ cup margarine, softened
⅓ cup shortening
⅔ cup sugar
3 egg yolks
1 teaspoon lemon juice
1 tablespoon whiskey

3 egg whites
⅓ cup sugar
1½ cups flour
¼ teaspoon baking powder
4 Granny Smith apples, cut
    into slices

Cream margarine and shortening in mixer bowl until light and fluffy. Add ⅔ cup sugar, egg yolks, lemon juice and whiskey; beat well. Beat egg whites in small bowl until soft peaks form. Add remaining ⅓ cup sugar gradually, beating until very stiff peaks form. Stir into creamed mixture. Add flour and baking powder; mix well. Spoon into greased and floured springform pan. Arrange apples in upright rows over batter. Bake at 325 degrees for 1 hour. Cool in pan. Place on serving plate; remove side of pan.

Mrs. Joe Mosso

Forget-Me-Not Carrot Cake
Yield: 16 servings

2 cups flour
2 teaspoons baking soda
2 teaspoons baking powder
2 teaspoons cinnamon
1 teaspoon salt
1¼ cups oil
1 cup firmly packed dark
  brown sugar
1 cup sugar
4 eggs
2 teaspoons vanilla extract
3 cups grated peeled carrots
½ cup chopped pecans
⅓ cup chopped dates
4 ounces cream cheese,
  softened
¼ cup butter, softened
2 cups confectioners' sugar
1 tablespoon (or more) lemon
  juice

Sift flour, baking soda, baking powder, cinnamon and salt together. Combine oil, brown sugar and sugar in mixer bowl. Beat until light. Beat in eggs and vanilla. Add flour mixture; mix well. Fold in carrots, pecans and dates. Spoon into greased 10-inch tube pan. Bake at 350 degrees for 1 hour or until cake tests done. Cool in pan on wire rack. Invert onto wire rack to cool completely. Combine cream cheese, butter, confectioners' sugar and lemon juice in bowl. Beat until of spreading consistency. Spread over top and side of cooled cake.

Helen W. Malcolm

Three-Chocolate Cake
Yield: 8 servings

1 2-layer package devil's food
   cake mix
1 4-ounce package chocolate
   instant pudding mix
½ cup brewed coffee
4 eggs
1 cup sour cream
½ cup oil
½ cup dark rum
2 cups semisweet chocolate
  chips

Combine cake mix, pudding mix, coffee, eggs, sour cream, oil and rum in mixer bowl. Beat at low speed until blended. Beat at medium speed for 2 minutes, scraping bowl once. Fold in chocolate chips. Spoon into greased and floured bundt pan. Bake for 55 minutes to 1 hour or until cake tests done. Cool in pan for several minutes. Invert onto serving plate.

Nancy Pruitt

SAND TRAP CHOCOLATE CAKE
Yield: 15 servings

1/2 teaspoon baking soda
1/2 cup buttermilk
2 ounces unsweetened
 chocolate
1/2 cup oil
1/2 cup margarine
1 cup water
2 cups flour
2 cups sugar

2 eggs
1 teaspoon vanilla extract
1/8 teaspoon salt
6 tablespoons melted margarine
3 ounces unsweetened
 chocolate, melted
6 tablespoons milk
1 1-pound package
 confectioners' sugar

Dissolve baking soda in buttermilk. Combine 2 ounces chocolate, oil, 1/2 cup margarine and water in saucepan. Cook for 1 minute, stirring frequently. Combine with flour, sugar, eggs, vanilla, salt and buttermilk mixture in bowl; mix well. Spoon into greased and floured 9x13-inch cake pan. Bake at 400 degrees for 25 to 30 minutes or until cake tests done. Combine melted margarine, remaining 3 ounces chocolate and milk in bowl; mix well. Stir in enough confectioners' sugar to make of spreading consistency. Spread over hot cake.

Louise S. Hunter

SURPRISE CUPCAKES
Yield: 2 dozen

1 2-layer package chocolate
 cake mix
8 ounces cream cheese, softened
1 egg

1/2 cup sugar
Pinch of salt
1 cup semisweet chocolate
 chips

Prepare cake mix using package directions. Line cupcake pans with paper liners. Combine cream cheese, egg, sugar and salt in mixer bowl. Beat until fluffy. Stir in chocolate chips. Drop 1 heaping teaspoonful into each cupcake. Bake at 350 degrees for 20 to 25 minutes or until cupcakes test done.

Janie Wilkerson

JAM CAKE

Yield: 16 servings

1 teaspoon baking soda
1 cup buttermilk
3 cups flour
1 teaspoon allspice
1 teaspoon cloves

1 teaspoon cinnamon
3/4 cup margarine, softened
1 cup sugar
1 cup blackberry jam
3 eggs, beaten

Dissolve baking soda in buttermilk. Sift flour and spices together. Cream margarine and sugar in mixer bowl until light and fluffy. Stir in jam and eggs. Add buttermilk mixture and flour mixture alternately to creamed mixture, beating well after each addition. Spoon into greased and floured tube pan. Bake at 350 degrees for 45 minutes. Cool in pan for several minutes. Invert onto serving plate.

Kaye Black

LAZY DAISY CAKE

Yield: 12 servings

1 cup cake flour
1 teaspoon baking powder
1/2 teaspoon salt
1 cup sugar
1 teaspoon vanilla extract
2 eggs
1 cup milk, scalded, cooled

1 tablespoon butter, softened
1/4 cup milk
5 tablespoons melted butter
9 tablespoons packed brown
  sugar
1/2 cup coconut

Sift flour, baking powder and salt together. Cream sugar, vanilla and eggs in mixer bowl until light and fluffy. Stir in scalded milk and 1 tablespoon softened butter. Spoon into greased 9-inch square cake pan. Bake at 350 degrees for 25 minutes. Combine remaining 1/4 cup milk, melted butter, brown sugar and coconut in bowl; mix well. Spread over warm cake. Toast lightly under broiler. Cool in pan.

Jane Moore

AUNT LIVEY'S ORANGE CAKE   *Yield: 8 servings*

¹/₂ cup sugar	2 eggs
Juice of 1 orange	2 cups sifted flour
1 teaspoon baking soda	1 teaspoon vanilla extract
³/₄ cup buttermilk	Grated rind of 1 orange
¹/₂ cup butter, softened	1 cup chopped raisins
1 cup sugar	¹/₂ cup chopped pecans

Dissolve ¹/₂ cup sugar in orange juice; set aside. Dissolve baking soda in buttermilk. Cream butter and remaining 1 cup sugar in mixer bowl until light and fluffy. Add buttermilk mixture and flour alternately to creamed mixture, beating well after each addition. Stir in vanilla, orange rind, raisins and pecans. Spoon into greased and floured tube pan. Bake at 325 degrees for 1 hour. Cool in pan. Invert onto serving plate. Drizzle with orange juice mixture.

Irene Kreeger

POPPY SEED CAKE   *Yield: 16 servings*

1 2-layer package yellow cake mix	³/₄ cup oil
	1 cup sour cream
4 eggs	¹/₄ cup poppy seeds

Combine all ingredients in mixer bowl. Beat until well blended. Spoon into buttered and sugared bundt pan. Bake at 350 degrees for 50 minutes to 1 hour or until cake tests done. Cool in pan for several minutes. Invert onto serving plate.

Andy Sonfield

BOURBON POUND CAKE

Yield: 16 servings

1 cup butter, softened
3 cups sugar
6 eggs
3 cups flour

1 cup whipping cream
1/4 teaspoon salt
3 tablespoons bourbon

Cream butter and sugar in mixer bowl until light and fluffy. Beat in eggs 1 at a time at low speed. Add flour alternately with cream, mixing at low speed after each addition and mixing in salt with last addition of cream. Beat in bourbon at low speed. Spoon into greased and floured bundt pan. Bake at 325 degrees for 1 1/2 hours or until cake tests done. Cool in pan for 10 minutes. Remove to wire rack to cool completely.

Connie D. Herrman

DADDY'S POUND CAKE

Yield: 16 servings

3/4 cup shortening
2 cups sugar
3 eggs
1 1/2 teaspoons vanilla extract

3 cups cake flour, sifted
2 teaspoons baking powder
1 teaspoon salt
1 cup milk

Cream shortening and sugar in mixer bowl until light and fluffy. Beat in eggs 1 at a time. Add vanilla; mix well. Sift flour, baking powder and salt together. Add to creamed mixture alternately with milk, mixing well after each addition. Spoon into greased and floured tube pan or into two 5x9-inch loaf pans. Bake at 350 degrees for 1 hour. Cool in pan for 10 minutes. Remove to wire rack to cool. Use no substitutions in this recipe. It was given to my father years ago by the head chef of the Dining Car Department of the Atlantic Coastline Railroad.

Jane S. Shortt

CHOCOLATE-POTATO POUND CAKE *Yield: 16 servings*

1 cup shortening
2 cups sugar
4 eggs
4 ounces unsweetened
 chocolate, melted
1 cup mashed cooked potatoes
2 cups flour

1 tablespoon baking powder
1 teaspoon cinnamon
1 teaspoon nutmeg
1 teaspoon cloves
1 cup milk
1 cup chopped nuts

Cream shortening and sugar in mixer bowl until light. Beat in eggs 1 at a time. Blend in chocolate and warm potatoes gradually. Sift flour with next 4 ingredients. Add to batter alternately with milk, mixing well after each addition. Stir in nuts. Spoon into greased tube pan. Bake at 375 degrees for 1 hour. Cool in pan for 10 minutes. Remove to wire rack to cool completely.

Emily Bond

SOUR CREAM POUND CAKE *Yield: 16 servings*

1 cup butter, softened
3 cups sugar
6 eggs
1¹/₂ teaspoons vanilla extract

1¹/₂ teaspoons butternut extract
3 cups cake flour
¹/₈ teaspoon baking soda
1 cup sour cream

Cream butter and sugar in mixer bowl until light and fluffy. Add eggs 1 at a time, beating well after each addition. Stir in vanilla. Add mixture of flour and baking soda; beat well. Stir in sour cream. Spoon into well greased tube pan. Bake at 325 degrees for 1 to 1¹/₂ hours or until cake tests done. Cool in pan for several minutes. Invert onto serving plate. May add 1 cup chopped, lightly floured nuts to batter and may use any flavoring.

Janice Horton

WEDDING CAKE

Yield: 16 servings

3 cups flour
¹/₄ teaspoon baking soda
1 cup butter, softened
2¹/₂ cups sugar

6 eggs
1 cup sour cream
¹/₂ cup sugar
Vanilla extract to taste

Sift flour and baking soda together. Cream butter and 2¹/₂ cups sugar in mixer bowl until light and fluffy. Add eggs 1 at a time, beating well after each addition. Add sour cream and flour mixture alternately to creamed mixture, beating well after each addition. Stir in remaining ¹/₂ cup sugar and vanilla. Spoon into greased tube pan, Bake at 315 degrees for 1³/₄ to 2 hours or until cake tests done. Cool in pan. Invert onto serving plate. This was Rebecca's, Carolina's and Janie's wedding cake.

Jane S. Clark

SEVEN-UP CAKE

Yield: 10 servings

1 2-layer package lemon cake
   mix
1 4-ounce package lemon
   instant pudding mix
³/₄ cup oil
4 eggs
1¹/₄ cups 7-Up

1¹/₂ cups sugar
2 tablespoons (heaping) flour
1 small can crushed pineapple
¹/₂ cup butter
2 eggs
1 can flaked coconut

Combine cake mix, pudding mix, oil, 4 eggs and 7-Up in bowl; mix well. Spoon into 3 greased and floured 9-inch cake pans. Bake at 325 degrees for 25 to 30 minutes or until layers test done. Cool in pans for several minutes. Remove to wire racks to cool completely. Combine sugar, flour, pineapple with juice, butter and 2 eggs in saucepan; mix well. Cook until thickened, stirring frequently. Stir in coconut. Spread between layers and over top and side of cake.

Ina Carpenter

PRUNE CAKE
Yield: 20 servings

2 cups flour
1 teaspoon baking soda
1/2 teaspoon salt
1/2 teaspoon baking powder
1 1/2 teaspoons cinnamon
1 teaspoon nutmeg
1/2 cup butter, softened
1 1/2 cups sugar
3 eggs

1 cup cooked pitted prunes
1 cup buttermilk
1 teaspoon vanilla extract
3 ounces cream cheese, softened
6 prunes, cooked, chopped
1   1-pound package
    confectioners' sugar
Half and half

Sift flour, baking soda, salt, baking powder, cinnamon and nutmeg together. Cream butter and sugar in mixer bowl until light and fluffy. Add eggs. Beat for 2 minutes or until creamy. Stir in 1 cup prunes. Add flour mixture and mixture of buttermilk and vanilla alternately to creamed mixture, beating well after each addition. Spoon into greased and floured 9x12-inch cake pan. Bake at 350 degrees for 50 minutes. Cool in pan. Combine cream cheese and remaining 6 prunes in bowl; mix well. Stir in confectioners' sugar and enough half and half to make of spreading consistency. Spread over cooled cake.

Dorothy Asnip Hilton

SHERRY CAKE
Yield: 16 servings

1   2-layer package butter-
    recipe yellow cake mix
1   4-ounce package vanilla
    instant pudding mix
1/2 cup butter, softened

5 eggs
1 teaspoon vanilla extract
1/4 teaspoon almond extract
1 cup cream sherry

Combine first 6 ingredients in mixer bowl. Beat for 4 minutes. Stir in sherry. Spoon into greased and floured bundt pan. Bake at 350 degrees for 50 minutes. Cool in pan for 10 minutes. Invert onto serving plate. Drizzle with favorite glaze.

Marion Johnson

CHOCOLATE ZUCCHINI CAKE   *Yield: 16 servings*

1/2 cup butter, softened
1/2 cup oil
1 1/4 cups sugar
2 eggs
1/2 cup sour milk
1 teaspoon vanilla extract
2 1/2 cups flour
6 tablespoons baking cocoa

1/2 teaspoon baking powder
1 teaspoon baking soda
1/2 teaspoon cinnamon
1/2 teaspoon cloves
2 cups grated zucchini
1/2 cup chopped walnuts
1/2 cup chocolate chips

Beat butter, oil and sugar in mixer bowl until light and fluffy. Blend in eggs, sour milk and vanilla. Mix flour, cocoa, baking powder, baking soda, cinnamon and cloves in bowl. Add to batter; mix well. Stir in zucchini, walnuts and chocolate chips. Grease bundt pan; dust with additional cocoa. Spoon batter into prepared pan. Bake at 350 degrees for 45 to 50 minutes or until cake tests done. Cool in pan for 10 minutes. Remove to wire rack to cool.

Sue Burden

BLUEBERRY CHEESECAKE   *Yield: 8 to 10 servings*

1 package pecan shortbread
  cookies, crushed
1/2 cup melted butter or
  margarine
8 ounces cream cheese,
  softened

2/3 cup sugar
3 eggs
1 teaspoon vanilla extract
2 cups fresh blueberries
Cinnamon to taste

Mix cookie crumbs with butter in bowl. Press into 8 or 9-inch springform pan. Beat cream cheese and sugar in mixer bowl until light. Beat in eggs 1 at a time. Mix in vanilla. Spoon into prepared springform pan. Spoon blueberries evenly over top; berries may sink into batter. Sprinkle with cinnamon. Bake at 350 degrees for 50 minutes or until set. Turn off oven; open oven door. Let cheesecake stand for 1 hour. Chill in refrigerator overnight. Place on serving plate; remove side of pan. May substitute fresh peaches for blueberries.

Sue West

HEAVENLY CHEESECAKE   *Yield: 12 servings*

1 cup graham cracker crumbs
1 teaspoon cinnamon
1/4 cup melted butter
4 eggs
1 1/2 cups sugar

24 ounces cream cheese, softened
1 teaspoon vanilla extract
16 ounces sour cream
1/2 cup sugar
1 teaspoon vanilla extract

Mix cracker crumbs, cinnamon and butter in bowl. Press over bottom of 10-inch springform pan. Combine eggs, 1 1/2 cups sugar, cream cheese and 1 teaspoon vanilla in mixer bowl. Beat for 20 minutes. Spoon into prepared pan. Bake at 350 degrees for 30 to 35 minutes or until cheesecake tests done. Cool in pan on wire rack. Blend sour cream, 1/2 cup sugar and 1 teaspoon vanilla in bowl. Spread over cheesecake. Bake for 10 minutes longer. Cool in pan on wire rack. Chill in refrigerator. Place on serving plate; remove side of pan. Top with favorite fruit topping if desired.

Vicki Rippeto

CAROL'S L.A. CHEESECAKE   *Yield: 12 servings*

1 recipe graham cracker crust
16 ounces cream cheese,
  softened
2 cups sour cream

2 eggs
1 cup sugar or honey
1 tablespoon flour
2 teaspoons lemon extract

Press graham cracker crumb mixture into lightly buttered spring-form pan. Beat cream cheese and sour cream in mixer bowl until smooth. Beat in eggs. Add sugar and flour gradually, mixing well after each addition. Mix in lemon extract. Spoon into prepared pan. Bake at 375 degrees for 25 minutes. Cool on wire rack for 2 hours. Chill in refrigerator. Place on serving plate; remove side of pan. Serve with warm strawberry or blueberry jam. For chocolate marble cheesecake, pour batter into pan and drizzle with 2 envelopes premelted milk chocolate; swirl gently with knife to marbleize.

Elaine Boone

KAHLUA CHEESECAKE

Yield: 10 to 12 servings

1¹/4 cups graham cracker
  crumbs
¹/4 cup sugar
¹/4 cup baking cocoa
¹/3 cup melted butter or
  margarine
16 ounces cream cheese,
  softened
³/4 cup sugar
¹/2 cup baking cocoa

2 eggs
¹/4 cup strong coffee
¹/4 cup Kahlua or other
  coffee-flavored liqueur
1 teaspoon vanilla extract
1 cup sour cream
2 tablespoons sugar
1 teaspoon vanilla extract
6 to 8 chocolate curls

Combine cracker crumbs, ¹/4 cup sugar, ¹/4 cup cocoa and melted butter in bowl; mix well. Press over bottom of 9-inch springform pan. Bake at 325 degrees for 5 minutes. Cool to room temperature. Beat cream cheese in mixer bowl until light and fluffy. Add ³/4 cup sugar and ¹/2 cup cocoa gradually, beating constantly. Beat in eggs 1 at a time. Stir in coffee, liqueur and 1 teaspoon vanilla. Spoon into prepared pan. Bake at 375 degrees for 25 minutes or until filling is set but still soft. Increase oven temperature to 475 degrees. Spread hot cheesecake with mixture of sour cream, 2 tablespoons sugar and 1 teaspoon vanilla. Bake for 5 to 7 minutes or until topping is set. Cool in pan on wire rack. Chill for 8 hours or longer. Place on serving plate; remove side of pan. Place 3 chocolate curls in center of cheesecake. Crush remaining chocolate curls and sprinkle over cheesecake.

Terry Hughes

ITALIAN CHEESECAKE

Yield: 10 to 12 servings

2 pounds ricotta cheese
5 eggs
1 cup (or less) sugar
2 cups sour cream

¹/4 cup cornstarch
1 teaspoon vanilla extract
3 tablespoons butter, softened

Combine all ingredients in bowl; mix well. Grease springform pan with additional butter. Spoon filling into prepared pan. Bake at 325 degrees for 1¹/2 hours. Cool in pan on wire rack. Chill in refrigerator. Place on serving plate; remove side of pan.

Franca Lotz

WHITE CHOCOLATE CHEESECAKE *Yield: 10 to 12 servings*

32 ounces cream cheese,
  softened
4 eggs
1 egg yolk
1/2 cup unsalted butter, softened
1 pound high-quality white
  chocolate, melted

3 tablespoons Frangelico
1 tablespoon vanilla extract
1 cup Hazelnut Praline
  (page 241)
Nutmeg to taste
Chocolate Hazelnut Crust

Beat cream cheese in large mixer bowl until light. Beat in eggs and egg yolk 1 at a time. Add 1/2 cup butter and white chocolate; mix well. Mix in Frangelico and vanilla. Stir in Hazelnut Praline and nutmeg. Spoon carefully into Chocolate Hazelnut Crust. Bake at 300 degrees for 1 1/4 hours. Sprinkle with reserved Chocolate Hazelnut Crust mixture. Bake for 15 minutes longer. Cool in pan on wire rack. Chill, covered, in refrigerator. Place on serving plate; remove side of pan. May substitute crushed peanut brittle for Hazelnut Praline.

Karen Laughlin

CHOCOLATE HAZELNUT CRUST *Yield: 10 to 12 servings*

1 8-ounce package chocolate
  wafers
1/4 cup toasted hazelnuts,
  skinned

2 tablespoons sugar
1 teaspoon cinnamon
5 tablespoons melted unsalted
  butter

Combine chocolate wafers, hazelnuts, sugar and cinnamon in food processor container. Process until finely crushed. Combine with 5 tablespoons melted butter in bowl; mix well. Reserve 3 tablespoons crumb mixture for topping. Press remaining crumbs over bottom and side of lightly buttered 9 1/2 or 10-inch springform pan. Chill in refrigerator.

Karen Laughlin

HAZELNUT PRALINE

Yield: 2 cups

1¹/₂ cups hazelnuts
¹/₂ cup sugar
2 tablespoons water

1 teaspoon vanilla extract
1 tablespoon unsalted butter

Spread hazelnuts on baking sheet. Toast at 250 degrees for 7 to 10 minutes or until light brown. Rub off skins with towel. Bring sugar and water to a boil in medium heavy saucepan over medium heat. Boil rapidly for 2 to 3 minutes, stirring occasionally with wooden spoon; remove from heat. Stir in hazelnuts until sugar begins to crystallize. Heat until sugar melts and nuts are caramelized and golden, stirring constantly. Stir in vanilla and butter. Spread on oiled foil; let stand until cool. Break into pieces. Process in food processor until finely ground. Store in airtight container.

Karen Laughlin

MACADAMIA CHEESECAKE

Yield: 8 to 10 servings

1 cup graham cracker crumbs
6 tablespoons melted butter
¹/₄ cup sugar
¹/₂ cup coarsely chopped
  macadamia nuts
24 ounces cream cheese,
  softened
1 cup packed light brown sugar

2 tablespoons flour
3 eggs
1 teaspoon vanilla extract
3 tablespoons butter
2 tablespoons light brown sugar
1 teaspoon Amaretto or
  Frangelico
Macadamia nut halves

Mix cracker crumbs, 6 tablespoons butter and sugar with fork in bowl. Press into 8-inch springform pan. Sprinkle with chopped macadamia nuts. Beat cream cheese, 1 cup brown sugar and flour in mixer bowl until light. Beat in eggs 1 at a time. Mix in vanilla. Spoon into prepared pan. Bake at 350 degrees for 50 minutes. Turn off oven. Let cheesecake stand in closed oven for 1 hour. Melt 3 tablespoons butter with 2 tablespoons brown sugar in saucepan; mix well. Stir in Amaretto. Arrange macadamia halves in circle on cheesecake. Drizzle with Amaretto mixture. Chill until serving time. Place on serving plate; remove side of pan. May use pecans for macadamia nuts to make praline cheesecake.

Sue West

Mrs. Punt's Pumpkin Cheesecake   *Yield: 12 servings*

32 ounces cream cheese,
  softened
1¼ cups sugar
3 tablespoons Cognac or
  brandy
1 teaspoon ginger
1 teaspoon cinnamon
½ teaspoon nutmeg
4 eggs, at room temperature

¼ cup heavy cream
1 cup cooked or canned
  pumpkin
Spicy Graham Cracker Crust
2 cups sour cream
¼ cup sugar
1 tablespoon maple syrup
1 tablespoon Cognac or brandy
¼ cup toasted almonds

Beat cream cheese in mixer bowl until light. Add 1¼ cups sugar gradually, beating constantly. Add 3 tablespoons Cognac, 1 teaspoon ginger, cinnamon and nutmeg; mix well. Beat in eggs 1 at a time. Mix in cream and pumpkin. Spoon into Spicy Graham Cracker Crust. Bake at 325 degrees for 45 minutes. Turn off oven. Let cheesecake stand in closed oven for 1 hour. Increase oven temperature to 425 degrees. Blend sour cream, ¼ cup sugar, maple syrup and 1 tablespoon Cognac in bowl. Spread over cheesecake. Bake for 10 minutes. Cool in pan on wire rack for 1 hour. Arrange toasted almonds in circle on cheesecake. Chill for 3 hours. Place on serving plate; remove side of pan. We enjoy our Thanksgiving dinner with a group of friends who also take the last swim of the year in the ocean on that day. We can then enjoy our cheesecake without guilt.

Mrs. Marc A. Puntereri

Spicy Graham Cracker Crust   *Yield: 12 servings*

1½ cups graham cracker
  crumbs
⅓ cup ground almonds

⅓ cup melted butter
½ teaspoon cinnamon
½ teaspoon ginger

Mix cracker crumbs, ground almonds, butter, cinnamon and ½ teaspoon ginger in bowl. Press over bottom of 10-inch springform pan. Bake at 425 degrees for 10 minutes. Cool on wire rack.

Mrs. Marc A. Puntereri

Cookies
& Confections

ALMOND MACAROONS
Yield: 3 dozen

1   8-ounce can almond paste
1 cup sugar

2 egg whites

Crumble almond paste in mixer bowl. Blend in ½ cup sugar. Add remaining sugar and egg whites, beating until smooth and stiff. Grease cookie sheet generously. Press dough through pastry tube with large star-shaped tip using slight upward swirling motion. Bake at 350 degrees for 15 to 18 minutes. Remove to wire rack immediately. Cool completely. Dough may be dropped by teaspoonfuls onto well-greased cookie sheet if desired.

Betsy Smith

CARAMEL BROWNIES
Yield: 3 dozen

1 package German chocolate
   cake mix
¾ cup margarine, softened

1 cup chopped pecans
1   5-ounce can evaporated milk
1 package caramels

Combine cake mix, margarine, pecans and ½ of the evaporated milk in mixer bowl; mix well. Pat ½ of the mixture into 9x13-inch baking pan. Bake at 350 degrees for 6 to 8 minutes or until brown. Combine remaining evaporated milk and caramels in saucepan. Cook over low heat until melted, stirring frequently. Pour over baked layer. Sprinkle remaining dry mixture over caramel layer. Bake for 15 to 18 minutes longer or until brownies test done. Cut into squares when cool.

Abby Builder

Strawberry Fans—Select large firm strawberries with caps. Cut several parallel slices from the tip of each berry to just below the cap with sharp knife. Spread slices gently to form fan.

CINNAMON BROWNIES

Yield: 2 dozen

1/2 cup butter
2 ounces unsweetened
  chocolate
1 cup sugar
2 eggs
3/4 cup flour

1/4 teaspoon salt
3/4 teaspoon cinnamon
1/2 teaspoon baking powder
1/2 cup chopped pecans
  (optional)
1/2 teaspoon vanilla extract

Melt butter and chocolate in saucepan over low heat. Stir in sugar. Let stand until cool. Add eggs 1 at a time to cooled chocolate mixture, beating well after each addition. Combine flour, salt, cinnamon, baking powder and pecans in bowl. Stir dry ingredients and vanilla into beaten mixture until moist. Spoon into greased 12-inch square baking pan. Bake at 325 degrees for 25 to 30 minutes or until brownies test done. Cut into squares when cool.

Paige Pruitt

DOUBLE SHOT BROWNIES

Yield: 1 1/3 dozen

1/3 cup butter
3/4 cup sugar
2 tablespoons water
1 cup chocolate chips
1 teaspoon vanilla extract
2 eggs

3/4 cup flour
1/4 teaspoon baking soda
1/4 teaspoon salt
1 cup chocolate chips
1/2 cup chopped pecans
  (optional)

Combine butter, sugar and water in saucepan over medium heat. Bring to boiling point. Remove from heat. Add 1 cup chocolate chips and vanilla, stirring until smooth. Transfer mixture to large bowl. Add eggs 1 at a time, mixing well after each addition. Stir in mixture of flour, baking soda and salt gradually. Let stand for 30 minutes. Stir in remaining 1 cup chocolate chips and pecans. Spoon into greased 9-inch square baking pan. Bake at 325 degrees for 30 to 35 minutes or until brownies test done. Cool completely. Cut into squares.

Jo Hagan Proffitt

VIENNESE BROWNIES

Yield: 1¹/₃ dozen

8 ounces cream cheese, softened
1 egg
¹/₃ cup sugar
2 eggs
1 cup sugar
2 ounces melted unsweetened
   chocolate

¹/₂ cup melted butter
³/₄ cup flour
¹/₂ teaspoon baking powder
¹/₂ teaspoon salt
Chopped walnuts

Blend cream cheese, 1 egg and ¹/₃ cup sugar in small bowl. Set aside. Beat 2 eggs in large bowl. Add remaining 1 cup sugar, chocolate and butter; mix well. Sift in flour, baking powder and salt; stir until blended. Spoon half the batter into greased 8-inch square baking pan. Spread with cream cheese mixture. Top with remaining batter; sprinkle with walnuts. Bake at 350 degrees for 50 minutes.

Katie Robertson

ZEBRA BROWNIES

Yield: 2 dozen

6 ounces cream cheese, softened
¹/₄ cup water
¹/₂ teaspoon vanilla extract
1 egg
1   23-ounce package brownie
   mix

¹/₃ cup very hot water
¹/₃ cup oil
1 egg
³/₄ cup chopped pecans

Beat cream cheese, ¹/₄ cup water, vanilla and 1 egg in small mixer bowl until smooth. Set aside. Combine brownie mix, hot water, oil and remaining egg in large bowl; mix with spoon. Spread half the brownie mixture in greased 9x13-inch baking pan. Cover with cream cheese mixture; sprinkle with pecans. Spoon remaining batter over top. Swirl through all layers with knife to create marbled appearance. Bake at 350 degrees for 35 minutes. Do not overbake. Cut into squares when cool. Store in airtight container in refrigerator.

Mae Ola Sanders

KAHLUA CHOCOLATE SQUARES

Yield: 2 dozen

1½ cups sifted flour
¾ teaspoon baking powder
½ teaspoon salt
½ cup butter, softened
¾ cup packed brown sugar
1 egg
¼ cup coffee liqueur
1 cup semisweet chocolate
  chips

⅓ cup chopped walnuts or
  pecans
1 tablespoon coffee liqueur
2 tablespoons butter
1 tablespoon coffee liqueur
2 teaspoons milk
1⅓ cups sifted confectioners'
  sugar
24 walnut or pecan halves

Resift flour with baking powder and salt. Cream softened butter, brown sugar and egg in mixer bowl until light and fluffy. Add ¼ cup liqueur and flour mixture alternately, stirring to blend. Fold in chocolate chips and chopped walnuts. Spoon into greased 7x11-inch baking pan, spreading evenly. Bake at 350 degrees for 30 minutes or until top springs back when touched lightly in center. Cool in pan for 15 minutes. Brush top with 1 tablespoon liqueur. Place 2 tablespoons butter in saucepan over low heat. Cook until butter is lightly browned. Remove from heat. Add remaining 1 tablespoon liqueur, milk and confectioners' sugar; beat until smooth. Spread over cooled cake. Let stand until icing is set. Cut into bars. Top each bar with walnut half.

Terry Hughes

FUDGE SQUARES

Yield: 3 dozen

6 ounces unsweetened
  chocolate
¾ cup margarine
1½ cups flour

6 eggs, well beaten
3 cups sugar
1 teaspoon vanilla extract

Melt chocolate and margarine in double boiler. Add flour, beaten eggs, sugar and vanilla, mixing well after each addition. Spoon into 8x12-inch baking pan coated with nonstick cooking spray. Bake at 325 degrees for 20 minutes. Cool completely. Cut into squares. Chopped pecans may be added to batter or pecan halves may be added to top before baking.

Betty Black

BUTTERSCOTCH COOKIES

Yield: 4 dozen

2 cups packed brown sugar
1 cup margarine, softened
2 eggs, well beaten
3¹/₂ cups flour
1 teaspoon baking powder

¹/₄ teaspoon salt
1 cup chopped almonds
Beaten egg whites
Almond halves

Combine brown sugar, margarine, eggs, flour, baking powder, salt and pecans in mixer bowl, mixing well after each addition. Shape into roll. Chill overnight. Cut into thick slices. Brush each slice with beaten egg whites; top with almond half. Place on lightly greased cookie sheet. Bake at 350 degrees for 12 to 15 minutes or until firm. Cool on wire rack.

Clare Fisher

CHINESE COOKIES

Yield: 2 dozen

1 cup Chinese noodles
1 cup margarine, softened
¹/₂ cup sugar

2 teaspoons vanilla extract
2 cups flour
¹/₂ teaspoon salt

Pulverize Chinese noodles in blender. Cream margarine, sugar, vanilla, flour and salt in bowl until smooth. Stir in Chinese noodles. Chill for 1 hour. Shape into curved finger-like rolls. Place on nonstick cookie sheet. Bake at 350 degrees for 15 minutes. Sprinkle warm cookies with confectioners' sugar.

Lorraine B. Sheldon

HERITAGE CHOCOLATE CHIP COOKIES   *Yield: 2 dozen*

1 cup plus 2 tablespoons flour
1 tablespoon wheat germ
1/2 teaspoon baking soda
1/2 teaspoon salt
1/2 cup butter, softened
6 tablespoons packed brown
  sugar

6 tablespoons sugar
1/2 teaspoon vanilla extract
1 egg
1 cup semisweet chocolate
  chips
1/2 cup chopped pecans
  (optional)

Combine flour, wheat germ, baking soda and salt in small bowl. Set aside. Beat butter, brown sugar, sugar and vanilla in large mixer bowl until creamy. Beat in egg. Add flour mixture gradually; mix well. Stir in chocolate chips and pecans. Drop by rounded tablespoonfuls onto ungreased cookie sheet. Bake at 375 degrees for 10 minutes. Cool on wire rack.

Andy Rose

COCOA-BANANA MUFFINETTES   *Yield: 1 dozen*

1 1/4 cups flour
1 cup oats
1/2 cup packed brown sugar
1/3 cup baking cocoa
1 tablespoon baking powder
1/4 teaspoon baking soda

2 small bananas, mashed
1/2 cup skim milk
1/3 cup melted margarine
2 egg whites, slightly beaten
1 teaspoon vanilla extract

Combine flour, oats, brown sugar, cocoa, baking powder and baking soda in large bowl; mix well. Stir in bananas, milk, margarine, egg whites and vanilla. Spoon into miniature muffin cups coated with nonstick cooking spray. Bake at 400 degrees for 10 to 12 minutes or until muffins test done. Cool in pan for 10 minutes. Remove to wire rack to cool completely.

Nancy Pruitt

COCONUT COOKIES

Yield: 3 dozen

3 eggs, well beaten
2 cups sugar
1 cup butter, softened
1 teaspoon baking soda
1/2 cup buttermilk

1 teaspoon cream of tartar
2 1/2 cups flour
1 teaspoon salt
2 cups coconut
1 teaspoon vanilla extract

Blend beaten eggs, sugar and butter in bowl. Stir in mixture of baking soda and buttermilk. Add mixture of cream of tartar, flour and salt; mix well. Stir in coconut and vanilla. Drop by tablespoonfuls onto greased cookie sheet. Bake at 350 degrees for 5 minutes or until lightly browned around edge. Cool on wire rack.

Lucille H. Davis

DATE WHEELS

Yield: 4 dozen

1 package dates, chopped
1 cup sugar
1 cup cold water
1 cup chopped pecans
1 cup shortening

2 cups packed brown sugar
3 eggs, well beaten
4 cups flour
1/2 teaspoon baking soda
1/2 teaspoon salt

Combine dates, sugar and water in saucepan. Cook over medium heat until thickened. Add pecans; mix well. Let stand until cool. Cream shortening and brown sugar in mixer bowl until light and fluffy. Beat in eggs. Sift in mixture of flour, baking soda and salt; stir until moistened. Divide dough into 4 rolls. Chill completely. Roll on lightly floured surface. Spread with date mixture. Roll as for jelly roll. Chill, tightly wrapped in waxed paper, overnight. Cut into thin slices. Place on nonstick cookie sheet. Bake at 400 degrees for 8 minutes or until lightly browned. Cool on wire rack.

Jo Gross

EVERYTHING COOKIES

Yield: 4 dozen

1 cup butter, softened
1 cup sugar
1 cup packed brown sugar
2 eggs
1 teaspoon baking soda
2 cups flour

³/₄ teaspoon salt
2 cups oats
2 cups wheat cereal
1 cup chocolate chips
1 cup chopped pecans
1 small package dates, chopped

Cream butter, sugar and brown sugar in mixer bowl until light and fluffy. Beat in eggs. Add baking soda, flour, salt, oats and cereal; stir until blended. Stir in chocolate chips, pecans and dates. Drop by teaspoonfuls onto nonstick cookie sheet. Bake at 350 degrees for 10 minutes. Cool on wire rack.

Barbara Leonard

GINGERSNAPS

Yield: 4 dozen

1 cup shortening
2 cups packed brown sugar
1 egg, well beaten
1 cup molasses
4 cups sifted flour

2 teaspoons baking soda
2 teaspoons ground ginger
¹/₂ teaspoon salt
1 teaspoon vanilla extract
1 teaspoon lemon extract

Cream shortening and brown sugar at medium speed in mixer bowl until light and fluffy. Blend in egg and molasses. Sift flour, baking soda, ginger and salt together. Add to creamed mixture gradually, beating well after each addition. Stir in vanilla and lemon flavorings. Chill dough for 4 hours. Dough will be soft. Shape into 1¹/₂-inch balls using lightly floured hands. Place on greased cookie sheet. Bake at 350 degrees for 12 to 15 minutes or until brown. Sprinkle with additional sugar. Cool on wire rack.

Geneva Patterson

HOME-STYLE GRAHAM CRACKERS
Yield: 4 dozen

4 cups whole wheat flour
1 cup butter
1 cup sugar
1 teaspoon baking soda

1 teaspoon cream of tartar
1 egg, lightly beaten
1/4 to 1/2 cup hot water
1 teaspoon vanilla extract

Place flour in bowl. Cut in butter until crumbly. Add sugar, baking soda, cream of tartar, egg and enough water to make soft dough. Roll 1/8 to 1/4 inch thick on lightly floured surface. Cut into 3-inch squares. Place on ungreased baking sheet. Bake at 350 degrees for 15 to 20 minutes or until lightly browned. Cool on wire rack.

Geneva Patterson

GRANDMA'S COOKIES
Yield: 3 dozen

2 cups margarine or butter,
   softened
1 1/2 cups sugar
3 cups flour

1/2 cup coconut
1/2 cup chopped pecans
1/4 teaspoon baking powder

Cream margarine and sugar in bowl until light and fluffy. Add flour, coconut, pecans and baking powder; mix well. Drop by teaspoonfuls onto greased cookie sheet. Bake at 350 degrees for 10 to 13 minutes. Cookies will be very light in color. Cool on cookie sheet for 5 minutes. Remove to wire rack to cool completely.

Barbara DeLoach

CRISPIE BARS

Yield: 2 dozen

3 tablespoons butter
³/₄ cup light corn syrup
³/₄ cup packed brown sugar
³/₄ cup peanut butter

3 cups crisp rice cereal
1¹/₂ cups peanuts
1 cup chocolate chips, melted

Combine butter, corn syrup, brown sugar and peanut butter in saucepan over medium heat. Bring to a boil. Remove from heat. Add cereal and peanuts; mix well. Spoon into buttered 9x12-inch pan. Chill until set. Spread melted chocolate chips over chilled cookies. Cut into squares.

Caneel Cotton

MOLASSES COOKIES

Yield: 2 dozen

³/₄ cup shortening
¹/₄ cup molasses
1 cup sugar
1 egg
2 cups flour

2 teaspoons baking soda
1 teaspoon ground ginger
1 teaspoon ground cloves
1 teaspoon cinnamon
Dash of salt

Cream shortening, molasses and sugar in bowl until light and fluffy. Add egg; mix well. Sift flour, baking soda, ginger, cloves, cinnamon and salt together. Add to creamed mixture; mix well. Shape dough into balls. Coat top of each ball with additional sugar. Place sugar side up on cookie sheet; flatten with fork. Bake at 350 degrees for 6 to 8 minutes or until brown. Cool on wire rack.

Sally Reeds

EASY PEANUT BUTTER COOKIES

Yield: 1 dozen

1 cup peanut butter	1 egg
1 cup sugar	1 teaspoon vanilla extract

Blend peanut butter and sugar in bowl. Stir in egg and vanilla. Shape into 1-inch balls. Place on ungreased cookie sheet. Flatten slightly with fork. Bake at 350 degrees for 15 minutes. Cool on wire rack.

Laura Fifer

PEANUT BUTTER-CHIP COOKIES

Yield: 2 dozen

3/4 cup shortening	1 teaspoon vanilla extract
3/4 cup sugar	1 3/4 cups flour
3/4 cup packed brown sugar	1/2 teaspoon baking soda
1 egg	1/2 teaspoon salt
1 cup peanut butter	1/2 package chocolate chips

Cream shortening, sugar and brown sugar in bowl until light and fluffy. Add egg and peanut butter, stirring well after each addition. Add vanilla, flour, baking soda and salt; mix well. Stir in chocolate chips. Shape by teaspoonfuls into balls. Place on ungreased cookie sheet. Bake at 375 degrees for 10 minutes. Cool on wire rack.

Coach Neil Gruber

Cookie Trimmers—Coat rolls of chilled cookie dough with minced candied fruit, chopped nuts or candy sprinkles before slicing and baking.

RUSSIAN ROCKS

Yield: 9 dozen

2 cups margarine or butter,
  softened
1 1-pound package brown
  sugar
6 eggs
2 teaspoons vanilla extract

6 cups (or more) flour
2 teaspoons baking soda
2 cups chocolate chips
1¹/₂ cups chopped walnuts
1 package raisins

Cream margarine and brown sugar in bowl until light and fluffy. Add eggs and vanilla; mix well. Add mixture of flour and baking soda gradually, mixing well after each addition. Stir in chocolate chips, walnuts and raisins. Drop by teaspoonfuls onto ungreased cookie sheet. Bake at 350 degrees for 15 minutes. Cool on wire rack.

Olga Dunnigan

SAND TARTS

Yield: 4 dozen

1 cup butter, softened
2 cups flour
6 tablespoons confectioners'
  sugar

2 teaspoons vanilla extract
¹/₂ cup chopped pecans
Additional sifted
  confectioners' sugar

Cream butter in bowl. Add flour gradually, mixing until smooth. Add 6 tablespoons confectioners' sugar and vanilla; mix well. Stir in pecans. Shape by teaspoonfuls into crescents on ungreased cookie sheet. Bake at 400 degrees for 8 to 10 minutes or until golden brown. Roll warm cookies in confectioners' sugar. Cool on wire rack. Roll cooled cookies in confectioners' sugar. Store in tightly covered container.

Vicki Rippeto

SNICKERDOODLES

Yield: 5 dozen

2³/₄ cups sifted flour
2 teaspoons cream of tartar
1 teaspoon baking soda
¹/₂ teaspoon salt
1 cup shortening

1¹/₂ cups sugar
2 eggs
2 tablespoons sugar
2 teaspoons cinnamon

Sift flour, cream of tartar, baking soda and salt together. Cream shortening and 1¹/₂ cups sugar in bowl until light and fluffy. Add eggs; mix well. Add dry ingredients; mix well. Chill dough. Shape by tablespoonfuls into balls. Roll in mixture of remaining 2 tablespoons sugar and cinnamon. Place 2 inches apart on ungreased cookie sheet. Bake at 400 degrees for 8 to 10 minutes or until lightly browned. Do not overbake. Cool on wire rack.

Laurel Smith

TARA'S COOKIES

Yield: 10 dozen

4 cups oats
1¹/₂ cups butter, softened
2 cups sugar
2 cups packed brown sugar
4 eggs
2 teaspoons vanilla extract
4 cups flour

1 teaspoon salt
2 teaspoons baking powder
2 teaspoons baking soda
4 cups chocolate chips
1   8-ounce chocolate candy
  bar, grated
3 cups chopped pecans

Pulverize oats in blender. Cream butter, sugar and brown sugar in mixer bowl until light and fluffy. Stir in eggs and vanilla. Mix ground oats, flour, salt, baking powder and baking soda in large bowl. Add to creamed mixture; mix well. Stir in chocolate chips, grated chocolate and pecans. Roll into 2-inch balls. Place on nonstick cookie sheet 2 inches apart. Bake at 375 degrees for 6 to 10 minutes or until light golden.

Tara's Beauty Salon

ICED ALMONDS
Yield: 4 servings

1 cup whole blanched almonds
2 tablespoons butter
1/2 cup sugar

1/2 teaspoon vanilla extract
3/4 teaspoon salt

Combine almonds, butter and sugar in heavy skillet over medium heat. Cook about 15 minutes or until almonds are toasted and sugar is golden brown, stirring constantly. Stir in vanilla. Spread mixture on foil; sprinkle with salt. Let stand until cool. Break into clusters.

Dale Kelly

CARAMEL CANDY
Yield: 50 servings

1 1-pound package light
   brown sugar
1 cup light corn syrup
1 cup butter

1 14-ounce can sweetened
   condensed milk
1 cup chopped pecans

Combine brown sugar, corn syrup, butter and condensed milk in saucepan over medium heat. Bring to a boil, stirring constantly. Cook to soft-ball stage. Stir in pecans. Pour into buttered 9x13-inch pan. Chill until firm. Cut into squares; wrap each square.

Ellen Taylor

MAN-MADE STRAWBERRIES
Yield: 20 servings

1/2 can sweetened condensed milk
1 3-ounce package strawberry
   gelatin

2 cups coconut
1 3-ounce package strawberry
   gelatin

Mix first 3 ingredients in bowl. Shape into strawberries. Roll in remaining gelatin. Garnish with mint leaves. Chill completely.

Leigh Glei

CHOCOLATE-COVERED FRUITCAKE   *Yield: 12 servings*

1 fruitcake	2 squares paraffin
¹/₂ cup favorite liqueur	¹/₄ cup favorite liqueur
2 cups chocolate chips	

Soak fruitcake in ¹/₂ cup liqueur. Cut into ¹/₂-inch squares. Melt chocolate chips and paraffin in double boiler. Stir in remaining ¹/₄ cup liqueur. Dip fruitcake squares 1 at a time into chocolate mixture. Place on waxed paper until hardened. Grand Marnier, Amaretto or peach schnapps would work nicely in this recipe.

Nancy Pruitt

MINI FRUIT CUPCAKES   *Yield: 84 servings*

8 ounces candied red cherries, chopped	1 16-ounce package dates, chopped
8 ounces candied green cherries, chopped	1 package golden raisins
16 ounces mixed candied fruit	4 eggs, beaten
3 tablespoons Grand Marnier	³/₄ cup sugar
4 cups chopped pecans	³/₄ cup self-rising flour

Combine red cherries, green cherries and mixed fruit in large bowl. Pour liqueur over fruit. Let stand, covered, overnight. Stir in pecans, dates and raisins. Combine eggs and sugar in bowl. Stir in flour. Add to fruit mixture; mix well. Spoon into greased miniature muffin cups. Bake at 300 degrees for 30 minutes. Cool in pan for 10 minutes. Remove to wire rack to cool completely.

Marguerite Gorman

BEST-EVER FUDGE
Yield: 36 servings

5 cups sugar
1   12-ounce can evaporated
    milk
1 cup butter
1 teaspoon salt
1 package German's sweet
    chocolate, crumbled

2 cups semisweet chocolate
    chips
1 jar marshmallow creme
1 cup chopped pecans

Mix first 4 ingredients in saucepan. Bring to a boil over low heat, stirring frequently. Boil for exactly 5 minutes, stirring constantly. Remove from heat. Stir in crumbled chocolate and chocolate chips until melted. Stir in marshmallow creme and pecans. Pour into buttered 9x13-inch glass dish. Chill overnight. Let stand at room temperature for 15 minutes before cutting.

Jo Anne Conner

PLANTATION PECANS
Yield: 8 servings

1 egg white
1 tablespoon water
3/4 cup sugar

1 teaspoon salt
1 1/2 teaspoons cinnamon
2 cups pecan halves

Beat egg white with water. Set aside. Mix sugar, salt and cinnamon in bowl. Brush pecans with egg white; coat with cinnamon mixture. Spread on greased baking sheet. Bake at 275 degrees for 30 minutes.

Cele Weidman

FONDANT

Yield: 1¹/₄ pounds

3 cups sugar
1¹/₂ cups water

¹/₄ teaspoon cream of tartar
1 teaspoon vanilla extract

Combine sugar, water and cream of tartar in saucepan. Cook over low heat until sugar dissolves, stirring constantly. Cook over medium heat until mixture comes to a boil. Cook, covered, for 5 minutes. Cook, uncovered, to 238 degrees on candy thermometer. Wipe platter or marble slab with cloth. Pour fondant onto surface. Do not scrape pan. Cool just enough to hold platter on palm of hand, or to 100 degrees on candy thermometer. Work fondant into circles from edges to center with spatula until white and creamy. Pile into ball; cover with bowl. Let rest for 20 to 30 minutes. Knead until soft and smooth. Place in airtight container. Let ripen for 24 hours or longer. Shape into small candies.

Jane Kennedy

BONBONS

Yield: 1¹/₂ pounds

1 recipe Fondant
Green food coloring
Several drops of pistachio
   flavoring

Red food coloring
Several drops of rose extract
Chopped nuts, coconut, raisins
   or candied fruit

Divide Fondant into 3 portions. Knead green food coloring and pistachio flavoring into 1 portion. Knead red food coloring and rose extract into 1 portion. Knead 1 or more remaining ingredients into 1 portion. Shape each portion into 1-inch rolls. Cut into pieces; flatten. Dry on waxed paper-lined surface for several days. Coat with chocolate if desired.

Jane Kennedy

Pies
& Pastries

AMBROSIA PIE

Yield: 8 servings

1 envelope unflavored gelatin
1/4 cup cold water
4 egg yolks
1/2 cup sugar
1/2 teaspoon salt
1/2 cup orange juice

1 tablespoon lemon juice
3/4 teaspoon grated orange rind
4 egg whites
1/2 cup sugar
1 cup finely chopped orange
1 baked 9-inch pie shell

Soften gelatin in cold water. Combine egg yolks, 1/2 cup sugar, salt, orange juice, lemon juice and orange rind in double boiler. Cook until thickened, stirring frequently. Stir in gelatin. Cook until gelatin is dissolved. Let stand until cool. Beat egg whites with remaining 1/2 cup sugar until stiff peaks form. Fold into cooled mixture gently. Add chopped orange, stirring gently. Spoon into prepared pie shell. Chill until serving time. Serve with whipped cream and coconut.

Connie D. Herrman

ANGEL PIE

Yield: 6 servings

4 egg whites
1/4 teaspoon cream of tartar
1 cup sugar
4 egg yolks
1/2 cup sugar
3 tablespoons lemon juice

2 teaspoons grated lemon rind
1 cup whipping cream
2 tablespoons confectioners'
   sugar
1 teaspoon vanilla extract

Beat egg whites in mixer bowl until soft peaks form. Stir in cream of tartar. Add 1 cup sugar gradually, beating until stiff peaks form. Spoon into buttered pie plate. Bake at 250 degrees for 1 hour. Turn off oven. Leave meringue in oven for 20 minutes longer. Let stand until cool. Beat egg yolks until thick and lemony. Add remaining 1/2 cup sugar, lemon juice and grated lemon rind gradually, beating well after each addition. Transfer mixture to double boiler. Cook until thickened, stirring frequently. Let stand until cool. Whip whipping cream in mixer bowl with confectioners' sugar and vanilla. Cover cooled meringue with half the whipped cream. Top with cooled lemon custard. Spoon remaining whipped cream over custard layer. Chill for 24 hours before serving.

Nancy C. Miller

OLD ENGLISH PIE

Yield: 6 servings

4 apples, chopped
1 cup sugar
1 teaspoon cinnamon
1/2 cup packed brown sugar
1/2 cup butter, softened

1/2 cup chopped pecans
1 teaspoon cinnamon
1 cup flour
3 tablespoons water (optional)

Toss apples with 1 cup sugar and 1 teaspoon cinnamon in pie plate. Combine brown sugar, butter, pecans, remaining 1 teaspoon cinnamon, flour and water in bowl; mix well. Spread over apples. Bake at 350 degrees for 45 minutes.

Kay Hammill

BRANDY ALEXANDER PIE

Yield: 8 servings

7 ounces chocolate cookies, crushed
1/2 cup melted butter
8 ounces marshmallows
1/2 cup milk

1 1/2 ounces Crème de Cacao
1 1/2 ounces brandy
1 cup whipping cream
Grated chocolate

Combine cookie crumbs and melted butter in bowl. Press onto bottom and side of buttered 8-inch springform pan. Bake at 350 degrees for 10 minutes. Let stand until cool. Combine marshmallows and milk in saucepan over low heat. Cook until marshmallows are melted, stirring constantly. Let stand until cool. Stir in Crème de Cacao and brandy. Whip whipping cream in mixer bowl. Fold into cooled marshmallow mixture gently. Pour into cooled crumb crust. Sprinkle with grated chocolate. Chill for 4 hours. May substitute 3 ounces very strong black coffee for brandy.

Nancy Stephens

CHEESE PIE

Yield: 8 servings

16 ounces cream cheese,
  softened
2/3 cup sugar
3 eggs

1 cup sour cream
3 tablespoons sugar
1/2 teaspoon vanilla extract

Beat cream cheese and 2/3 cup sugar in mixer bowl until smooth and creamy. Add eggs one at a time, beating well after each addition. Pour into large buttered pie plate. Bake at 325 degrees for 50 minutes. Center of pie will rise. Let stand for 10 minutes. Center will fall, creating crust. Mix sour cream, remaining 3 tablespoons sugar and vanilla in bowl. Spoon into crust. Bake for 10 to 15 minutes or until set. Cool before serving.

Linda Jenkins McConnell

MOCK CHERRY PIE

Yield: 6 servings

2 cups fresh cranberries
1/4 cup flour
2 cups (scant) sugar
1 cup boiling water
1 cup seedless raisins, cut into
  halves

1 tablespoon butter
1/2 teaspoon salt
1/2 teaspoon vanilla extract
1 recipe 2-crust pie pastry

Cut cranberries into halves. Rinse with cold water to remove seeds; drain. Blend flour and sugar in bowl. Add boiling water gradually, stirring constantly. Add cranberries, raisins, butter, salt and vanilla; mix well. Pour mixture into pastry-lined pie plate. Top with remaining pastry, sealing edge and cutting vents. Bake at 425 degrees for 10 minutes. Reduce temperature to 350 degrees. Bake for 1 hour longer. This is a very old New England recipe and has been served as a holiday dessert in our family for five generations.

Terry Hughes

CHOCOLATE PECAN CREAM PIE   *Yield: 6 to 8 servings*

1/2 cup chopped pecans	3/4 cup sugar
1 baked 9-inch deep-dish pie shell	1/4 teaspoon salt
	1 3/4 cups half and half
2 tablespoons butter	1/2 cup butter
2 ounces semisweet chocolate	1/2 teaspoon vanilla extract
1/4 cup cornstarch	Nutmeg
1/4 cup half and half	

Sprinkle pecans in bottom of pie shell. Melt 2 tablespoons butter and chocolate in saucepan over low heat. Drizzle over pecans. Combine cornstarch and 1/4 cup half and half in bowl, stirring until blended. Combine sugar, salt, remaining 1 3/4 cups half and half and remaining 1/2 cup butter in double boiler. Stir in cornstarch mixture. Cook until thickened, stirring constantly. Stir in vanilla. Pour over pecans and chocolate in pie plate. Sprinkle with nutmeg. Bake at 400 degrees for 10 minutes. Chill before serving.

Phyllis Modell

BLACK JOKE PIE   *Yield: 6 servings*

1 cup chocolate chips, melted	1 cup chopped pecans
1 9-inch pie shell	1/2 cup melted margarine
2 eggs, beaten	1 cup sugar
1/2 cup flour	1 teaspoon vanilla extract

Pour melted chocolate chips into pie shell. Let stand until hardened. Combine eggs, flour, pecans, margarine, sugar and vanilla in bowl; mix well. Pour over hardened chocolate in pie shell. Bake at 350 degrees for 30 minutes or until golden brown. Serve with whipped topping.

Lynn Clanton

FRENCH SILK PIE
Yield: 8 servings

1 cup butter, softened
1 cup sugar
3 ounces unsweetened
   chocolate, melted and cooled

1 teaspoon vanilla extract
4 eggs
1 baked 9-inch pie shell
Whipped cream

Cream butter and sugar in mixer bowl until light and fluffy. Stir in chocolate and vanilla. Add 2 eggs. Beat at high speed for 5 minutes. Add remaining 2 eggs. Beat for 5 minutes longer. Pour into pie shell. Chill for 6 hours to overnight. Serve with whipped cream.

Allyson Harden

HARRIS' BIRTHDAY PIE
Yield: 6 servings

1/2 cup butter
1 ounce unsweetened chocolate
1 cup sugar
2 eggs, slightly beaten

1 teaspoon vanilla extract
Dash of salt
1 unbaked 9-inch pie shell
Whipped cream

Melt butter and chocolate in medium saucepan over low heat. Remove saucepan from heat. Add sugar, eggs, vanilla and salt, mixing well after each addition. Pour into pie shell. Bake at 350 degrees for 25 to 30 minutes or until set. Top with whipped cream. This has been Harris' choice for a birthday "cake" every year.

Carolyn Robinson

ICE CREAM PIE

Yield: 10 to 12 servings

1¼ cups chocolate wafers,
  finely crumbled
3 tablespoons sugar
¼ cup finely ground walnuts
  or almonds
6 tablespoons melted unsalted
  butter
1 cup sugar
¾ cup baking cocoa, sifted
1 teaspoon instant coffee
  powder

1 cup whipping cream
¼ cup unsalted butter
1 quart vanilla ice cream,
  softened
1 quart chocolate ice cream,
  scooped into balls
½ cup whipping cream,
  whipped
½ cup coarsely chopped pecans
Maraschino cherries

Combine crumbled wafers, 3 tablespoons sugar and walnuts in bowl. Cut in 6 tablespoons melted butter until well mixed. Press mixture on bottom and side of 9 or 10-inch pie plate. Chill, covered, for 30 minutes. Combine remaining 1 cup sugar, cocoa and coffee powder in saucepan. Stir in ½ cup whipping cream until smooth. Add remaining whipping cream; blend well. Cook over medium heat until sugar is dissolved, stirring constantly. Add butter. Cook for 5 to 8 minutes or until smooth and thickened. Keep chocolate sauce warm. Spread half the softened vanilla ice cream over crust. Freeze until firm. Drizzle half the hot fudge sauce over top. Spread remaining vanilla ice cream over fudge sauce. Freeze until firm. Arrange chocolate ice cream scoops over vanilla layer. Drizzle with remaining hot fudge sauce. Spoon whipped cream into pastry bag fitted with star tip. Pipe flowers around scoops. Garnish with pecans and cherries.

Gloria Carmines

COFFEE PIE
Yield: 6 servings

1/2 cup butter, softened
3/4 cup sugar
2 teaspoons instant coffee
   powder

2 eggs
1 baked 9-inch pie shell
Whipped cream

Cream butter in mixer bowl. Add sugar and coffee powder. Beat until light and fluffy. Add 1 egg. Beat for 5 minutes. Add remaining egg. Beat for 5 minutes longer. Pour into baked pie shell. Top with whipped cream. I add 1/4 teaspoon almond extract, 1 teaspoon un-flavored gelatin and about 2 tablespoons sugar to 1 cup whipping cream while whipping.

Lynn Ruggles

FUZZY NAVEL PIE
Yield: 6 servings

25 Oreo cookies, crushed
26 marshmallows
1/2 cup orange juice
1 6-ounce can sliced peaches
1 envelope unflavored gelatin

2 tablespoons peach schnapps
2 tablespoons Grand Marnier
2 cups whipping cream,
   whipped

Press cookie crumbs into pie plate. Combine marshmallows and orange juice in microwave-safe bowl. Microwave on Low for 2 minutes or until melted, stirring frequently. Set aside until cool. Drain peaches, reserving liquid. Dissolve gelatin in peach liquid. Purée peaches in blender. Stir in reserved peach liquid, peach schnapps and Grand Marnier. Pour into marshmallow mixture; mix well. Fold in whipped cream gently. Pour into pie shell. Garnish with cookie crumbs and whipped cream. May be frozen.

Richard Adams

LEMON-SOUR CREAM PIE

Yield: 6 servings

1 cup sugar
3 tablespoons cornstarch
Dash of salt
1 cup milk
3 egg yolks, slightly beaten
1/4 cup butter

1 teaspoon grated lemon rind
1/4 cup lemon juice
1 cup sour cream
1 baked 9-inch pie shell
1 recipe meringue

Combine sugar, cornstarch and salt in saucepan. Add milk gradually, stirring constantly. Cook over medium heat until thickened, stirring constantly. Stir a small amount of hot mixture into beaten egg yolks; stir eggs into hot mixture. Cook for 2 minutes, stirring constantly. Stir in butter, grated lemon rind and lemon juice. Cover mixture; cool. Fold in sour cream gently. Pour into cooled pie shell. Top with meringue. Bake at 400 degrees until golden brown.

Connie D. Herrman

KEY LIME PIE

Yield: 8 servings

1 package graham crackers, crushed
1/2 cup butter, softened
4 eggs yolks

1 14-ounce can sweetened condensed milk
3 ounces Key lime juice

Combine graham cracker crumbs and butter in bowl; mix well. Press into 9-inch pie plate. Whip egg yolks and condensed milk in mixer bowl. Add Key lime juice gradually, whipping constantly. Pour into prepared pie plate. Chill for 2 hours or longer before serving.

Joe Carter

CHRISTMAS MINCE CHIFFON PIE   *Yield: 6 servings*

1   3-ounce package lemon
    gelatin
1/4 cup sugar
1 cup boiling water
1 cup mincemeat

1/4 cup sherry
3 egg whites
1/4 cup sugar
1/2 cup whipping cream
1 baked 9-inch pie shell

Dissolve gelatin and 1/4 cup sugar in boiling water. Stir in mincemeat and sherry. Chill until partially set. Beat egg whites in bowl until soft peaks form. Add remaining 1/4 cup sugar gradually, beating until stiff peaks form. Whip whipping cream in mixer bowl. Add stiffly beaten egg whites and gelatin mixture, folding gently after each addition. Spoon into cooled pie shell. Chill until serving time. Serve with additional whipped cream. This is a new variation of our Christmas mincemeat pie. Add a sprig of holly for a festive look.

Nancy Pruitt

MOUTH-WATERING PIE   *Yield: 6 servings*

1/4 cup chopped pecans
1 unbaked 9-inch deep-dish
  pie shell
1 1/2 cups sifted confectioners'
  sugar

4 ounces cream cheese, softened
2 cups whipped topping
Banana slices
1/2 can blueberry pie filling

Press pecans into bottom of unbaked pie shell. Bake using package directions. Let stand until cool. Beat confectioners' sugar and cream cheese in mixer bowl until smooth. Fold in whipped topping gently. Arrange banana slices in bottom of cooled pie shell. Pour cream cheese mixture over bananas. Top with blueberry pie filling. Chill before serving.

Lynn Clanton

MAPLE PECAN PIE

Yield: 6 servings

1 cup maple syrup
1 cup packed dark brown sugar
1/3 cup melted butter
1 cup (heaping) pecans

3 eggs, beaten
1 teaspoon vanilla extract
Dash of salt
1 unbaked 9-inch pie shell

Combine first 7 ingredients in bowl; mix well. Pour into pie shell. Bake at 350 degrees for 45 to 50 minutes or until knife inserted near center comes out clean. Turn off oven. Leave pie in oven for 5 to 10 minutes. Serve cooled pie with ice cream or whipped topping. A chocolate crumb pie shell may be substituted for unbaked pie shell.

Margaret D. Jones

REAL SOUTHERN PECAN PIE

Yield: 6 servings

3/4 cup sugar
3 eggs, well beaten
3/4 cup corn syrup
3 tablespoons butter, softened

1 cup pecans
1 teaspoon lemon juice or
  vinegar
1 unbaked 9-inch pie shell

Combine first 6 ingredients in mixer bowl; mix well. Beat for 2 minutes or longer. Pour into pie shell. Bake at 325 degrees for 45 minutes.

Janie Wilkerson

RUM PIE

Yield: 6 servings

6 egg yolks
1 cup (scant) sugar
1 envelope unflavored gelatin
1/2 cup cold water

2 cups whipping cream
1/2 cup rum
1 baked 9-inch pie shell
Shredded semisweet chocolate

Beat egg yolks with sugar in bowl. Soften gelatin in cold water in double boiler. Heat over hot water until gelatin is dissolved, stirring frequently. Add to egg mixture; mix well. Beat whipping cream in mixer bowl until stiff. Fold into egg mixture. Stir in rum. Pour into pie shell. Garnish with chocolate. Chill completely.

Mary Moss

MILE-HIGH STRAWBERRY PIES
Yield: 12 servings

16 ounces frozen unsweetened
  strawberries
2 egg whites
1 cup sugar

1/2 teaspoon salt
1 envelope whipped topping
  mix
2 baked 9-inch pie shells

Thaw strawberries partially. Beat egg whites in bowl until soft peaks form. Add sugar and salt gradually, beating constantly. Add undrained strawberries. Beat at high speed for 20 minutes. Prepare whipped topping using package directions. Fold into strawberry mixture gently. Mound mixture into cooled pie shells. Freeze until firm. May substitute graham cracker pie shells for pastry pie shells.

Marianne Smith

STRAWBERRY CREAM PIE
Yield: 6 servings

8 ounces cream cheese, softened
1/4 cup sugar
1/2 teaspoon vanilla extract
Dash of nutmeg
1 cup sliced strawberries

1 cup whipping cream
1/4 cup sifted confectioners'
  sugar
1 baked 9-inch pie shell

Beat cream cheese in mixer bowl. Add sugar gradually, mixing constantly. Add vanilla and nutmeg; mix well. Stir in drained strawberries. Whip whipping cream in bowl until soft peaks form. Add confectioners' sugar gradually, whipping constantly after each addition. Fold into strawberry mixture gently. Spoon into cooled pie shell. Chill until serving time.

Elaine Fulton

STRAWBERRY PIE
Yield: 6 servings

3 egg whites
1/2 teaspoon baking powder
1 cup sugar
10 saltines, crushed

1/2 cup crushed pecans
4 cups unsweetened
　strawberries
Sweetened whipped cream

Beat egg whites with baking powder in mixer bowl until soft peaks form. Add sugar gradually, beating until stiff peaks form. Fold in cracker crumbs and crushed pecans gently. Pour into buttered pie plate. Bake at 300 degrees for 30 minutes. Fill with strawberries. Top with whipped cream to serve.

Betsy Pratt

SWEET POTATO PIE
Yield: 6 servings

2 cups mashed cooked sweet
　potatoes
1/2 cup packed brown sugar
3 tablespoons melted butter
3 eggs, beaten
1/2 cup milk

1/2 teaspoon nutmeg
1/4 teaspoon ground cloves
1/4 teaspoon cinnamon
1/2 teaspoon salt
1 unbaked 9-inch pie shell

Combine sweet potatoes, brown sugar, butter, eggs, milk, nutmeg, cloves, cinnamon and salt in bowl; mix well. Spoon into pie shell. Bake at 400 degrees for 40 to 50 minutes or until set. Cool on wire rack. May omit spices if desired.

Jill Bradley

MINIATURE CINNAMON PASTRIES   *Yield: 48 servings*

1/2 cup butter, softened	2 1/2 cups flour
1/2 cup margarine, softened	2 teaspoons cinnamon
8 ounces cream cheese, softened	1/2 cup sugar
1/4 cup sugar	1/2 cup chopped pecans

Combine butter, margarine and cream cheese in bowl; mix well. Add 1/4 cup sugar and flour; mix well. Shape into ball. Chill, covered, in refrigerator for 24 hours. Divide dough into 4 portions. Roll each portion into a 12-inch circle on lightly floured surface. Mix cinnamon, remaining 1/2 cup sugar and pecans in bowl. Sprinkle over each circle. Cut each circle into 12 wedges. Roll as for jelly roll, starting at widest end. Place seam side down on greased baking sheet. Bake at 325 degrees for 20 minutes. Pastries may be frozen before baking. Thaw completely at room temperature before baking.

Carol M. Wilson

PEACH COBBLER ROLL   *Yield: 8 servings*

1/2 cup butter	1 1/2 cups sifted self-rising flour
2 cups sugar	1/3 cup milk
2 cups water	1 teaspoon cinnamon
1/2 cup shortening	2 cups finely chopped peaches

Melt butter in 9x13-inch baking dish. Heat sugar and water in saucepan until sugar is dissolved, stirring frequently. Cut shortening into flour in bowl until crumbly. Add milk, stirring with fork until dough leaves sides of bowl. Turn dough onto lightly floured surface. Knead just until smooth. Roll dough onto large rectangle 1/4-inch thick. Sprinkle cinnamon over peaches in bowl; mix well. Spread peaches over dough. Roll as for jelly roll to enclose filling, sealing edges. Cut into 16 slices; place in prepared baking dish cut side down. Pour sugar syrup carefully around slices. Bake at 350 degrees for 35 to 40 minutes or until most of syrup is absorbed and pastry is light brown.

Mary Coleman

BAVARIAN APPLE TART
Yield: 8 servings

½ cup butter	1 egg
⅓ cup sugar	½ teaspoon vanilla extract
¼ teaspoon vanilla extract	4 cups sliced, peeled apples
1 cup flour	⅓ cup sugar
8 ounces cream cheese,	½ teaspoon cinnamon
softened	½ cup chopped walnuts
¼ cup sugar	

Cream butter and ⅓ cup sugar in bowl until light and fluffy. Add ¼ teaspoon vanilla and flour; mix well. Spread over bottom and 2 inches up side of greased 9-inch springform pan. Combine cream cheese and ¼ cup sugar in bowl; mix well. Add egg and remaining ½ teaspoon vanilla; mix well. Spread over pastry. Combine apples, remaining ⅓ cup sugar and cinnamon in bowl; toss to mix. Spread over filling; sprinkle with walnuts. Bake at 450 degrees for 10 minutes or until brown. Cool in refrigerator before serving.

Sue Burden

BAKEWELL TARTS
Yield: 18 servings

1 10-ounce package pie crust	¼ teaspoon almond extract
mix	1 4-ounce can whole blanched
¼ cup cold water	almonds, ground
½ cup butter	3 tablespoons raspberry
½ cup sugar	preserves
½ teaspoon salt	½ cup blanched almond halves
2 eggs	

Prepare pie crust mix using package directions with ¼ cup cold water. Roll to ¼-inch thickness on lightly floured surface. Cut eighteen 4-inch circles from pastry. Line fluted pans or muffin cups with circles. Cream butter, sugar and salt in mixer bowl until light and fluffy. Add eggs; beat at high speed until well mixed. Stir in almond extract and ground almonds. Place ½ teaspoon raspberry preserves in bottom of each pastry cup; top with 1½ tablespoons almond mixture. Place almond half on top. Bake at 375 degrees for 25 minutes or until golden brown and filling tests done. Cool on wire rack.

Gillian Burr

CHEESE TARTS

Yield: 10 servings

4 ounces cream cheese, softened
1/2 cup butter, softened

1 cup flour
Jam, mincemeat or pie filling

Combine cream cheese and butter in bowl; mix well. Add flour; mix well. Shape into ball. Chill, covered, in refrigerator overnight. Roll to 1/8-inch thickness on lightly floured surface. Cut into rounds. Place 1 teaspoon jam, mincemeat or pie filling on 1 side of each round; fold to enclose filling, sealing edges. Place on baking sheet. Bake at 375 degrees for 12 minutes or until brown.

Louise Levzow

CHEESECAKE CUPCAKES

Yield: 2 to 2 1/2 dozen

8 ounces cream cheese, softened
1/2 cup sugar
3/4 teaspoon almond extract
2 eggs
Vanilla wafers

1 cup sour cream
1/4 cup sugar
1/2 teaspoon almond extract
Raspberry preserves

Combine cream cheese, 1/2 cup sugar and 3/4 teaspoon almond extract in food processor container. Process until well mixed. Add eggs 1 at a time, processing until well blended. Line muffin cups with paper liners. Place 1 vanilla wafer in each. Fill 2/3 full with cream cheese mixture. Bake at 300 degrees for 20 to 25 minutes or until brown. Cool in pan for 15 minutes. The tops will fall. Combine sour cream, remaining 1/4 cup sugar and 1/2 teaspoon almond extract in food processor container. Process until well mixed. Place 1 teaspoon topping on each cupcake; top with 1/4 teaspoon raspberry preserves. Bake at 300 degrees for 10 minutes longer. Cool on wire rack.

Trisha Hughes

GRANDMOTHER'S TARTS
Yield: 24 servings

1 cup graham cracker crumbs	1/2 cup sugar
1/4 cup melted butter	1 egg
8 ounces cream cheese, softened	1/2 teaspoon vanilla extract
	1 can cherry pie filling

Combine graham cracker crumbs and butter in bowl; mix well. Press into miniature muffin cups. Combine cream cheese, sugar, egg and vanilla in bowl. Beat until fluffy. Spoon into prepared muffin cups. Bake at 350 degrees for 20 minutes or until firm. Let stand until cool. Top with pie filling.

Marianne Smith

PECAN TASSIES
Yield: 12 servings

3 ounces cream cheese, softened	3/4 cup packed brown sugar
1/2 cup butter, softened	1 tablespoon melted butter
1 cup whole wheat flour	1 teaspoon vanilla extract
1 egg	1 cup chopped pecans

Combine cream cheese and butter in mixer bowl; mix well. Add flour; mix well. Chill, covered, in refrigerator for 1 hour. Shape into 24 small balls, adding a small amount of flour if needed. Place in buttered miniature muffin cups, pressing to flatten. Combine egg, brown sugar, melted butter and vanilla in mixer bowl; beat well. Fill pastry cups 3/4 full; top with pecans. Bake at 325 degrees for 25 minutes. Remove to wire rack to cool.

Mrs. Holland B. Clark

LINZERTARTS

Yield: 24 servings

1 cup butter, softened
1 cup sugar
2 eggs
1 teaspoon almond extract
3 cups flour

1/2 teaspoon salt
1 1/2 teaspoons baking powder
1 cup raspberry preserves
Confectioners' sugar

Cream butter and sugar in mixer bowl. Add eggs 1 at a time, beating well after each addition. Add almond extract; mix well. Mix flour, salt and baking powder together. Add to batter; mix well. Chill, covered, in refrigerator for 1 hour. Roll to 1/8-inch thickness on lightly floured surface. Cut with round cookie cutter. Cut thimble-sized hole in center of half the cookies. Place on baking sheet. Bake at 350 degrees for 10 minutes. Cool on baking sheet for several minutes. Remove to wire rack to cool completely. Spread raspberry preserves on whole cookies. Sprinkle confectioners' sugar on cookies with holes; place over preserve-topped cookies.

Dorothy Boyd

RUSSIAN MINT PIES

Yield: 18 servings

1 cup butter, softened
2 cups sifted confectioners'
  sugar
4 ounces unsweetened
  chocolate, melted
4 eggs
1 tablespoon peppermint
  extract

2 teaspoons vanilla extract
18 vanilla wafers
1 cup whipping cream,
  whipped
Chopped pecans
Maraschino cherries

Cream butter and confectioners' sugar in mixer bowl until light and fluffy. Add melted chocolate; mix well. Add eggs, peppermint and vanilla extracts; beat well. Place 1 vanilla wafer in each paper-lined muffin cup. Fill 3/4 full with chocolate mixture; top with dollop of whipped cream. Sprinkle with pecans; top with maraschino cherry. Freeze, covered, in muffin cups until firm. Remove to plastic bags to store. Serve frozen.

Allyson Harden

NUTRITIONAL PROFILE

Persons with dietary or health problems or whose diets require close monitoring should not rely solely on the nutritional information provided; they should consult their physicians or a registered dietitian for specific information. We hope to encourage you to look at these and other favorite recipes in light of current nutritional recommendations. Keep in mind that almost every recipe can be adjusted to meet individual needs and tastes.

Nutritional information for these recipes is computed from information derived from many sources, including materials supplied by the United States Department of Agriculture, computer databanks, and journals in which the information is assumed to be in the public domain. Because of new products and changes in familiar products as well as the trend to supply more information on packages, we strongly urge you to read package labels.

Abbreviations for Nutritional Profile

Cal — Calories   Fiber — Dietary Fiber   Sod — Sodium
Prot — Protein   T Fat — Total Fat   g — gram
Carbo — Carbohydrates Chol — Cholesterol   mg — milligrams

Measurement and Ingredient Guidelines

The analysis of the recipes in *Hilton Head Cooks* were based on the following premises unless otherwise stated.

- **MEASUREMENTS**—All volume measurements are level. All eggs are large.

- **YIELDS**—When a yield appears as dozens i.e. cookies, the analysis is for 1 cookie. When a variable yield is given i.e. 6–8 servings, the number on which the analysis is based is always the smaller number.

- **OPTIONAL INGREDIENTS** are not included in the analysis. Ingredients without measurements that are listed in the nature of "serve withs" or garnishes i.e. corn chips with dips or parsley sprigs are not included in the analysis.

- **TO TASTE**—Salt and other seasonings or ingredients to taste have not been included in the nutritional analysis.

- **ALTERNATIVE INGREDIENTS**—If a choice of ingredients has been given, the analysis reflects the first option.

- **VARIABLE AMOUNTS**—If a choice of amounts has been given i.e. 3 to 4 cups flour, the analysis reflects the greater amount.

- **GENERIC CHOICE**—In recipes in which the choice of nuts has been left to the cook, the analysis was based on pecans; where the choice of cheese is not specified, the analysis is based on Cheddar cheese.

- **FLOUR**—Unless otherwise specified all flour used is unsifted all-purpose flour.

- **MARINADES**—The analysis has been based on the entire amount of marinade since it is impossible to determine the amount absorbed by the food during marinating or cooking.

- **DAIRY PRODUCTS**—The percentage of fat in commercial dairy products may vary across the country to accommodate regional tastes and state laws. In this book, unless otherwise specified, the following guidelines were used for analysis:

Product	Butterfat Content
whole milk	3.5%
low-fat milk	1.0%
whipping cream	37.6%
half and half	11.7%
cottage cheese, cream-style	4.2%
cottage cheese, dry curd	<1.0%
yogurt	3.5%

The analysis for cheeses is not based on low-fat or low-sodium versions currently available. If these versions are used, make the proper adjustments in the analysis by using the label information. Yogurt is plain, produced from whole milk. See carton for additional information.

- **FATS**—Oils and shortening used in recipes and analyses are vegetable oils and hydrogenated vegetable shortening made from vegetable oils. Butter and margarine are regular, not whipped or pre-softened products. Whenever large amounts of shortening or oil are used for frying, the analysis does not include these since it is impossible to determine the amount that would be absorbed by the food.

- **PREPARED FOODS**—Foods such as canned soups are generic averages rather than brand specific or dietetic versions now entering the marketplace. Can or package sizes are average, popular sizes unless specified. Such ingredients as breads and pie crusts are generic averages. When using special diet or especially rich versions, be sure to recognize that the nutritional analysis information supplied must be altered.

- A few recipes are noted "nutritional information is not available." No nutritional analysis was possible if information regarding measurements was not included, choices of ingredients and amounts varied greatly, no yield was given or appropriate, or a major ingredient of the recipe was not included in available computer databanks.

Pg #	Recipe Title (Approx Per Serving)	Cal	Prot (g)	Carbo (g)	Fiber (g)	T Fat (g)	% Cal from Fat	Chol (mg)	Sod (mg)
22	Vidalia Onion Dip (1 c.)	519	3	46	2	38	63	39	984
22	Chicken and Rice Salad	444	18	25	3	30	61	58	277
22	Superb Baked Crab	222	20	7	<1	12	49	170	599
23	Patio Beans	284	13	49	6	6	17	14	871
23	Eggplant Parmigiana	196	11	15	4	10	47	53	871
23	Onion Pie	360	13	20	1	26	65	145	614
24	Bran Bread	209	4	28	1	10	40	18	181
24	Hummingbird Cake	734	6	86	2	43	51	71	290
26	Cheese Log	326	13	5	1	30	79	67	737
26	Tang Cheese Ball	202	3	13	2	16	69	31	86
26	Smoked Salmon Roll	114	7	1	<1	9	72	30	233
27	Shrimp Cheese Balls	150	8	3	1	13	73	48	142
27	Artichoke Hors d'Oeuvres	178	4	3	<1	17	84	16	365
27	Hot Cheese Dip	214	5	1	<1	21	88	40	214
28	Crab Meat Dip	87	6	3	4	5	55	41	143
28	Oven-Baked Crab Dip	208	9	2	<1	19	80	73	315
28	Luscious Layered Crab Dip	94	7	<1	0	7	67	46	150
29	Hot Crab Meat Appetizer	315	16	5	1	27	75	100	317
29	Eggplant Appetizer	87	1	6	2	7	69	0	358
30	Guacamole	60	1	4	3	5	70	0	143
30	Layered Mexican Dip	126	4	5	3	11	75	17	118
30	Shrimp Butter	179	8	<1	<1	17	82	115	114
31	Spinach Dip	203	2	8	1	19	81	19	352
31	Smoky Vegetable Dip	132	4	4	<1	11	75	27	199
31	Apricot-Peach Spread	212	2	41	1	5	22	16	56
32	Artichoke Spread	176	4	3	0	17	85	16	324
32	Avocado-Crab Meat Spread	136	3	4	4	13	80	16	101
32	Crab Mold	101	4	2	<1	9	77	28	182
33	Chipped Beef Spread	148	4	3	<1	14	84	38	328
33	Artichoke Squares	143	8	5	2	11	65	91	351
34	Bacon Roll-Ups	116	5	5	0	9	67	23	304
34	Baked Brie Bites	333	15	30	<1	18	47	52	493
34	Brie in a Pastry	341	11	16	<1	26	68	55	433
35	Cheese Straw Crispies	148	4	9	<1	11	66	31	156
35	Crab Meat Ravigote	167	17	2	<1	10	55	117	476
35	Hilton Head Crabgrass	82	5	2	1	6	66	29	149
36	Kelly Buffalo Wings	257	18	1	<1	20	70	75	170
36	Cocktail Puffs	33	1	2	<1	2	66	23	22
36	Chex Party Mix (1 c.)	223	3	28	2	12	46	28	578

Pg #	Recipe Title (Approx Per Serving)	Cal	Prot (g)	Carbo (g)	Fiber (g)	T Fat (g)	% Cal from Fat	Chol (mg)	Sod (mg)
37	Chili Meatballs	104	5	11	<1	5	40	25	311
37	Sausage-Stuffed Mushrooms	123	8	3	1	9	65	27	183
38	Stuffed Mushrooms	301	9	5	2	28	81	41	378
38	Olive Cheese Balls	68	2	3	<1	5	68	14	154
38	Scalloped Oysters	122	5	7	3	42	88	180	194
39	Exceptional Pâté	30	1	<1	<1	2	74	42	42
39	Liver Pâté Mold	35	1	<1	<1	3	81	12	59
40	Rum Sausages	158	5	10	0	10	59	0	611
40	Stupendous Sausage Balls	32	2	4	<1	1	25	10	74
41	Marinated Shrimp	416	17	3	<1	38	80	158	620
41	Tasty Marinated Shrimp	298	18	4	1	24	71	158	450
42	Shrimp Mousse	1522	55	32	3	133	77	484	2264
42	Spinach Balls	45	2	3	<1	3	62	28	113
43	Straw and Hay	430	18	24	1	29	61	149	708
43	Deviled Pecans	235	2	6	2	24	87	0	67
43	Oyster Crackers	195	2	17	1	14	62	0	381
44	Roast Beef Sandwiches au Jus	432	44	31	<1	14	29	94	1142
44	Sicilian Sandwiches	872	56	43	3	56	56	146	740
45	Sloppy Joes for-a-Crowd	334	16	37	2	13	36	37	1429
45	Chicken and Peppers in Pitas	413	32	24	2	21	46	72	1008
46	Chicken Salad Sandwiches	407	21	30	1	22	49	133	758
46	Croque Monsieur	569	19	41	1	36	58	35	766
47	Cherry Sandwiches	87	2	8	<1	5	54	16	86
47	Cheese and Olive Sandwiches	576	17	43	2	38	59	54	912
48	Pimento Cheese Spread (1 c.)	588	26	3	1	53	80	121	764
48	Raisin Nut Spread (1 c.)	959	6	91	5	68	61	94	360
48	Strawberry Sandwiches (1 c.)	927	11	118	2	50	47	124	352
49	Gingered Fruit Sandwiches (1 c.)	824	13	57	5	65	68	181	673
49	Strawberry Blintz Sandwiches	659	24	91	4	24	32	116	679
50	Double-Decker Tea Rounds	109	3	13	1	5	40	12	255
51	Open-Faced Sandwiches	Nutritional informaton for this recipe is not available.							
52	Tea Sandwiches	Nutritional informaton for this recipe is not available.							
53	Ribbon Sandwich Fillings	Nutritional informaton for this recipe is not available.							
56	Champagne Punch	110	1	21	<1	<1	1	0	10
56	Cherry Ice Ring (1 ring)	605	1	156	1	1	1	0	41
56	Christmas Punch	62	<1	16	<1	<1	0	0	7
57	Cranberry Ice Ring (1 ring)	808	1	209	13	<1	0	0	144
57	Coffee Punch (1 gal.)	210	6	28	<1	9	37	35	114
57	Rich Coffee Punch	153	2	16	<1	10	56	38	39

Pg #	Recipe Title (Approx Per Serving)	Cal	Prot (g)	Carbo (g)	Fiber (g)	T Fat (g)	% Cal from Fat	Chol (mg)	Sod (mg)
58	Hot Cranberry Tea (1 gal.)	227	<1	58	1	<1	0	0	4
58	Simple and Easy Punch	116	<1	29	<1	<1	1	0	19
58	Teahouse Punch	8	<1	2	<1	<1	4	0	9
59	Wassail Bowl (1 gal.)	134	<1	34	<1	<1	1	0	8
59	Carol's Daiquiri	181	<1	30	<1	<1	0	0	12
60	Eggnog	338	9	34	0	15	40	252	147
60	Holiday Eggnog	529	8	36	0	35	59	322	89
60	Mimosas	87	1	11	1	<1	2	0	5
61	Orange Julius	410	6	89	1	4	9	17	55
61	Café Brûlot	52	<1	10	<1	<1	0	0	3
61	Café Suisse Mocha Mix	53	1	12	<1	1	16	0	32
62	Carolina Iced Coffee	144	2	3	<1	15	87	52	29
62	Irish Coffee	170	<1	1	<1	<1	0	0	4
62	Italian Coffee	76	4	6	<1	4	47	17	54
62	Latin American Coffee	114	4	16	<1	4	33	17	85
63	Mexican Coffee	376	<1	28	<1	<1	0	0	7
63	Pecan Coffee	129	1	12	<1	5	32	0	8
63	Debutante's Tea (1 c.)	162	<1	42	1	<1	1	0	3
64	Friendship Tea Mix (1 c.)	445	1	111	<1	<1	0	0	81
64	Instant Russian Tea Mix (1 c.)	715	1	181	0	<1	0	0	83
64	Russian Tea (1 qt.)	122	<1	31	<1	<1	0	0	6
65	Sangria Tea (1 qt.)	142	<1	27	1	<1	0	0	15
65	Summertime Tea (1 c.)	64	<1	17	<1	<1	1	0	2
65	Hot Cocoa Mix (1 c.)	756	26	147	0	14	15	6	723
66	Cinnamon Hot Chocolate Mix (1 c.)	689	4	68	2	50	61	109	39
66	Instant Hot Chocolate Mix	245	21	38	0	3	9	10	311
68	Polish Borscht	146	17	7	2	5	32	48	775
68	Broccoli Chowder	327	22	13	4	22	59	75	1284
68	Chilled Broccoli Soup	209	7	17	2	13	55	35	824
69	Chicken and Corn Soup	403	50	19	4	14	32	214	188
69	Quick Corn Chowder	427	17	54	4	17	35	42	1290
70	Crab Bisque	537	23	14	<1	44	73	227	373
70	She-Crab Soup	480	18	16	<1	37	71	235	407
71	Crab Soup	331	17	19	1	20	55	94	1298
71	Carl's Chowder	185	12	20	1	7	34	52	649
72	Low-Calorie Gazpacho	51	2	12	3	<1	5	0	415
72	Mom's Italian Soup	597	47	61	3	18	27	214	678
73	Chilled Mushroom Velvet Soup	286	7	13	4	24	74	57	481
73	Mexican Oatmeal Soup	275	10	20	4	18	58	42	1089

Pg #	Recipe Title (Approx Per Serving)	Cal	Prot (g)	Carbo (g)	Fiber (g)	T Fat (g)	% Cal from Fat	Chol (mg)	Sod (mg)
73	Black Olive Soup	94	5	3	<1	8	71	65	414
74	Mother's Pea Soup	138	6	17	4	5	33	46	336
74	Peanut Soup	437	18	11	3	38	75	50	1010
75	Vegetable Soup	381	15	45	7	17	39	55	675
75	Shin Bone Vegetable Soup	254	12	32	3	9	30	31	259
76	Watercress Soup	263	5	22	1	18	60	122	1171
76	Watercress-Meatball Soup	111	11	9	1	3	27	22	706
77	Beef Continental	643	49	24	2	34	51	131	133
77	Easy Beef Burgundy	379	40	10	1	13	30	102	835
77	Easy Tender Beef Stew	382	45	8	<1	15	35	128	857
78	Boeuf Bourguignon	427	35	14	2	22	47	119	499
79	Three-Dog Chili	367	26	9	1	24	61	93	377
79	Gang Chili	488	33	54	5	18	31	74	3698
80	Southern Chili	163	11	13	4	8	42	27	325
80	Fish Stew	218	23	17	2	6	27	120	927
81	Williston Catfish Stew	593	31	41	4	45	58	418	486
81	Uncle Remus' Fish Stew	286	25	35	2	5	17	70	450
82	Shrimp Stew	82	9	6	1	3	28	68	206
82	Shrimp Creole	258	28	19	5	9	30	221	664
84	Angel Salad	196	2	30	1	8	37	63	32
84	Cran-Orange Wreath Salad	508	6	70	5	26	43	23	180
85	Exotic Salad	327	2	22	4	27	72	0	<1
85	Fresh Fruit Salad	125	2	29	5	1	5	0	8
86	Coconut Fruit Salad	259	2	34	3	14	47	13	29
86	Holiday Fruit Salad	210	3	29	2	11	43	68	44
87	Fruit Stack Salad	53	1	14	2	<1	2	0	2
87	Hot Wine Fruit Salad	180	1	29	2	6	31	16	55
87	Watergate Salad	409	3	50	2	24	51	0	115
88	Seven-Up Holiday Salad	243	5	36	1	10	35	10	117
88	Holiday Salad Topping (1 c.)	562	5	51	<1	39	61	200	119
89	Strawberry-Banana Salad	319	6	46	3	15	39	17	113
89	Corned Beef Salad	510	21	17	1	41	71	177	965
90	Pasta Salad	307	8	39	3	16	42	5	430
90	Taco Toss	770	32	46	8	57	62	117	891
91	Chicken and Pasta Salad	802	41	33	4	58	64	109	846
91	Congealed Chicken Salad	409	19	13	3	31	68	61	567
92	Cranberry-Chicken Salad	286	9	21	2	20	60	32	275
92	Chicken and Lobster Salad	1023	29	13	2	96	84	302	1458
93	Curried Chicken-Rice Salad	661	27	30	2	48	66	84	581

Pg #	Recipe Title (Approx Per Serving)	Cal	Prot (g)	Carbo (g)	Fiber (g)	T Fat (g)	% Cal from Fat	Chol (mg)	Sod (mg)
93	Crab and Olive Salad	139	10	2	1	11	69	50	660
93	Marinated Crab Salad	253	24	4	1	16	56	113	317
94	Fisherman's Salad	913	45	60	6	55	54	318	1292
94	Shrimp Remoulade	340	25	3	1	26	67	246	749
95	Sea Island Pickled Shrimp	495	30	11	2	38	68	263	305
95	Artichoke Rice Salad	204	3	21	3	13	55	5	703
96	Pecan-Asparagus Salad	177	4	7	2	19	80	0	97
96	Asparagus Vinaigrette	98	5	20	4	2	13	0	874
96	Asparagus Salad	81	4	5	2	6	57	0	3
97	Marinated Broccoli	272	3	7	3	28	87	0	1444
97	Brown Derby Cobb Salad	1145	14	8	4	120	93	108	2288
98	Carol's Caesar Salad	449	7	6	1	45	89	35	294
98	Caesar Salad	222	9	10	1	17	66	50	433
99	Copper Pennies	224	2	35	4	10	38	1	772
99	Hilton Head Layered Salad	288	6	8	2	27	82	29	297
100	Three-Lettuce Salad	57	2	6	2	3	45	0	20
100	Sweet and Sour Dressing	189	<1	16	<1	14	65	0	189
100	Love This Salad	85	3	6	4	6	59	3	452
101	Pea Salad	461	6	14	4	44	83	11	557
101	Layered Potato Salad	327	4	30	2	22	59	28	419
102	Radicchio Pecan Salad	948	7	10	3	101	93	113	156
102	Waldorf Coleslaw	390	2	33	3	30	66	22	573
103	Coleslaw	21	1	5	1	<1	4	0	6
103	Coleslaw Dressing (1 c.)	757	<1	74	<1	55	62	0	68
103	Hot Slaw	79	1	14	1	2	27	23	43
104	Seven-Day Slaw	176	1	17	1	13	62	0	192
104	Tabouli	277	3	19	5	22	69	0	433
104	Tomato Cream Cheese Aspic	479	5	21	<1	43	79	63	693
105	Fresh Tomato Aspic	35	3	6	2	<1	6	<1	895
105	Vegetable Salad	83	5	7	2	5	48	53	798
106	Marinated Vegetable Salad (1 c.)	226	6	26	4	13	47	0	369
106	Mustard-Celery Seed Dressing (1 c.)	1191	8	13	2	127	93	87	2277
106	Sour Cream Fruit Dressing (1 c.)	439	7	62	<1	20	40	176	89
108	Beef Stroganoff	711	58	27	2	41	52	216	941
108	Grand Marnier Roast Beef	774	66	75	3	22	26	181	455
109	Lobster-Stuffed Tenderloin	473	49	1	<1	28	56	148	415
109	London Broil	244	28	1	<1	13	50	85	451
110	Barbecued Pot Roast	370	44	13	0	13	34	128	1160
110	Roast on the Rocks	302	43	1	<1	13	40	128	1136

Pg #	Recipe Title (Approx Per Serving)	Cal	Prot (g)	Carbo (g)	Fiber (g)	T Fat (g)	% Cal from Fat	Chol (mg)	Sod (mg)
111	Steak in a Bag	562	45	13	1	36	58	144	827
111	Hamburger Quiche	555	21	17	1	45	73	149	575
112	Baked Spaghetti	509	28	33	3	31	53	86	965
112	Burrito Pie	506	26	25	5	35	61	79	955
113	Shepherd's Pie	305	18	34	3	12	34	49	726
113	The Recipe	534	29	33	2	32	54	120	1238
114	Three-Bean Beefy Casserole	314	17	49	7	7	20	24	851
114	Island Palms en Cauchette	131	17	5	<1	5	34	31	1406
115	Heritage Peachy Baked Ham	276	32	20	<1	7	23	70	1696
115	Ham and Turkey Pie	488	19	33	2	31	57	52	1099
116	Luscious Lamb	522	75	0	0	22	40	243	186
116	Butterfly Lamb	1138	100	6	1	77	62	324	1227
116	Grilled Lamb	1157	104	6	0	78	61	324	3472
117	Wausetti	390	30	29	1	17	40	132	589
117	Saltimbocca alla Romana	389	48	<1	0	19	47	200	936
118	Veal with Lemon and Brandy	247	24	15	<1	9	34	107	106
118	Vermouth Veal	328	18	2	0	23	64	140	173
118	Elephant Stew	Nutritional information for this recipe is not available.							
120	Bird of Paradise	247	28	1	0	12	43	129	142
120	Chicken in-a-Blanket	406	47	8	<1	14	32	115	2219
121	Chicken Caruso with Rice	347	20	36	1	14	35	66	449
121	Chicken Elegant in Crust	707	27	25	0	55	71	220	677
122	Apricot-Ginger Chicken	286	27	9	<1	16	50	88	371
122	Chicken Hawaiian	358	24	22	2	20	50	64	1170
123	Chicken Monterey	465	38	13	<1	28	56	205	258
123	Chicken Scallopini	140	26	0	0	3	20	72	63
124	Chicken Supreme	336	14	21	2	23	59	43	911
124	Chicken in Wine	347	31	10	1	19	51	90	468
125	Pan-Barbecued Chicken	133	21	7	1	2	16	54	428
125	Fried Chicken	375	52	6	<1	15	37	160	171
126	Oven-Fried Chicken	283	30	12	0	12	39	129	581
126	Grilled Chicken	608	47	6	<1	46	66	146	412
127	Marinated Chicken Breasts	196	29	8	<1	5	23	80	598
127	Poulet Garni aux Champignons	373	29	13	1	21	53	119	768
128	Olé Poulet	310	28	4	3	22	61	72	1429
128	Lemon Tarragon Chicken	226	33	2	<1	9	35	101	228
129	Chicken in Artichoke Sauce	467	33	18	<1	29	56	134	845
129	Sesame Chicken Drumettes	441	49	8	<1	22	46	157	1877
130	Spicy Ginger Chicken	330	30	19	3	15	40	72	284

Pg #	Recipe Title (Approx Per Serving)	Cal	Prot (g)	Carbo (g)	Fiber (g)	T Fat (g)	% Cal from Fat	Chol (mg)	Sod (mg)
130	Swiss Chicken Cutlet	606	43	26	1	34	53	214	621
132	Steamed Fish with Vegetables	113	22	2	<1	1	12	62	95
132	Fresh Fish Oriental	359	30	3	<1	25	63	112	1506
132	Great Gobs of Grouper	539	46	52	1	15	26	49	909
133	Lemon Burger Mackerel	626	30	12	<1	53	74	174	555
133	Salmon with Ginger Sauce	414	33	14	<1	25	54	136	183
134	Sea Pines Seafood Casserole	250	14	7	1	19	67	100	441
134	Pasta with Seafood	599	42	53	2	24	36	189	576
135	Seafood Kabobs	160	26	4	4	4	22	140	263
135	Crab Meat-Stuffed Lobster	484	63	13	<1	19	36	322	2313
135	Crab Casserole	488	17	13	1	41	76	242	548
136	Sherried Crab Casserole	341	22	8	1	23	63	103	672
136	Daufuskie Deviled Crabs	610	35	22	2	42	62	262	1246
137	Crab Chesapeake	285	30	12	<1	13	41	228	1162
137	Sautéed Oysters	170	6	3	4	14	76	78	192
137	Maggie's Scalloped Oysters	822	17	40	10	66	73	289	1165
138	Spinach and Oyster Pie	441	19	25	12	30	60	176	696
138	Scallop-Artichoke Casserole	307	19	15	<1	16	46	57	537
139	Scallops in Garlic Sauce	515	40	47	1	19	33	141	356
139	Scalloped Scallops	343	22	5	0	23	60	121	204
139	Barbecued Shrimp	628	38	1	<1	52	75	416	734
140	Shrimp and Saffron Linguine	915	34	76	7	49	50	299	475
140	Saucy Shrimp Casserole	376	35	9	<1	22	53	411	511
141	Shrimp Etouffée	492	36	14	2	33	59	357	874
141	Shrimp Delight	376	26	13	2	23	57	218	868
142	Shrimp and Rice Elegante	267	15	23	1	13	43	133	644
142	Shrimp and Spinach Casserole	408	39	17	5	22	47	250	1558
144	Company Venison Stroganoff	643	73	31	1	21	31	167	407
144	Smoked Venison	424	53	1	<1	22	48	116	125
145	Marinade for Leg of Venison (1 c.)	157	1	6	1	9	52	0	11
145	Dove Pie	822	60	49	12	35	38	273	2385
146	Southern Dove With Rice	374	13	30	1	22	54	48	432
146	Connie's Wild Duck Skewers	343	24	10	1	23	60	82	1448
147	Ducks Burgundy	354	19	12	1	23	58	94	1045
147	Fruited Stuffed Wild Goose	344	32	18	1	17	43	193	349
148	Marinated Goose	330	14	3	<1	28	78	98	24
148	Roast Grouse with Sour Cream	749	56	7	0	32	38	274	807
148	Quail in Mushroom Sauce	283	16	9	1	19	63	26	727
150	Breakfast Casserole	538	36	23	1	33	56	327	2379

Pg #	Recipe Title (Approx Per Serving)	Cal	Prot (g)	Carbo (g)	Fiber (g)	T Fat (g)	% Cal from Fat	Chol (mg)	Sod (mg)
150	Egg Casserole for Brunch	417	28	4	0	32	70	296	709
151	Brunch Eggs	461	32	4	0	35	69	422	827
151	Deviled Egg Casserole	281	11	6	<1	24	76	243	564
152	Crab Meat-Stuffed Eggs	115	9	2	<1	8	63	227	135
152	Heat and Hold Eggs	202	11	4	<1	16	70	341	436
153	Egg and Sausage Puff	430	22	19	0	29	61	273	944
153	Calibogue Shrimp and Grits	588	21	26	4	45	68	237	368
153	Carolina Cheese Grits	417	14	22	3	30	65	154	391
154	Cheese Grits-Sausage Casserole	302	12	17	2	20	61	105	599
154	Super Breakfast Pizza	357	15	18	<1	25	63	164	799
155	Breakfast Quiches	324	13	16	1	23	64	172	663
155	Crab Quiche	467	20	21	1	33	65	176	750
156	Sausage Quiche	529	19	15	1	43	74	197	1261
156	Breakfast Soufflé	255	7	20	1	16	57	144	151
156	Simple Cheese Soufflé	360	16	10	<1	29	71	282	900
157	Sausage Casserole	287	13	25	1	15	46	37	2020
157	Sausage-Egg Casserole	286	16	13	<1	19	59	151	726
158	Sausage and Wild Rice	212	8	20	<1	11	48	22	969
158	Strawberry Cheese Ring	322	8	18	1	25	69	38	256
158	Spicy Welsh Rarebit	380	17	4	<1	33	78	148	535
160	Asparagus Puff Casserole	420	11	8	1	40	83	118	1232
160	Cheesy Green Bean Casserole	432	13	18	4	36	72	64	1134
161	Green Bean Casserole	168	4	25	2	7	34	21	163
161	Creole Lima Beans	140	7	24	8	2	15	3	229
161	Broccoli Casserole	338	8	10	2	31	79	88	584
162	Carrot Casserole	199	1	9	2	19	81	11	356
162	Glazed Carrots and Grapes	79	1	16	4	<1	3	0	64
163	Sea Pines Corn Pudding	253	8	32	6	13	42	112	228
163	Eggplant Parmesan	511	21	63	6	20	35	117	1180
164	Baked Okra	36	2	8	2	<1	4	0	5
164	Fried Okra	96	4	21	3	<1	3	0	6
164	Fried Onion Rings	147	6	22	2	4	22	30	435
165	Sautéed Peas	90	7	14	5	1	9	<1	323
165	New Potatoes and Carrots	208	3	31	3	9	37	23	359
165	Potato Puff Casserole	357	6	36	3	22	54	59	156
166	Twice-Baked Potatoes	492	12	53	5	27	48	70	714
166	Ratatouille	227	3	15	5	19	70	0	13
167	Spinach Chausson	553	12	45	5	37	59	167	404
168	Creamy Ranch Spinach Soufflé	343	15	7	5	29	75	243	1227

Pg #	Recipe Title (Approx Per Serving)	Cal	Prot (g)	Carbo (g)	Fiber (g)	T Fat (g)	% Cal from Fat	Chol (mg)	Sod (mg)
168	Creamed Spinach Casserole	273	7	9	4	25	78	41	367
168	Spinach Casserole	167	6	21	2	7	37	42	530
169	Sour Cream Squash	205	4	11	3	17	73	35	75
169	Squash and Corn Soufflé	272	11	26	3	14	46	20	634
170	Honey Cranberry Squash	287	3	74	8	<1	1	0	42
170	Squash Supreme	357	8	37	2	20	50	42	1113
170	Sweet Potato Supreme	555	4	63	2	34	53	62	305
171	Southern Sweet Potatoes	116	2	17	2	5	38	15	50
171	Sweet Potato Casserole	234	4	34	3	10	38	8	208
172	Fresh Tomato Tart	797	27	45	4	57	64	92	1264
172	Tomato Casserole	102	5	13	3	4	32	10	133
173	Tony's Tomatoes Rockefeller	215	8	12	2	16	65	140	653
173	Pepperoni and Cheese Zucchini	485	23	19	4	36	66	65	1386
174	Monterey Zucchini	204	7	11	2	15	66	39	627
174	Zucchini Fritters	18	1	3	<1	<1	15	9	4
175	Zucchini and Tomato Bake	77	4	7	1	4	43	11	128
175	Vegetable Casserole	376	9	31	4	27	60	24	1322
176	Tossed Vegetables	124	3	16	3	6	42	6	47
176	Mixed Vegetable Casserole	554	11	33	7	45	70	67	759
177	Kaye's Macaroni and Cheese	500	15	36	2	33	59	52	638
177	Pasta Primavera	530	19	55	6	27	45	84	355
178	Noodle Pudding	551	15	71	1	24	38	227	521
178	Rolled Lasagna	488	27	36	3	27	49	134	813
179	Marinara Sauce	247	16	13	2	15	54	57	580
179	Spinach Pesto	343	9	36	3	18	48	4	222
180	Brown Rice	135	5	28	1	<1	2	<1	426
180	Chinese-Style Rice	145	4	27	1	2	13	71	25
180	Green Rice	329	12	21	1	22	61	73	560
181	Crunchy Sweet and Sour Rice	152	4	31	2	2	10	<1	58
181	Ravishing Rice	284	13	28	1	13	42	32	2461
182	Baked Wild Rice	188	6	29	1	6	29	0	975
182	Wild Rice with Wine	239	6	35	1	8	31	21	80
182	Barbecue Sauce (1 c.)	587	5	71	1	34	50	0	1749
183	Another Barbecue Sauce (1 c.)	249	3	25	3	17	58	41	1104
183	Béarnaise Sauce	236	2	1	<1	26	96	169	331
183	Curry Sauce (1 c.)	615	5	12	1	62	89	64	1085
184	Currant Jelly Sauce	99	1	21	<1	2	18	22	24
184	Hollandaise Sauce	146	3	2	<1	15	89	138	236
184	Easy Hollandaise Sauce	160	1	1	<1	17	94	112	132

Pg #	Recipe Title (Approx Per Serving)	Cal	Prot (g)	Carbo (g)	Fiber (g)	T Fat (g)	% Cal from Fat	Chol (mg)	Sod (mg)
185	Mushroom Asparagus Sauce (1 c.)	219	3	14	2	17	69	45	115
185	Sweet and Hot Mustard (1 c.)	633	21	97	0	25	32	213	100
185	The Sauce	269	1	2	<1	30	97	37	270
186	Raisin Sauce (1 c.)	403	2	104	3	1	2	0	35
186	Tingle's Red Sauce for Fish	19	1	4	1	<1	8	0	93
186	Teriyaki Marinade (1 c.)	295	8	55	<1	1	2	0	8255
187	Diet Teriyaki Marinade (1 c.)	156	3	37	1	<1	2	0	2094
187	Basic White Sauce (1 c.)	410	10	23	<1	31	68	95	829
187	Cheesed Apples	384	8	44	1	21	47	58	505
188	Scalloped Apples	313	1	40	2	19	51	10	274
188	Spiced Fruit	269	1	57	2	6	19	0	82
188	Baked Pineapple	482	5	66	1	24	43	113	414
189	Cranberries and Rice	198	2	47	2	<1	1	0	17
189	Cranberry Sauce (1 c.)	431	<1	111	4	<1	0	0	4
189	Melrose Conserve (1 c.)	582	0	150	0	0	0	0	4
190	Pickled Peaches (1 pt.)	582	3	158	8	<1	1	0	274
190	Pear Relish (1 pt.)	560	3	146	14	2	3	0	540
192	Onion Crescent Crunch Sticks	69	1	5	<1	5	64	15	147
192	Jiffy Biscuits	82	2	11	<1	3	35	4	175
192	Low Country Biscuits	141	2	14	<1	9	57	1	154
193	Sour Cream Biscuits	114	3	16	1	4	33	9	235
193	Scones	121	2	13	<1	7	51	1	352
193	Carolina Corn Bread	179	6	33	0	2	12	54	620
194	Corn Bread Casserole	243	7	24	2	14	51	60	455
194	Mexican Corn Bread	318	11	22	2	21	59	89	498
195	Corn Bread	351	5	17	1	30	75	92	272
195	Spinach Spoon Bread	293	7	17	1	23	69	104	457
196	Doughnut Holes	109	2	21	<1	2	15	21	154
196	Applesauce Raisin Bread	300	5	51	3	9	3	43	351
197	Fool-Proof Banana Bread	297	4	47	1	11	3	67	421
197	Banana-Blueberry Bread	332	5	44	2	16	4	43	151
198	Banana-Strawberry Bread	339	4	48	2	15	4	43	285
198	Buttered Beer Loaves	242	4	33	1	10	4	25	484
198	Garlic-Cheese Sourdough Bread	204	5	23	0	11	5	25	449
199	Bishop's Bread	102	1	15	1	5	4	13	26
199	Golden Cheese Bread	210	7	22	2	11	5	36	290
200	Onion-Cheese Supper Bread	226	7	18	<1	14	56	51	442
200	Poppy Seed Bread	185	2	24	0	9	4	17	102
201	Irish Soda Bread	205	5	45	2	1	3	1	283

Pg #	Recipe Title (Approx Per Serving)	Cal	Prot (g)	Carbo (g)	Fiber (g)	T Fat (g)	% Cal from Fat	Chol (mg)	Sod (mg)
201	Swiss Braided Bread	158	4	27	1	4	2	3	168
202	Sally Lunn Bread	200	6	32	1	5	24	38	243
202	Sourdough Bread	200	5	41	1	2	1	0	323
203	Whole Wheat Bread	183	5	37	5	3	1	0	216
203	Banana Muffins	183	2	31	1	6	28	32	234
204	Yogurt Bran Muffins	60	1	8	1	3	39	1	100
204	Pineapple Muffins	69	1	11	<1	3	32	12	42
205	Applesauce Pancakes	374	13	49	2	14	34	237	279
205	Yummy Pancakes	533	5	100	1	13	22	36	573
206	Blender Croissants	155	3	18	1	8	47	34	70
206	Potato Rolls	96	2	13	<1	4	37	8	69
207	Refrigerator Yeast Rolls	116	2	16	1	5	37	9	48
207	Refrigerator Rolls	135	2	18	1	6	41	12	64
208	Coffee Cakes	266	3	49	1	7	23	43	140
208	Poppy Seed Coffee Cake	255	3	34	<1	12	42	53	262
209	Quick Caramel Coffee Ring	255	3	35	1	12	42	2	516
209	Tennis Ball Bread	262	3	41	1	10	33	17	523
210	Gingerbread Squares	369	4	47	1	19	46	36	142
210	Yuletide Coffee Cake	735	7	112	2	30	36	106	590
212	Fresh Apple Crumble	305	2	49	2	13	36	21	115
212	Apricot After All Dessert	999	14	87	7	70	61	221	837
213	Bananas Foster	227	1	33	1	6	24	16	57
213	Biscuit Tortoni	219	3	19	<1	15	60	103	78
214	Caramel Custard	627	6	37	0	52	73	447	56
214	Cheese Flan	554	14	71	<1	25	39	277	443
215	Easy and Elegant Cream	266	4	33	1	14	47	33	42
215	Chocolate Chip Eggnog Ball	612	5	80	2	34	47	38	267
216	Caterpillar	811	7	47	0	67	73	217	464
216	Chocolate Mousse Cake	737	11	75	2	45	54	188	108
217	Wendy's Chcoolate Lush Pie	421	5	42	1	27	56	28	270
217	Luscious Chocolate Squares	545	7	51	1	36	58	35	327
218	Fruit Pizza	693	9	608	2	32	10	46	531
218	Crêpes in Fruit Sauce	88	2	9	<1	5	50	52	54
219	Orange Dessert Crêpes	52	2	5	<1	3	45	45	34
219	Christmas Grape Dessert	306	3	29	2	22	61	75	32
220	Baked Grapefruit Alaska	470	6	72	2	7	14	30	112
220	Churned Peachy Ice Cream	462	13	70	1	14	27	113	186
221	Ice Cream Liqueur Dessert	365	5	44	0	14	35	59	117
221	Apricots and Sherbet	360	3	78	1	4	10	14	93

Pg #	Recipe Title (Approx Per Serving)	Cal	Prot (g)	Carbo (g)	Fiber (g)	T Fat (g)	% Cal from Fat	Chol (mg)	Sod (mg)
221	Homemade Sherbet	398	2	102	2	1	1	0	4
222	Frozen Pineapple Dessert	138	2	32	<1	1	4	2	65
222	Frozen Grand Marnier Mousse	459	6	47	<1	28	54	143	56
223	Frozen Lemon Mousse	364	5	39	<1	22	53	177	136
223	Orange Icebox Cake	460	8	72	<1	16	31	41	77
224	Peachy Dessert	695	8	92	3	35	44	35	578
224	Great Grandma's Pudding	298	7	48	2	10	30	85	47
225	Bread Pudding	322	8	53	2	9	25	90	394
225	Brandy Sauce	87	2	7	0	6	60	65	54
226	Strawberry Delight	365	3	41	1	22	53	57	101
226	Trifle	512	7	74	2	23	39	11	303
228	Apple Drabble Cake	584	5	65	2	35	53	41	275
228	German Apple Cake	214	2	26	1	11	47	40	83
229	Forget-Me-Not Carrot Cake	494	4	62	2	27	47	69	355
229	Three-Chocolate Cake	795	9	91	2	44	50	119	677
230	Sand Trap Chocolate Cake	528	4	79	2	24	40	30	192
230	Surprise Cupcakes	243	3	35	<1	11	40	19	136
231	Jam Cake	285	4	45	1	10	31	41	183
231	Lazy Daisy Cake	240	3	39	1	9	32	55	194
232	Aunt Livey's Orange Cake	497	7	80	3	19	33	85	245
232	Poppy Seed Cake	290	4	28	<1	18	56	60	222
233	Bourbon Pound Cake	418	5	56	1	19	42	131	163
233	Daddy's Pound Cake	282	3	42	1	11	36	42	195
234	Chocolate-Potato Pound Cake	392	5	43	2	24	52	56	126
234	Sour Cream Pound Cake	383	4	55	1	17	39	117	138
235	Wedding Cake	392	5	56	1	17	38	117	145
235	Seven-Up Cake	786	7	102	3	40	45	153	518
236	Prune Cake	300	3	57	1	7	22	50	179
236	Sherry Cake	305	3	41	<1	11	31	82	237
237	Chocolate Zucchini Cake	318	5	37	2	18	50	43	125
237	Blueberry Cheesecake	499	7	50	2	32	56	157	363
238	Heavenly Cheesecake	510	8	44	<1	34	60	160	305
238	Carol's L.A. Cheesecake	432	6	37	<1	29	60	94	303
239	Kahlua Cheesecake	398	6	36	2	26	58	99	256
239	Italian Cheesecake	346	12	23	<1	23	59	152	137
240	White Chocolate Cheesecake	794	13	47	2	62	70	214	415
240	Chocolate Hazelnut Crust	153	2	17	<1	9	52	13	136
241	Hazelnut Praline (1 c.)	789	11	63	6	60	64	16	4
241	Macadamia Cheesecake	585	9	48	1	41	62	166	397

Pg #	Recipe Title (Approx Per Serving)	Cal	Prot (g)	Carbo (g)	Fiber (g)	T Fat (g)	% Cal from Fat	Chol (mg)	Sod (mg)
242	Mrs. Punt's Pumpkin Cheesecake	673	12	46	2	50	66	191	406
242	Spicy Graham Cracker Crust	152	3	13	1	10	60	14	136
244	Almond Macaroons	50	1	8	1	2	29	0	3
244	Caramel Brownies	166	2	21	<1	9	47	2	207
245	Cinnamon Brownies	99	1	12	<1	6	49	28	67
245	Double Shot Brownies	209	2	26	1	12	49	37	90
246	Viennese Brownies	219	3	23	1	14	54	71	181
246	Zebra Brownies	199	3	22	<1	11	50	26	122
247	Kahlua Chocolate Squares	199	2	26	1	10	44	22	104
247	Fudge Squares	154	2	22	1	7	40	36	57
248	Butterscotch Cookies	133	2	19	1	6	39	9	71
248	Chinese Cookies	132	1	13	<1	8	55	<1	153
249	Heritage Chocolate Chip Cookies	123	1	16	<1	7	47	19	100
249	Cocoa-Banana Muffinettes	188	4	31	2	6	28	<1	178
250	Coconut Cookies	147	2	20	1	7	43	32	136
250	Date Wheels	169	2	27	1	6	33	13	41
251	Everything Cookies	160	2	23	1	7	40	19	102
251	Gingersnaps	132	1	22	<1	4	30	4	64
252	Home-Style Graham Crackers	85	2	11	1	4	42	15	51
252	Grandma's Cookies	176	1	17	1	12	59	0	122
253	Crispie Bars	223	5	26	2	13	47	4	98
253	Molasses Cookies	137	1	18	<1	7	44	9	72
254	Easy Peanut Butter Cookies	198	7	20	1	12	49	18	93
254	Peanut Butter-Chip Cookies	231	4	25	1	14	51	9	112
255	Russian Rocks	114	2	15	1	6	45	12	62
255	Sand Tarts	65	1	5	<1	5	65	10	32
256	Snickerdoodles	73	1	9	<1	4	45	7	34
256	Tara's Cookies	137	2	18	1	7	46	14	63
257	Iced Almonds	360	7	32	4	25	59	16	452
257	Caramel Candy	126	1	18	<1	6	41	13	48
257	Man-Made Strawberries	98	2	16	1	3	29	3	41
258	Chocolate-Covered Fruitcake	370	3	48	2	17	43	20	72
258	Mini Fruit Cupcakes	118	1	21	1	4	30	10	16
259	Best-Ever Fudge	333	2	51	1	16	40	17	121
259	Plantation Pecans	254	3	24	2	18	61	0	273
260	Fondant (1 lb.)	2325	0	599	0	0	0	0	15
260	Bonbons	Nutritional information for this recipe is not available.							
262	Ambrosia Pie	280	6	42	2	10	33	106	301
262	Angel Pie	394	5	54	<1	18	41	196	55

Pg #	Recipe Title (Approx Per Serving)	Cal	Prot (g)	Carbo (g)	Fiber (g)	T Fat (g)	% Cal from Fat	Chol (mg)	Sod (mg)
263	Old English Pie	539	3	86	3	23	36	41	140
263	Brandy Alexander Pie	451	4	47	0	27	54	74	317
264	Cheese Pie	371	7	24	0	28	66	155	209
264	Mock Cherry Pie	660	5	120	4	20	27	5	566
265	Chocolate Pecan Cream Pie	500	4	41	1	37	65	61	364
265	Black Joke Pie	754	8	74	3	51	58	71	390
266	French Silk Pie	506	6	38	2	39	67	169	366
266	Harris' Birthday Pie	464	5	48	1	30	56	112	336
267	Ice Cream Pie	560	7	52	2	39	60	106	150
268	Coffee Pie	563	5	44	1	42	66	167	351
268	Fuzzy Navel Pie	641	6	69	1	38	53	109	257
269	Lemon-Sour Cream Pie	679	9	77	1	38	50	150	499
269	Key Lime Pie	424	8	51	1	22	45	154	348
270	Christmas Mince Chiffon Pie	410	6	55	1	18	41	28	295
270	Mouth-Watering Pie	487	4	59	2	27	49	21	279
271	Maple Pecan Pie	716	7	95	2	36	45	134	332
271	Real Southern Pecan Pie	583	6	73	2	32	48	122	286
271	Rum Pie	661	7	49	1	45	64	322	223
272	Mile-High Strawberry Pies	255	3	36	2	12	41	1	291
272	Strawberry Cream Pie	475	6	30	1	38	71	96	311
273	Strawberry Pie	254	3	46	3	8	26	2	119
273	Sweet Potato Pie	453	7	63	2	20	38	125	476
274	Miniature Cinnamon Pastries	94	1	8	<1	6	60	10	53
274	Peach Cobbler Roll	526	3	76	2	25	42	32	335
275	Bavarian Apple Tart	436	6	45	2	27	55	89	191
275	Bakewell Tarts	213	4	18	1	15	61	38	214
276	Cheese Tarts	184	2	15	<1	13	64	37	112
276	Cheesecake Cupcakes	91	1	10	<1	5	52	28	46
277	Grandmother's Tarts	114	1	15	<1	6	46	24	85
277	Pecan Tassies	271	3	26	2	19	59	49	107
278	Linzertarts	200	2	30	1	8	37	39	137
278	Russian Mint Pies	257	3	18	1	20	69	96	122

INDEX

Hilton Head Entertains
8 Fox Grape Road
Hilton Head Island, South Carolina 29928
(803) 671-2286

Please send me _____ copies of *Hilton Head Entertains*
    @ $15.95 each   _____

Plus sales tax of 80¢ per book   _____

Plus postage and handling of $2.00 per book   _____

                           TOTAL   _____

Make checks payable to: **Hilton Head Preparatory School**

Name _____

Address _____

City _____ State _____ Zip _____

VISA and MasterCard accepted

Card # _____

Expiration _____ VISA or MasterCard

Proceeds for the sale of this book will benefit the Hilton Head Preparatory School.

Hilton Head Entertains
8 Fox Grape Road
Hilton Head Island, South Carolina 29928
(803) 671-2286

Please send me _____ copies of *Hilton Head Entertains*
    @ $15.95 each   _____

Plus sales tax of 80¢ per book   _____

Plus postage and handling of $2.00 per book   _____

                           TOTAL   _____

Make checks payable to: **Hilton Head Preparatory School**

Name_____

Address _____

City _____ State _____ Zip _____

VISA and MasterCard accepted

Card # _____

Expiration _____ VISA or MasterCard

Proceeds for the sale of this book will benefit the Hilton Head Preparatory School.